# INDIAN ECONOMY & BUSINESS

# – OVERVIEW OF RECENT

# TRENDS & EVENTS

I0390398

**A MUST READ FOR -**

> ➤ STUDENTS PREPARING FOR MANAGEMENT, BANKING AND CIVIL SERVICES EXAM.

> ➤ STUDENTS OF BUSINESS, FINANCE AND ECONOMICS.

> ➤ ALL RECENT GRADUATES AND OTHER NON-FINANCE ENTHUSIASTS.

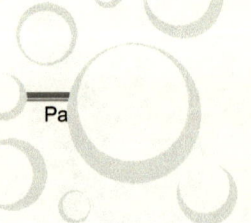

What they said about the Book…

The book titled "Indian Economy & Business" presents a complex situation relating to the Indian Economy, Policies and Regulations in a very simple and lucid manner. The book also relates the effect of these policy measures on the corporate world through various cases. **The book is a must for all students who are studying Management, Economics as a subject at the undergraduate or post graduate level.** We wish Mr. Ashish all the best and hope he writes many more books on such important topics.
**Dr. R Gopal**, Director, D.Y.Patil Univ., School of Management.

I finished reading the book two days back with lot of interest and found it very engaging. The topics chosen are highly relevant and practical and would certainly give youngsters a better understanding of these complex issues. The coverage of financial sector is worth mentioning as it provides a holistic view of many diffused issues and trends in an easy to learn manner. Looking forward to many such contributions from the Author in the future.
**Dr Bigyan Verma,** Director - GNIMS Business School, Mumbai.

The book authored by an IIM graduate does not disappoint at all. I managed to read all the articles but could not find fault in any of them. The book provides practical insights on economic and business happenings to compliment the classroom learning. Cases on Corporate strategies gone wrong provides unique insights on how management fails. **A must read for all management professionals...**
**Dr Atul Pandey,** Dean, Faculty of Management Studies, APS University Rewa & Chairman, Central Board of Studies (Management), MP.

The book makes a good reading since it presents overview of the Indian Economy in an easy to read and simple to understand language. The cases and examples presented are apt and relevant for students and professionals alike. All the best!!
**Dr Prashant Gundawar,** Director - Sterling Institute of Management Studies, Navi Mumbai.

**Are you still waiting..??!!**

## Letter from the Author

Dear Reader,

It is matter of great pleasure for me to present this book to you. Briefly, I am an IIT Roorkee-IIM Calcutta graduate with over 25 years of professional experience. This book is a culmination of my quest to find purpose of my life.

The book is a collection of articles analysing recent developments and key features of Indian economy & business. The articles are sourced from the portal https://www.indiaeconomyandbusiness.com/ founded by the author and have been compiled in a book form to give readers a better reading experience. The book also contains brief case studies on corporate failures of recent times, analysis of mergers & acquisitions, Industry analysis and analysis of key international developments. The book attempts to reach out to all youngsters, particularly, those appearing in Management, Banking, Civil Services and similar entrance exams. I am sure this would go a long way in helping you prepare for these exams. Apart from that, the book would also be an extremely useful read for those are already in various management institutes or studying Economics, Finance, Business etc. This would not only prepare them for their job interviews but also because it is important for all the youngsters to have a broad understanding of these issues to evolve as smarter professionals.

Other than the articles on Economy, Policy, Banking etc, the book also delves on corporate failures and decisions gone wrong. As Former President, Late APJ Abdul Kalam had said, "Don't read success stories, you will only get a message. Read failure stories, you will get some ideas to get success". I believe the "Corporate" section can provide considerable insights on how things go wrong. This, together with the section on "Policy", also throws light on practical aspects of business and policy decision making. This is a modest attempt to achieve what former President Late Pranab Mukherjee said, "Adjunct faculty from the industry and research institutions can provide practical orientation to course modules". The endeavour is to keep the articles simple and focus on broad trends/ insights rather than on numbers.

So, friends, here is the book for you. Would be happy to hear from you. My Mail id - ashish8012@gmail.com.

Happy Learning!
Ashish Agrawal

# Table of Contents

# SECTION - I
# ECONOMY

# Budget - Revenue & Expenditure Analysis. Part I

The Budget proposal projects total expenditure of Rs 45 lakh crore against receipt of Rs 27.1 lakh crore for the year 2023-24 or FY24. This implies fiscal deficit of Rs 17.9 lakh crore or 5.9% of projected GDP. The revised estimates (RE) for the current year (2022-23, FY23) shows an increase in receipts but even greater increase in expenditure. Yet, deficit as a percent of GDP in RE remains the same as budget estimates (BE) due to higher nominal growth in GDP. Here is a look at RE vis-à-vis BE for FY23 and proposals for FY24.

Government's total receipt comprises of two items – revenue receipt and capital receipt. Revenue receipt is further classified as tax revenue and non-tax revenue with tax revenue accounting for almost 90% of revenue receipt. Tax revenues are further classified as direct taxes and indirect taxes. Direct taxes comprises of corporation tax and income tax whereas indirect taxes primarily comprise of GST, customs and excise duty.

Direct taxes receipt for FY23 as per RE is projected at Rs 16.5 lakh crore, 17% higher than FY22, a reasonably strong growth rate. Projection for FY24 is Rs 18.2 lakh crore, increase of 11%. The projection is quite conservative considering the growth momentum and actual should surpass this level. Indirect tax stands at Rs 13.8 lakh crore for FY23 RE, 4% higher than BE and 7% higher than FY22. For FY24, it is projected to grow to Rs 15.3 lakh crore, increase of 10%. Within indirect taxes, GST accounts for over 60% whereas excise is about 25% and the rest, customs. Even though growth projection for FY24 is higher than growth estimate for FY23, it is still modest at 10% and doesn't look over-optimistic. This is because, in FY23, excise duty declined by as much as 19% because of excise duty cut in petroleum products. This dampened the strong growth of 22% in GST collection. For FY24, there should not be any such surprises in excise which is projected to increase by 6%. GST growth is projected at 12% against 22% in FY23.

Total tax revenue for FY23 RE stands at Rs 30.3 lakh crore, 10% higher than BE and 12.3% higher than FY22. A significant increase over BE implies fiscal prudence as an over-ambitious projection of revenue at the time of budget presentation helps paint a rosy picture. However, a lower collection leads to significant deviation towards the end and higher deficit which disturbs government finances and financial market. For FY24, total tax revenue is projected to reach Rs 33.5 lakh crore, 10% increase over FY23, lower than 12.3% growth recorded in FY23. The figure implies tax/GDP ratio of 11.1% for FY24, same as FY23, but lower than 11.4% in FY22. A ratio same as FY22 could mean additional mobilization of over Rs 1 lakh crore.

While the central government is collecting these taxes, it has to transfer a part of this to states as per the recommendation of the Finance Commission (FC). For FY23 RE, amount being transferred is Rs 9.5 lakh crore, about 31% of total revenue. This is projected at Rs 10.2 lakh crore for FY24, 30% of total taxes. The share is significantly lower than FC's mandated share of 41% because of greater mobilization of funds through cess etc which central government doesn't have to share with states. FC had raised concern in its report regarding increasing use of cess for tax mobilization. Net revenue available with central government is Rs 20.8 lakh crore in FY23 RE, projected at Rs 23.3 lakh crore for FY24.

Other than tax revenue, government also mobilizes resources as dividends & profits, interest receipt, license fees etc. Since these are recurring in nature, these are called non-tax revenue. Receipts under this stands at Rs 2.6 lakh crore for FY23 RE, 3% lower than BE and 28% lower than FY22. The decline is due to lower dividends & profits. For FY24, the figure is Rs 3 lakh crore, 15% increase over FY23.

The second category is called capital receipt which includes primarily receipt from disinvestments. Budget estimates under this head used to be in the range of Rs 1.5-2 lakh crore for several years but failed to meet the target. For instance, disinvestment receipt was only Rs 15,000 crore against BE of Rs 1.75 lakh crore for FY22. FY23 budget took a conservative view for the first time, projecting only Rs 65,000 crore of disinvestment receipt and Rs 79,000 crore of total capital receipt. Capital receipt is projected at Rs 83,500 crore for FY23 RE and almost the same at Rs 84,000 crore for FY24.

In terms of expenditure, FY23 RE stands at Rs 41.9 lakh crore, up from Rs 39.5 lakh crore BE. Even though the expenditure is Rs 2.4 lakh crore higher than BE, the slippage is less than the slippage in FY22. A part of this gets compensate with higher tax revenues helping cap the deficit increase at Rs 17.6 lakh crore against Rs 16.6 lakh crore in BE. For FY24, expenditure is projected at Rs 45 lakh crore, 7.5% increase over FY23.

*****

# Budget - Revenue & Expenditure Analysis. Part II

Against total receipt of Rs 27.1 lakh crore, central government is projected to spend nearly Rs 45 lakh crore in FY24. Other than interest payments, broad areas which account for maximum expenditure are Defence, Subsidies and rural & agriculture sector. Here is a look at the details of various government expenses.

Government's expenditure classification is more complicated than the income classification. These are classified in several ways, the most important being revenue and capital expenditure since capital expenditure is expected to increase the productive capacity. As per the budget, government would be spending Rs 10 lakh crore towards capex which is 33% higher than RE for FY23. Among the major heads of capex are Roads & Highways at Rs 2.6 lakh crore, Railways at Rs 2.4 lakh crore, 56% increase for both together and Defence at Rs 1.62 lakh crore.

The revenue expenditure is classified as A) General services which includes government expenditure such as interest, pension, defence, salaries etc; B) Social services such as education, health, housing which are for the benefit of people and does not give any return; C) Economic services such as agriculture, rural, railways, roads etc which generate revenue or provide tangible economic outcome and D) Grants-in-aid to state governments and UTs. General services expenditure is budgeted at Rs 18.4 lakh crore in FY24, up about 8% over FY23. The same was higher by 5% in FY23 RE over BE and up about 15% over FY22. Within this, interest payments is projected at Rs 11 lakh crore (almost 25% of total budget), increase of 13%, lower than 17% in FY23. The other item within this is Defence Services (revenue expenditure only) accounting for Rs 2.8 lakh crore, projected to increase only marginally by 1.5%. FY23 RE figure for this is 11% higher than BE and 14% higher than FY22 actuals. Pension expenditure also comes under this head which is projected at Rs 2.6 lakh crore, lower than FY23 RE. FY23 RE is 17% higher than BE and 23% higher than FY22 actuals. FY23 RE being significantly higher than BE implies that actual expenditure could be higher than BE.

Major expenditure under social services is water supply at Rs 64,000 crore, education & youth services at Rs 57,000 crore and health at Rs 39,000 crore. Total expenditure under this head is only about Rs 2.2 lakh crore which corresponds to just 0.7% of GDP. The expenditure is very low and infrastructure needs to be built to improve the delivery capacity of the system. Economic services are budgeted at Rs 11.1 lakh crore, lower by 11% over FY23 RE. FY23 BE was also lower by 5% over FY22 but RE is 20% higher than BE. Within this, agriculture plus rural expenditure is estimated at Rs 4.2 lakh crore, lower than Rs 5.6 lakh crore in FY23 RE. The expenditure under this head had risen sharply over last three years due to additional free food provided to minimize the adverse impact of Covid and higher outgo due to increase in demand under MGNREGA. The same was only Rs 3.1 lakh core in FY20, rising to Rs 7 lakh crore in FY21 and Rs 5.8 lakh crore in FY22. (However, a part of FY21 expenditure was due to accounting adjustment as government took over loans from the account books of Food Corporation of India (FCI)). Other expenditure within this are Rs 2.7 lakh crore towards transport (mostly, Railways) and Rs 1.9 lakh crore to industries, primarily as subsidy to fertilizer industry.

The last, Grants-in-aid to state governments and UTs, comprises of grants for creation of capital assets, grants mandated by finance commission, grants for projects aided by foreign bodies etc (and does not include states' share in total taxes as stated in Part I). Amount under this corresponds to Rs 3.5 lakh crore almost the same as FY23 RE. Central government transfers funds to states in yet another way which is for the implementation of central scheme such as MGNREGA. Total funds transfer to states is projected at Rs 18.6 lakh crore, 9% higher FY23 RE.

In terms of subsidy, projection for FY24 is Rs 3.7 lakh crore, 28% lower than FY23 RE. FY23 RE, in turn, is 64% higher than BE and 17% higher than FY22 actuals. FY23 RE has risen sharply due to more than doubling of fertilizers subsidy, a fall-out of Russia-Ukraine war whereas food subsidy was higher by about 40% due to increase in prices.

*****

# Budget – Understanding Deficit Terminology

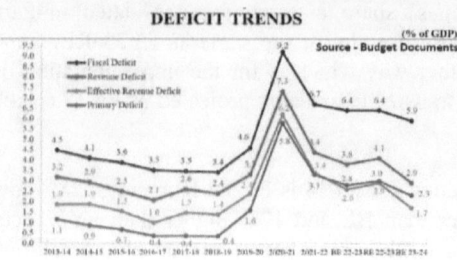

The budget proposal projects a decline in fiscal deficit (FD) from 6.4% of GDP in FY23 to 5.9% in FY24 whereas revenue deficit is projected to decline more sharply from 4.1% to 2.9% of GDP. Another deficit indicator, primary deficit (PD), is projected to decline from 3% to 2.3%. But what do all these deficits indicate and what is their importance?? Here is a brief look.

FD is the highest of all the deficits, which is the difference between the sum total of all government earnings minus sum total of all government's expenses. FD is the amount that government has to borrow from the market and receives maximum focus as high borrowings may lead to higher cost of funds and may reduce the funds available for private investment, called 'crowding-out'. For FY23 (RE), FD stands at Rs 17.6 lakh crore or 6.4% of GDP. While in absolute terms, FD RE is higher than FD BE, as a percent of GDP, it remains the same since GDP projection in RE is higher than BE. FD as a percent of GDP had reached a level of 9.2% in FY21, the peak of Covid, when government expenses had risen sharply even as the revenues had fallen sharply.

However, not all the deficit is funded from market borrowings as government also receives significant amount of money through National Small Savings Funds (NSSF), Provident fund etc. As per the budget documents, government would be borrowing Rs 12.3 lakh crore from the market and Rs 22,000 crore as external debt whereas the rest, Rs 5.4 lakh crore would be mobilized from NSSF, PF etc. Market borrowings is largely unchanged from FY23 RE at Rs 11.96 lakh crore as a result of which, yield on government bonds declined after the budget. Covid-19 has disturbed government finances immensely with FY20 borrowings, the pre-Covid period, being just about half at Rs 6.24 lakh crore.

The next item in the budget statement is revenue deficit (RD) which is the difference between revenue receipt and revenue expenditure. The deficit removes capital items - both on the receipt and expenditure side since these are investments and are expected to provide benefits in future. The number helps understand whether government is able to finance its recurring/non-asset creating expenditure from its recurring earnings or not. The FRBM Act stipulates that RD should come down to less than 1%. FY23 RE is Rs 11.1 lakh crore or 4.1%, higher than BE of Rs 9.9 lakh crore or 3.8% of GDP. Major reason for this is sharp increase in fertilizer and food subsidy. It is interesting to note that while FD as a percent of GDP remains the same, RD has gone up which means that capital expenditure has got squeezed.

Central government also provides funds to state government as grants for creation of capital assets. These are classified as revenue as per the norms but are actually adding to the productive capacity of the economy. To take this into account, a new number was introduced in 2008 called effective revenue deficit (ERD). For FY24, government is projected to provide Rs 3.7 lakh crore through this route, 14% higher than FY23 RE and double that of FY20 figure at Rs 1.85 lakh crore. Reducing this from RD, ERD works out to 1.7% in FY24, down from 2.9% in FY23 RE and 3.3% in FY22.

The final item in the deficit terminologies is primary deficit (PD), the most dangerous of all and source of what is called "debt trap". It is equal to total expenditure excluding cost of servicing debt or interest payments minus total receipts, eliminating the impact of interest burden on government deficit. PD, thus, reflects the underlying strength of government budgeting as to whether it is able to meet its current expenditure or not. Running a primary deficit means that the government is not able to do so, putting more stress on finances of the government. FRBM Act stipulates that primary deficit of the government should be zero. PD for FY24 is projected at Rs 7.1 lakh crore or 2.3% of GDP, down from Rs 8.1 lakh crore or 3% in FY23 RE. Japan, with government debt to GDP ratio of over 250%, had primary deficit of as much as 8% in 2020, the peak of Covid.

Point to Ponder. What is better – Increasing or decreasing gap between FD and RD?

*****

# The Mass Exodus – Understanding the Characteristics

The nationwide lockdown to prevent the spread of Covid-19 had led to an unexpected fallout - mass exodus of people from urban centers to their home town. While it is a common knowledge that most of these people come to cities in search of jobs, exactly how significant is the number. A brief look.

Migration refers to movement of people from their place of birth/place of last residence to another place within the nation. As per the Census of 2011, India had as many as 45.6 crores migrants, close to 37% of its population. The figure stood at 31.5 crores in 2001, implying annual increase of 4.6%, much higher than population growth. However, the figure over-states the intensity of the challenge as over 30 crores of total migrants are females and more than 80% have migrated after marriage. There is a degree of inevitability attached to it and can't be stopped even if all regions attain sufficient prosperity. So, it would be better to focus on migration characteristics of male population who largely move for economic reasons. (Figures below relate to male migration unless stated otherwise).

Migration can be at three levels – within the same district, outside the district but within the state and outside the state. Of the total 14.5 crores migrants, only 16% or 2.4 crores migrated to areas outside their states. Migration within the district forms the largest proportion at 8.3 crores or 58% of migrants. Within the overall context of balancing economic needs with minimal social displacement, the first two migration should be acceptable.

Migration is also classified based on the direction of flow - rural to rural, rural to urban, urban to urban and even urban to rural. While rural to rural and urban to rural migration do not pose much of a stress, the other two put pressure on city infrastructure and affect the quality of life. Of the total migrants, while 8.1 crores migrated to urban area, 6.5 crores migrated to rural areas also, mostly from other rural areas. This is contrary to perception that only cities attract migrants. The significance of the number is that in the absence of opportunities in rural areas, these people could have added to the number of people moving to cities putting even greater pressure on urban centers. Only half of the migrants in urban area are from rural are with the other half coming from other urban areas.

A positive development between 2001-2011 is the decline in share of people migrating for economic reasons (in search of job). While 28% of migrants in 2001 moved for economic reason, the share declined to 24% in 2011. The decline is even greater in case of rural to urban movement from 37% to 31%. Yet, the data needs greater scrutiny as 34% are classified as "Others" and 20% as "moved with households" where ultimate objective could be economic. Another positive trend within this is increase in share of female migrants although marginally, from 1.7% to 2.1%.

The statistics on migration is also divided on the basis of period of migration which helps understand the possibility of reverse migration. Of 2.4 crores males who have migrated to other states, 1.04 crores have migrated within last ten years who are more likely to come back to their home town given an opportunity. (Based on the growth rate recorded between 2001-2011, this could have risen to nearly 1.5 crores). It is this population which would have possibly responded to the lockdown in the manner as seen over last few days.

In terms of state, maximum migration has occurred within Maharashtra at 2.4 crores, almost half of the male population. However, most of it is from within the state and inflow from outside the state is only 49 lakhs (2011 figures). UP and Karnataka accounts for the largest migrants at 17.6 lakh and 5.9 lakhs. Surprisingly, inflow from Bihar is quite low at only 3.9 lakh. Other states with high migrants are Andhra Pradesh and Tamil Nadu at 1.5 crores and 1.3 crores (mostly Intra-state). In case of Delhi, the other centre which witnessed huge exodus after the lockdown, migrants' inflow stood at 37.5 lakhs (including females, 72 lakhs). Within this, UP and Bihar accounted for maximum inflow at 15.1 lakh and 6.6 lakhs.

However, the figure does not reflect the gravity of the issue and a comparison would put this in proper perspective. Capacity of an unreserved train is close to 2,000 which may carry 4,000 at peak load. Carrying people from Mumbai to UP alone would require as many as 440 trains.

*****

# Agriculture Sector – Issues & Challenges

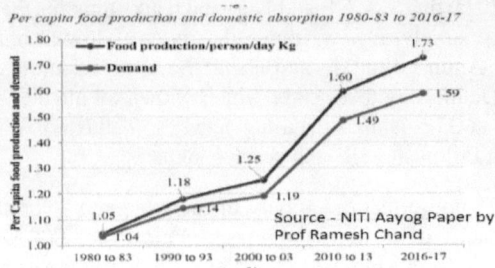

Per capita food production and domestic absorption 1980-83 to 2016-17

India's rural economy remains an area of significant concern due to low level of income and high population dependent upon the same. Income of a farmer, which was about 35% of an urban worker in 1980s, has further declined to 30% now. Despite all the efforts and large spending, the sector just does not seem to budge. So, what are the issues? A brief attempt to understand some of them.

Agriculture production can be classified into two groups – food grains and commercial crops. Food grains can be further classified into cereals (rice, wheat etc or subsistence food) and pulses. India's agricultural policies date back to 1960s and 70s when the nation faced huge shortage of even subsistence food items. The policies did yield results in increasing the production of these items and attaining self-sufficiency. After reaching sufficiency in subsistence food items, the natural progression should have been to reduce thrust on these and increase on nutritious items such as pulses (and then, to commercial crops such as oilseeds). However, the policies could not catch up with the changes leading, paradoxically, to shortage and excess at the same time. As per a paper by Prof Ramesh Chand, Member, NITI Aayog, while total production has increased from about 1 kg per person per day in 1980s to 1.73 kg now, the consumption has increased to only 1.59 kg. On the other hand, there is significant shortage of pulses and oilseeds, which continue to be imported. Imports of pulses and oilseeds stand at $11 bn in FY19, with trend-line showing increase of more than 75% over FY10. Clearly, farmers have not been able to switch to other crops production in the absence of adequate incentives.

An option to absorb the excess production of food grains would be exports. However, global prices are lower than MSP (minimum support price) which not only makes Indian produce uncompetitive but also leads to a tendency of undesirable imports. While focus of supply through MSP has helped meet the demand over the years, the mechanism, in its current form, has distorted the market as the supply now exceed the demand.

An alternative to safeguard farmers' income without distorting the market is to allow the farmers to sell in the open market and pay the difference between MSP and open market price. The scheme, called *bhavantar yojna*, would help create a free-flowing market. It can also help integrate Indian supply chain with global market as traders would be able take a view of global supply dynamics and procure from the farmers if terms of trade are favourable. Even more important is the fact that it would save huge cost that government agencies (largely FCI) incur in procurement, storage, transportation, leakages, spoilage etc. As per FCI website, it incurs almost Rs 1,500 per quintal of food grain procured over and above the procurement price. With average stock of over 50 mn tons, it is easy to estimate the loss. Government can, over a period of time, also start selective disbursement, to small and marginal farmers only, leaving aside the big farmers. The scheme, was implemented in Madhya Pradesh recently but seems to be losing its efficacy in pollical muddle.

The other important need is to supplement famers' income through diversification into horticulture, fisheries etc where there is still a significant gap. A comparison with China shows that even though the per capita availability of cereals is nearly same, availability of vegetables is only 1/3rd and eggs/meat/fish nearly 1/6th, as per the paper quoted above. Even after considering the vegetarian dietary preference of Indians, the difference in second category is very high providing huge scope for growth. While there has been a realization of the same in recent years, the scheme is still to take-off in a big way.

While these factors can help increase the income, there is a nother way to increase the same, by reducing the denominator. That is by reducing the number dependent upon agriculture. Share of population dependent upon agriculture is still almost 45%, although down from over 60% in early 1990s. The only option available to absorb excess agricultural labour force in large scale commercialization of agriculture and establishment of food processing industry and this cannot be achieved without the involvement of private players, possibly, foreign players also. A classic example of public-private partnership is Maruti Udyog where Indian government provided much of the risk capital and the foreign collaborator provided know-how and managed operations, a JV that changed the landscape of Indian automobile industry.

There are several other issues such as low capital investment, low yield, excessive and inefficient use of water leading to longer-term problems, inadequate marketing and supply chain network. However, resolution of these issues would become easier if agriculture sector is treated as any other sector of free market economy and allowed to evolve on its own. Yet, the vulnerable sections would need protection and that should be done by direct benefit transfer rather than by distorting the market.

*****

# Agricultural Marketed Surplus - Analyzing Inter-State Variation

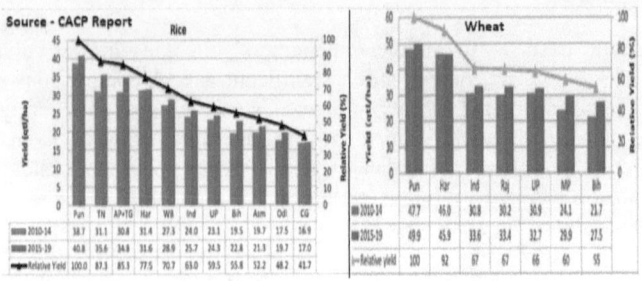

While agriculture, as a whole, remains an under-developed sector, the inter-state variation is even starker. This is reflected in the 'marketed surplus' of different states. Marketed surplus is the quantity that farmer sells in the market after keeping aside the produce for own consumption, to be used as seeds for the next season and other such purposes. So, how does it vary across states and what does it depend on? Here is a brief look.

The primary factor on which marketed surplus depends is the farm yield as higher the production, higher the ability of a farmer to sell it off. As per the Commission for Agricultural Costs and Prices (CACP), the agency tasked with setting the minimum support price (MSP), while Punjab and Haryana have yield close to 4,500 kg/hectare for wheat, it is just about 2,000 kg/ha for Bihar and MP and close to 3,000 kg/ha for UP. While Punjab and Haryana have achieved 90% of the potential yield, the figure is less than 70% for other major wheat producing states.

The disparity leading to significant difference in marketed surplus. Marketed surplus as a percent of production stands at 89% and 81% for Punjab and Haryana, whereas it is only 55% for UP, the largest wheat producing state, and somewhat better at 74% for MP. Tis also helps Punjab and Haryana become the largest collection centre for food procurement operation of FCI (Food Corporation of India). Out of the total wheat procured by FCI, Punjab and Haryana together account for more than 60% (with only 28% share in production). In contrast, procurement stands at less than 10% for UP despite accounting for almost 30% of domestic wheat production.

The yield difference is even greater in case of rice. While Punjab has yield of close to 4,000 kg/ha, Andhra and Haryana stand close to 3,000 kg/ha whereas Chhattisgarh, considered the rice bowl of India, has yield of 1,700 kg/ha, a little over 40% of the yield in Punjab! Marketed surplus as a percent of total production stands at 90% for Punjab, same as in case of wheat, and 85% for Haryana. In contrast, it is less than 70% for UP and West Bengal, the two largest rice producing states.

However, the difference in yields is only one of the problems facing domestic agriculture. Another one being differential access to the government procurement centre between large and small producers. As per an IIM Ahmedabad 2015 report based on field survey, while medium and large farmers (> 4 ha) managed to sell over 90% of the marketed surplus to government agencies - which offer greater price protection - small farmers could sell only about 25% to government agencies for both wheat and rice. This is largely because small farmers borrow money from these village level traders and are under obligation to sell majority of their crop to them.

As a mitigation measure, CACP recommends increasing procurement from small and marginal farmers and review open ended procurement policy from other farmers (such as a ceiling of procurement of up to 2 hectares). This would also help FCI, grappling with total food stock almost four times the minimum, manage its stock better. A point to note is that medium and large farmers account for 36% of farmers in Punjab as per the IIMA report against 10-12% for rest of the country. Indeed, it is time to classify small and large farmers separately, much like in case of manufacturing sector, design incentives to protect the small farmers and let others evolve as per the market. It is quite likely that the farmer bills appeared as a threat to assured procurement, leading to widespread protest in the state and eventually, repeal of the bills.

A comforting result of IIMA's report is that there isn't much variation in yields based on the size of landholding. (In fact, in some cases, large fields have recorded lower yields than small fields). While this is contrary to perception, there could be reasons for the same such as more intensive cropping in small fields, more careful monitoring etc. This helps small farmers also generate significant amount of marketed surplus. While small and marginal farmers managed to sell nearly 70% of their produce, the figure stood at 77% for semi-medium (2-4 ha), medium and large farmers.

While capping the procurement is an important recommendation, another important recommendation of CACP is giving greater thrust to PDPS and PPSS, (Price Deficiency Payment Scheme and Private Procurement & Stockist Scheme). Under PDPS, the difference between market price and MSP is directly paid to farmers and under PPSS, private agency procures crops from farmers at MSP and fixed service charges is paid to the agency. The schemes are similar to PPP (public Private Partnership) model introduced for execution of infrastructure project and can save government from having to procure large amount of food grains as well as reduce the burden of administering the entire process.

| | Yield (qtl/ha) | Yield/ potential | Production (mn tons) | Surplus (mn tons) | Surplus/ production | Share in total FCI procurement |
|---|---|---|---|---|---|---|
| Punjab | 49.9 | 94% | 18.2 | 16.1 | 89% | 33% |
| Haryana | 46.2 | 90% | 12.1 | 9.7 | 81% | 19% |
| Rajasthan | 33.4 | 66% | 10.5 | 8.2 | 78% | 6% |
| U.P. | 32.7 | 68% | 32.0 | 17.6 | 55% | 9% |
| M.P. | 29.9 | 60% | 18.6 | 13.7 | 74% | 33% |

The five states account for 85% of wheat production. Source – CACP

*****

# Indian Rupee – Is It Appreciating or Depreciating?

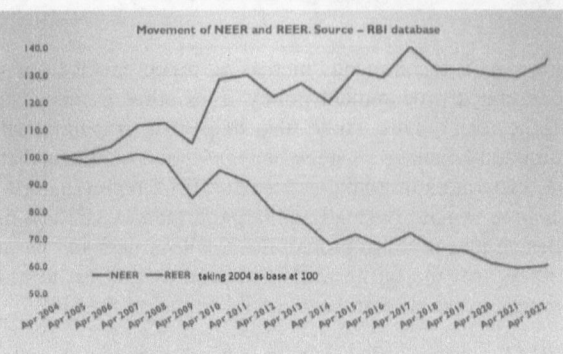

The rupee has depreciated by about 6% against the dollar in the first six months of 2022. Over last ten years, it has depreciated by over 35%. This is against the hypothesis that Indian currency is overvalued reducing the competitiveness of Indian exports. However, there is a point in what they say. An attempt to understand that.

In a free market economy, markets are expected to auto-correct and if a currency is overvalued, price of the goods produced by the country in terms of global currency would increase. This would lead to decline in exports and increase in imports leading to a trade deficit. This would increase the cost of foreign currency (say, dollar) or depreciation of the local currency. This would stabilize at a level so that domestic prices are aligned with global prices.

The other factor which dictates the exchange rate is difference in inflation rate between the trading economies. Assume exchange rate of Rs 70 per dollar on a particular day and a product costing one dollar or Rs 70. A year later, due to inflation, the product costs Rs 77 in India but costs only $1.02 in US (assuming inflation of 10% and 2% respectively). This implies an arbitrage opportunity whereby a trader can import the product from the US at Rs 71.4 ($1.02* 70) and sell at Rs 77. So, for an equilibrium, the exchange rate should move to Rs 75.5 per dollar (77/1.02).

However, things are not that simple. Other than the trade, currency flow also happens on capital account which is transaction in the form of FDI, FII, ECB etc. If inflow on capital account is more than trade deficit, there would actually be an appreciation of local currency. For instance, over five years between FY15-19, India received net capital inflow of $312 bn against trade deficit (current account deficit) of about $170 bn implying excess of dollars which would drive up the rupee. The two opposite forces lead to an exchange rate which shows a depreciation from year ago but is actually an appreciation after excluding the impact of inflation on product price or on real price basis.

This forms the crux of Nominal Effective Exchange Rate (NEER) and Real effective Exchange Rate (REER), widely used by RBI to track exchange rate movement. NEER is derived by calculating the composite value of rupee against the basket of currencies with which the country trades with each currency getting a weight equal to its share in the total trade. REER is calculated by taking the price of basket of product in each market and then calculating the exchange rate. In the above example, assuming a single product trade, REER after one year would be price of product in rupee terms divided by price in dollars terms which is 77/1.02 or 75.5.

However, if exchange rate settles at Rs 74 per dollar, then in nominal terms, the rupee has depreciated by 5.7% (74/70-1) but REER has actually appreciated by nearly 2% (74/75.5 - 1). Thus, the cost of pen would become $1.04 (77/74) in the international market, costlier than global price of $1.02, reducing its competitiveness. In other words, it has not depreciated as much as it should have, to maintain the product competitiveness.

This brings us to the actual performance of the rupee. As per RBI data, since 2004, 6-currecny NEER has depreciated by as much as 40% whereas REER has appreciated by about 35%. Over last ten years, even though rupee has depreciated by about 35% against dollar, REER has actually appreciated by 11% (the product price has increased by 13% in global currency terms) implying the pressure on exports.

Yet, trade performance is not completely aligned with REER movement. There are a large variety of other factors such as price movement of individual product, improving productivity, tariff barriers etc. Further, companies exporting services actually quote the price on dollar basis which protects their competitive edge from exchange rate movement. In the longer run, India's inflation rate should come down to global average which would arrest the divergent movement of NEER and REER.

*****

# Food Corporation of India – Managing Inefficiencies

Actual stocks of grains (as on July 1st) with public agencies vis-a-vis Buffer stock norms  Source - HLC on restructuring FCI

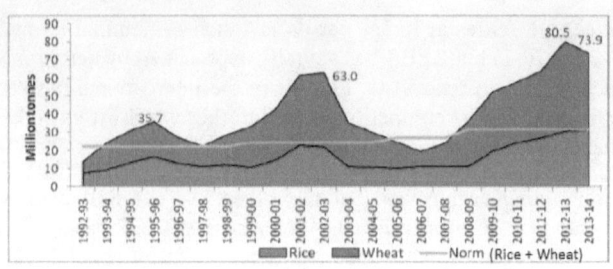

The FY21 budget increased allocation to FCI (Food Corporation of India) to Rs 3.44 lakh crore as subsidy against initial allocation of Rs 78,000 crore. The objective was to clear part of its past overdue. The financial management adds to the woes of the behemoth on top of the mammoth operation of food procurement, storage, and distribution. A look at the economics of FCI's operations.

FCI was set up in 1965 to tackle the huge food scarcity India was facing. Its key objective is procurement of food grains from the farmers at the minimum support price (MSP) and its distribution through PDS (Public Distribution System) as per government's policies and programmes. Other than that, it is also required to maintain a strategic buffer stock to meet any exigency. This buffer stock helped it step up distribution of additional food grains during Covid-19 lockdown months with total sales of close to 750 lakh tons against sales of less than 500 lakh tons in a usual year. Even though it is managing a critical task, it faces significant revenue gap because of high cost of procurement, additional cost of handling & distribution and subsidized sale. For FY21, as per the data available on its site, while procurement cost (MSP) of wheat was Rs 1,865 per quintal (100 kg), it incurred additional cost of Rs 874 per qtl during procurement and distribution. In case of rice, the additional cost was Rs 1,320 per qtl on top of MSP of Rs 2,790, implying other expenses accounting for a significant share of 32% in total cost of procurement.

FCI realises only Rs 457 in case of wheat and Rs 392 for rice as per the government mandated price, implying realisation of only 17% and 10%. The realisation is down from about 22% in FY15, adding to the burden on FCI. As a result, it faces revenue gap of Rs 2,283 and Rs 3,607 for wheat and rice. With total sales as stated above, total subsidy works out to Rs 2.22 lakh crore, which needs to be provided by the central government. The revenue gap has risen sharply from less than Rs 90,000 crore in FY14, after the passage of National Food Security Act (NFSA) which mandates subsidized food grains to 67% of total population.

The sharp increase in funds requirement for food management has forced government to meet the needs through off-balance sheet sources. Instead of government budgetary support, FCI is provided financial support from NSSF in the form of loan. FCI's outstanding loan has increased from less than Rs 90,000 at the end of FY16 to Rs 4.1 lakh crore by 31st Jan'21, almost 80% of this coming from NSSF. (However, a significant part of this would get paid back before the end of current financial year with the revised outlay as stated above).

Other than procurement and distribution, FCI is also incurring significant cost in holding excess buffer stock. Government mandates FCI to maintain a minimum stock of food grains to ensure food security. The norms currently stand at 41 million tons in July every year and 21 mn tons during other quarters. Against this, FCI had a stock of over 100 mn tons (including un-milled paddy) in Jul'20. Even after all the additional food grains distributed last year, the lowest stock level reached was 71 mn tons before the fresh procurement began and has crossed 95 mn tons again in Feb'21. (All figures as per FCI's website). This is a serious deficiency leading to significant cost of holding and also deterioration in quality of food grains. Government shows reluctance to sell this stock, either in open market or through exports, since open market prices are low. However, a sensible decision would be to off-load this even if it involves a revenue gap just as in case of sale through PDS. A suggestion on these lines was made by the rice exporters association recently. A rough calculation means government could fetch about Rs 1 lakh crore by off-loading half of this stock.

However, not all is well with FCI. As per a high-level committee (HLC) set up in 2014 to recommend ways to reduce FCI's losses, huge amount of food grains allotted for PDS is being diverted for open market sale. HLC estimates the leakages to the tune of 46% at national level going up to as much as 88% in some states. HLC has suggested reducing the coverage from current 67% of population to 40% who are actually vulnerable. HLC has also suggested removal of subsidized sale altogether and cash transfer through direct benefit transfer (DBT) in a phased manner which could have even more far-reaching consequences.

Other than this, FCI also suffers from considerable inefficiency arising as a result of being an unwieldy, mammoth organizational structure. HLC has recommended handing over the task of procurement to some of the state governments and only take possession of surplus grains to be transported to other regions. HLC further makes note of the fact that FCI's procurement is benefiting only about 6% of small farmers and recommends focusing on eastern states where most small farmers live. With huge amount of buffer stock already lying with it, it would have to reduce its procurement from Northern region for this, a fear, possibly, behind the farmers' agitation.

\*\*\*\*\*

# Government Debt – Analyzing the Movement

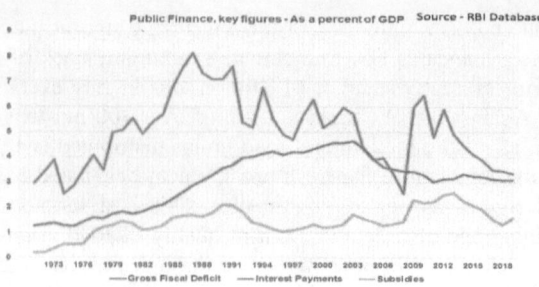

Public Finance, key figures - As a percent of GDP   Source - RBI Database

Apart from the loss of lives and livelihood, the pandemic has also impacted government finances immensely. By the end of FY23, central government's debt is projected to be higher by over Rs 50 lakh crore over its level at the end of FY20. As a percent of GDP, a critical parameter to gauge the capability of a nation to manage its debt, this would shoot up from 51.5% to 58.9% during this period. A look at the status of government's borrowings and related issues.

As per the budget documents, central government's total liabilities would reach Rs 152 lakh crore by the end of FY23. This comes about with fiscal deficit or excess of expenditure over revenue of Rs 18.2 lakh crore, Rs 15.9 lakh crore and Rs 16.6 lakh crore (projected) during FY21 to FY23, total of Rs 50.7 lakh crore in three years. In contrast, combined fiscal deficit for FY13 to FY20 stood at about the same level of Rs 52.4 lakh crore. (However, a more correct assessment would be to take note of the fact that about Rs 4 lakh crore of pre-FY20 off-budget deficit has been added to government deficit in FY21-23). The current debt movement, although unavoidable, is a reminder of the government finances before 2000s, a period of profligacy. During FY80-90, central government's debt rose by as much as 19.4% CAGR, which came down to 14% in FY90-2000 and 12% and 11% in subsequent decades. The increase for FY20-23 stands at 13.9%, close to Pre-2000 level.

Higher government's borrowings have been aided by the fact that there is limited demand for loans from the private sector (both retail and corporate). As per RBI database, total loans extended by banking sector to the private sector stood at Rs 103 lakh crore at the end of FY20 which is same as total government debt in that year. This has increased only marginally to Rs 114 lakh crore at the end of Jan'22. Based on current growth rate, this may remain around Rs 120 lakh crore at the end of FY23 in contrast with government debt of more than Rs 150 lakh crore.

This raises an important question – does government borrowings 'crowd-out' private investment? While literature keeps talking about the same, the critical determinant is to understand whether private investment is happening in the economy or not during that time. So, if private investment is not happening (as is the case now), government borrowings actually act as a support and may 'crowd-in' private investment by boosting demand/ consumption. The problem would occur if private borrowings start increasing and government is not able to manage its finances.

Increasing government debt affects four related parameters - government's interest payments, interest payments as a percent of government's total expenditure, total debt as a percent of GDP and average cost of borrowings. (However, the last parameter would be affected by other factors also). During the 80s, interest payments rose by 22.7% CAGR which declined to 17.7% in 90s and further to 9% and 11% in the subsequent decades. Interest payments as a percent of total government expenditure stood at 14% in 1980s, which rose to as much as 30% by late 90s and currently stands at about 23%. It may be noted that higher outgo on interest payments severely constrains government ability to spend on productive projects. The impact of reduced spending on interest rate is evident from the fact that tighter government spending after 2000 helped bring down rate of interest in the economy. Average cost of government borrowings had risen to as much as 8.3% in late 90s which is not down to about 6.5%. While the difference doesn't look too much, it may be noted that government would have paid additional interest of nearly Rs 3 lakh crore based on the interest rate of 1990s!

Government's indiscriminate spending and the foreign exchange crisis of 1991 led to implementation of some tough measures. Two of these were discontinuation of printing of money to finance government's deficit also called monetization of deficit and FRBM Act (Fiscal Responsibility and Budget Management). The Act mandates central government to limit its fiscal deficit to 3% by end of FY21 and reduce its debt to 40% of GDP by end of FY25. In view of the pandemic, FY21 budget invoked the clause allowing government to breach the limit.

Other than central government, state governments also borrow a significant to meet its needs. As per RBI database, this was budgeted at Rs 60 lakh crore at the end of FY21, almost half of central government debt. While state governments were less profligate till 80s, their debt started to rise faster after that, possibly a result of rise in state level leaders and greater friction between center and state. Share of state governments in total debt has risen from less than 30% till 90s to 36% now. The finance commission has expressed serious reservation about freebies being extended by state governments and has recommended punitive measures in case of breach of debt ceiling.

Other than restricting the aggregate debt, government's performance in managing external borrowings has been more impressive. External borrowings, which were rising at 18-20% rate till mid-90s, fell sharply to single digit subsequently and is less than 5% now. As a share of total debt, it now stands at less than 5%, sharp reduction from a high of 26% in 1992.

*****

# Analyzing Jobs Lost During Covid-19 - PLFS Survey

The periodic labour force survey (PLFS) data for April-June'20 quarter, the peak lockdown months, gives a comprehensive view of the extent of job losses. As per the survey, urban unemployment rate reached a level of 20.9% during the quarter. The dis-aggregated figures reveal that stress was as high as 59% for specific segment at state level. A look at some of the details.

PLFS is a quarterly report based on actual survey, started in April'17, done by NSO (National Statistical Office) to assess the actual status of employment. Other than quarterly report which gives details of urban area only, the annual report gives status across both urban and rural India. The latest survey, conducted during April-June'20 was unusual since part of the survey was done telephonically due to Covid-19 restrictions.

Before looking at the data, it would be pertinent to understand some of the terminologies. The first is *Labour force participation rate (LFPR)* which refers to the percent of the population which is employed or is looking for a job opportunity. The second is *Unemployment rate (UR)* defined as the percentage of unemployed persons as a percent of LFPR. As per PLFS definition, a person is unemployed if he/she did not get work for even one-hour duration over previous one week. Worker Population Ratio (WPR), defined as the percentage of workers in the total population, can be deduced from the above two ((1-UR)*LFPR). Only current weekly status (CWS) has been estimated and usual status which taken into account one-year period is not included in this survey.

The unemployment rate (UR) for the quarter at 20.8% with UR for females being marginally higher than males. This implies one out of every five urban individual seeking employment did not get a job. (All figures for population above 15 years of age). The figure is more than double the average of 8.5% in the previous four quarters. Not only did UR increase sharply, even LFPR fell, although slightly from 48.1% to 46%. Lower LFPR is also a reflection of economic stress as lesser individuals seek job when they perceive that chances of getting a job are low. (An unusual feature of Indian economy is that female LFPR is very low, averaging around 20% against 73% for males). With an increase in UR and decline in LFPR, WPR ratio came down sharply from 43.7% to 36.4%. Assuming average life-span of 65 years and population evenly distributed, population above 15 years of age works out to 100 crores. Change in WPR implies more than 7 crore people lost their jobs during the quarter. It must also be noted that as per the definition, a person is considered employed if he/she got even one-hour of job during the previous seven days. If the definition is made more rigorous to consider at least one day of employment, UR rate could worsen considerably.

The high UR figure, still, does not reveal the complete picture. For the age group 15-29 years, UR was as high as 34.7%, meaning every third person in this group was unemployed. Worst hit among major states in this age group for males were Jharkhand with UR going up from 21% to 52%, Maharashtra – 12 to 47%, Telangana – 28% to 41% and Andhra Pradesh - 33% to 49%. Only state to offer some relief was Gujarat where UR went up only marginally from 8.5% to 12%. For Females, worst hit was Karnataka with UR going up from 14% to 45% and Kerala from 48% to as high as 59%. Job losses is higher for this group possibly because of higher temporary engagement as trainees/ interns etc. However, unemployment within this groups is bigger concern as this, possibly, is the most productive age-group as far as blue-collared jobs are concerned. Not finding suitable avenue to channelize this resource is a great loss for the economy.

The report analyses data from many dimensions offering important insights. One of them is employment category and status in the current quarter vis-à-vis previous quarter giving information on group-wise job losses. The data shows that within males, casual workers were the worst hit with 58% of them either losing their jobs or going out of labour force. For other two groups, salaried and self-employed, share was 13% and 12%. Figures are worse for females at 65%, 19% and 31% respectively.

The inter-state analysis of data shows some more insights. LFPR fell significantly for industrialized states such as Gujarat, from 66.4% to 59.5%, possibly reflecting migration of labour. (It may be noted that industries' share in total employment in Gujarat is significantly high at 46% as compared to national figure of 34% (pre-Covid)). For Karnataka and Maharashtra, it fell from 58.8% to 53.1% and 54.2% to 50.9%. Some states such as Madhya Pradesh and Telangana saw increase in LPFR, possibly, as a result of returnees seeking jobs in their home state.

*****

# Has The Unemployment Rate Come Down? - Analyzing PLFS Report

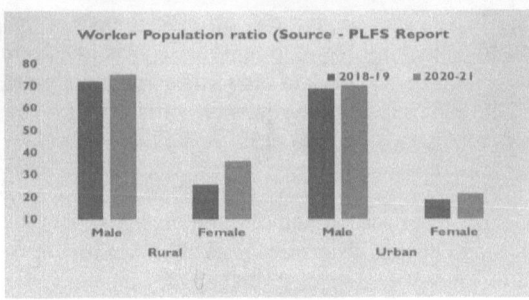

Periodic labour force survey (PLFS) for 2020-21 (July-June) shows that unemployment rate (UR) has declined over previous years. Amidst the raging pandemic, this appears counter-intuitive. So, has UR really declined or there is more to it than meets the eye. A look at the details explaining the same.

PLFS was started just four years back and is done by NSO (National Statistical Office) to gauge actual status of employment in India. The current survey is fourth in the series and covered over 4.1 lakh respondents. As per the report totaling over 750 pages, UR stood at 4.2% in 2020-21, lower than 4.8%, 5.8% and 6.1% respectively in previous three years. UR is defined as number of people seeking jobs but unemployed divided by number employed plus those seeking jobs but unemployed. While the aggregate figure may look reasonable, the segregated data across male/females, rural/urban, youths and educational level shows that there are pockets with significantly higher stress. All figures are for population above 15 years of age.

Urban India faces greater stress with UR at 6.7% against 3.3% in rural area. Even within this, urban females face higher UR at 8.6% in contrast with 2.1% for rural females. Similarly, educated workforce (highest level of education secondary and above) faces UR of 9.1%, more than double the national average. The biggest concern is the high unemployment rate of 12.9% among the youths (age 15-29 years). In urban area, this goes up to 16.6% for males and as high as 25% for females. This means one out of four females belonging to 15-29 age group and living in urban India is unable to get a job. Interestingly, while urban female youths have higher UR than their male counterpart, it is reverse in case of rural female youths.

However, the bigger question is - has the aggregate UR really come down? A look at the distribution across three types of employment – self-employed, salaried and casual labour gives some hint at that. Between 2018-19 and 2020-21, percentage of self-employed has gone up from 51.7% to 54.8% in rural area and from 31.8% to 33.2% in urban area. On the other hand, salaried jobs have seen a dip, although marginally. This means whatever additional jobs have been created during the period, it is largely in the self-employed group. Further, higher share of self-employed jobs also affects the average earnings as total buying power of the economy would be largely constant. As per the report, while average earning of a self-employed person has risen by only 3.5% between 2019-21, it has increased by 11.7% for salaried people. (Adjusting for inflation, this implies a decline). Average earning of self-employed, which was 65% of the earning of salaried person, has further come down to 60% in 2021. This is the fallacy of declining unemployment. Even though UR has come down, it has come with a decline in quality of jobs with more people taking up self-employment and also, a decline in earnings.

Despite the decline in quality of job, greater number of people are seeking jobs now. This is reflected in increasing *Labour force participation rate (LFPR)* which refers to the percent of the population which is employed or is seeking a job. Between 2019-21, LFPR (for age 15 years and above) has increased from 50.2% to 54.9%, a sharp increase of 4.7%. This is a positive development as lesser individuals seek job when they perceive those chances of getting a job are low. Even though LFPR is a slightly complex term to understand, it is widely used to gauge actual unemployment. An easier term is Worker Population Ratio (WPR) defined as the percentage of workers in the total population. WPR for Indian economy (for age 15 years and above) rose from 47.3% to 52.6% during 2019-21. This means nearly 7.3 crores more person started earning in the economy (including self-employed) between 2019-21. (Assuming population of 135 crores in 2018-19, growing at 1% annually and 74% being above 14 years of age). With total households at 33.6 in 2021, average person employed per household goes up from 1.44 to 1.60.

A unique characteristic of Indian economy is that female participation in the labour force is very low. LFPR for males stands at 77% against only 32.5% for females. This is even worse in the urban area at 23.2% against 36.5% in rural area. As stated earlier, a higher UR for urban females implies lack of opportunities for them which pushes more females out of the labour force.

The survey gives lot of other information also. For instance, self-employment forms as much as 55% of employment in rural households against only 33% in urban area. Jobs with regular salary accounts for only 13% of jobs in villages against 42% in cities. This is another reason for greater distress in rural area. About 61% of rural workers are engaged in agriculture, either working on own farm or as casual labour, with the share going up to 75% for females. The figure is higher than 57.8% in 2018-19 implying increasing dependency on agriculture which is worrisome. Biggest employer in urban area is Trade, hotel and restaurant accounting for 25% share followed by manufacturing with 20% share.

In terms of salary, while salary of a rural male stands at Rs 14-16,000 per month, almost 30% lower than that for urban male at Rs 21,200. For females, salaries are much lower, Rs 9,400-10,700 for rural and Rs 16-16,700 for urban. The level of earnings for other two groups, casual labour and self-employed is significantly lower than salaried. A self-employed female in rural India earns only Rs 4,500 whereas male earns Rs 10.200.

Salary level of casual workers in rural India is also nearly same at Rs 8,400 for male and Rs 5,500 for females (assuming 25 days of work). Salary level of an urban female is nearly 80% that of males and only about 68% in rural India. The ratio is even worse in case of self-employed at 40-50%. While females are certainly underpaid, a part of the disparity is also because of the fact that many females work for smaller hours. Average hours worked by a female worker in a week stood at 37.8 hours, nearly 20% less than males at 47.2 hours.

Trivia - More than 57% of males worked for more than 48 hours in a week in urban India against 49% in rural India.

*****

# Inflation - Understanding the Constituents & Drivers

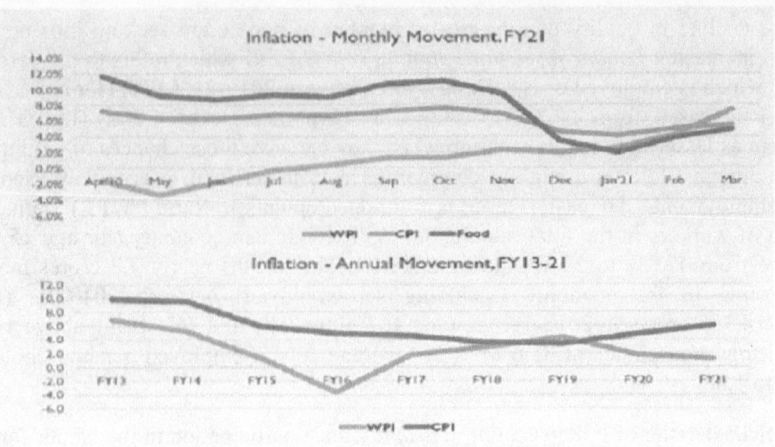

Domestic inflation remained high for second consecutive year with CPI inflation averaging 5.5% in FY22. WPI hit a record averaging almost 13%, not seen in over a decade. Russia-Ukraine war has completely disrupted food and fuel supply chain causing significant inflationary pressure. How things pan out over next few months and how policy makers handle growth-inflation trade-off would be keenly watched. A look at the movement of the inflation and its various components.

Inflation is measured by two main indices - CPI (Consumer price Index) and WPI (Wholesale price Index). While CPI primarily measures the price movement of consumption goods & services, WPI measures price movement of all goods produced in the economy. For FY22, average CPI inflation stands at 5.5%, lower than 6.2% in FY21 but still close to upper tolerance level of 6%. (Annual inflation is calculated as average value of monthly index divided by average value during the previous year). Monthly inflation for March'22 jumped to 6.95% from 6,07% in Feb'22, a result of the war. CPI inflation was relatively moderate in FY19-20 at 3.4% and 4.8%.

CPI index comprises of groups such as Food, Fuel & Light, Housing, Miscellaneous which includes health, education, transport etc. Food & fuel account for almost 60% of weightage in calculation. An important difference in inflation trajectory for the year was moderation in food prices (which, however, moved up sharply in March'22). Average food inflation for FY22 is down to 4.2% from 7.3% in FY21. However, Fuel group has played spoilsport, rising by 11.2% against 2.7% in FY21. Other items, though smaller in weightage, that have contributed to FY22 inflation are clothing, transport etc.

The bigger upset for the year is WPI which rose sharply to almost 13% from less than 2% for previous two years and almost double the previous peak of last nine years. All the three components of WPI - primary articles (PA), manufactured products (MP) and fuel & power

(F&P) recorded significant increase. While inflation in PA went up from 1.7% to 10.2%, MP rose from 2.7% to 11% and F&P, sharply from -8% to 33%. PA comprises of food, non-food (Oilseeds etc) and crude oil. Even though food prices haven't risen much at 4.1% against 3.1% last year, other items recorded very high inflation with oilseeds groups at 33%, up from 7% and crude oil group at 57%, reversal from -18% in FY21.

In contrast with CPI which is driven by food & fuel, WPI is primarily driven by MP which has a weightage of 65%. The increase in inflation for this group is more worrying as prices across this group were considerably stable with average inflation over last seven years being just 1.9%. That is more so as most of its components are considered as part of core inflation. Among the biggest contributor is basic metals at 26%, up from 5%, Textiles at 15%, against -0.1% last year and chemicals at 13%. Even though most manufactured products face lower demand and lower capacity utilization, prices have recorded significant increase due to cost push led by commodity prices. For instance, iron ore prices have risen by as much as 55% against 13% last year.

A look at the monthly inflation rate shows a rather stable trend in both CPI and WPI. Monthly CPI inflation moved within a band of 2.7% against average of 4% over previous two years. WPI moved within a band of 4%, 10.7% to 14.9% against as high as 11% band, -3.4% to 7.9% in Fy21.

The longer-term trend (FY13-22) shows re-emergence of price pressure which remained subsided till FY20. CPI, which stood at over 9.5% in FY13-FY14, came down to average of 4.2% during FY16-20 and has moved up again to 5.8% over last two years. WPI, which averaged 6% in FY13-FY14, came down sharply to 1.4% during FY15-21 but has surged back to 13% in FY22. Under the current environment of a still existing ultra-loose global monetary policy environment, exacerbated by the war, it may be tough time for Indian, indeed, global policy makers.

*****

# Purchasing Power Parity (PPP) – An Overview

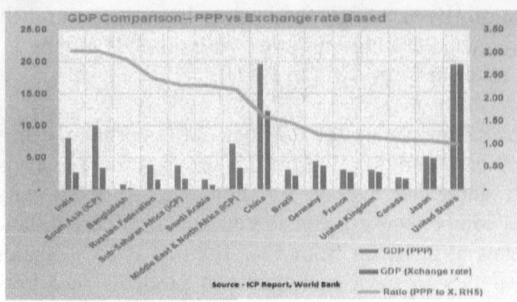

Purchasing Power Parity (PPP) is an important economic concept, requiring significant efforts to arrive at an authentic value. World Bank carries out an extensive exercise, called International Comparison Program (ICP), to get a fair value and understand where different economies are placed. As per the latest report released in May'20, covering economic performance for year 2017, global GDP stood at $119.5 trillion, nearly one and half time the exchange rate based GDP of $79.7 trillion. Here is a brief analysis of the report and issues surrounding PPP.

The concept of PPP originates from the fact that purchasing power of a dollar is different across different economies as price of a good or service (especially, services) is different. This does not get captured in GDP converted from local currency to dollar based on market exchange rate. For instance, a doctor's fees in India could be say, Rs 1,000 which would translate to about $13 on exchange rate basis. However, the fees in US or other developed economies would be much higher than that. This necessitates a measure which could capture the 'value' each dollar provides. ICP attempts to do the same by eliminating the impact of price differential. Apart from measuring relative size of the economy, this also helps in measuring the level of well-being of population.

As per the ICP report, China had the highest GDP at $19.6 tr, marginally higher than USA at $19.5 tr. Exchange rate based (termed nominal in this article) GDP for China stood at $12.3 tr implying that aggregate prices in China are 0.63 times that calculated by exchange rate (12.3/19.6). Nominal GDP for USA is same as PPP as the dollar serves as the benchmark. India stands as third largest economy with GDP PPP of $8.05 tr. Nominal GDP for India during 2017 was only $2.65 tr, implying price level of 0.33 times only. That is essentially the reason why India is an attractive destination for variety of services. India is followed by Japan, Germany and Russia in PPP ranking.

The ICP is one of the largest data collections initiative involving 176 countries. The last exercise was carried out in 2011. The exercise collected price level of as many as 17 expenditure components across all countries and standardized it to one scale to arrive at the purchasing power parity of each currency. *As per the report, among all the expenditure items, health and education showed maximum contrast being cheapest at 0.26 and 0.38 times the global average in South Asia against 1.76 and 2.61 times in North America.* As per the report, even though Gini Coefficient, the measure of inequality, has come down marginally, 74% of world population lives in countries where per capita consumption expenditure is less than the global average, increase from 70% in 2011.

But why does the price level differ so significantly. A reason is that developing and under developed economies operate with lower level of wages & salaries. This gets built into the prices of services such as medical, education, even real estate and so on. As economy grows and income level increases, cost of services also increase, leading to overall increase in price level. As a result, variation between PPP and exchange rate based GDP diminishes as the economy grows. For Japan, third largest economy by nominal measure, PPP GDP is only 1.06 times the nominal GDP whereas for UK, it is 1.14 times. The underpriced market of developing economies is also reflected in the fact that, middle income economies, which accounted for only 36% of global GDP in exchange rate terms, have a higher share of 50% in PPP terms.

However, despite this, the difference in per capita income between developed, developing and under-developed remains significantly high. Per capita income for upper-middle, lower-middle and low-income countries stands at 33%, 13.5% and 3.5% of high-income countries respectively. (The ratio is 20%, 5% and 1.7% on exchange rate basis). In terms of individual countries, Luxembourg had the highest GDP per capita at over $112,700, 6.8 times the world average whereas Burundi had the lowest at $784, 0.05 times the world average.

As a result of low level of income, under-developed countries have to spend most of it on basic needs such as food and are left with very little resource to spend on social or physical investment. For instance, Sub-Saharan Africa, having 45 countries, accounted for 3.1% of global GDP but their share in global expenditure on food & non-alcoholic beverages was as high as 8% whereas the share in capital formation was only 1.9%. The region could spend only 15% of its GDP on capital formation against global average of 24%.

*****

# Producer Price Index (PPI) - Is It Better Than WPI?

Inflation is core of any discussion on economic & policy issues. This also prompts economists to strive to find as precise a measure of inflation as possible. While India still follows WPI (Wholesale Price Index) as the benchmark, most of the developed economies follow another index called Producer Price Index (PPI). To align with global best practices, a committee was constituted to look at the issue and help economy transition to PPI. Here is a look at the same and its utility based on the committee's report.

The concept of PPI is not new as it has been adopted across most of the developed nations for decades now. PPI, as the name suggests, is the price that producer gets or the price of the product as it leaves the factory. In contrast, WPI measures the price of the product as it reaches the market which includes freight cost, trade margins, taxes etc. As a result, even if the core price of product does not change, WPI gets impacted if there is a change in cost/rate of these items. For instance, a reduction in tax rate to boost production would give a false sense of decline in WPI. However, this will not impact PPI.

Another gain from PPI is that it eliminates the problem of double counting inbuilt in WPI calculation. For instance, consider a price index consisting of price of steel and machinery. Assume a machine is sold for Rs 80,000 after using 1 ton of steel priced at Rs 40,000. If the price of steel goes up by 10% to Rs 44,000 per ton, cost of machine will go up to Rs 84,000 assuming everything else remains same. The price index in this case will incorporate 10% change in steel as well as 5% change in machine thus leading to double counting of same price change. PPI will only count price change of machinery (PPI final) and price change of steel will be reflected in PPI input only. The anomaly is similar to 'tax on tax' issue which existed before GST as taxes paid during procurement gets added to the cost and was also taxed at subsequent stages.

While PPI has a number of methodologies for calculations, the one being proposed in India involves calculation of two PPIs - PPI input and PPI final. Some of the developed countries also have PPI Intermediate. Goods which are used only in the input stage do not find place in PPI final (unlike in case of WPI). Thus, if rise in PPI final is same as PPI intermediate, it would imply price pressure at intermediate stage and not final stage. There are several other PPIs calculated across the world such as PPI Investment goods, PPI consumer durable goods, PPI consumer non-durable, PPI energy etc. PPI would also include services such as banking, airways, insurance, wholesale and retail trade, road transport, postal etc which are not included in WPI.

Still, the most important use of PPI is in calculation of GDP and Gross Value Added (GVA). As per the current practice, GVA at constant prices is derived by dividing GVA at current prices (which is gathered from the market) with a relevant price index. The method assumes that input and output prices for an industry change at the same rate called single deflation approach. However, this is rarely so and correct method is to divide output at current price by output PPI and input by input PPI. This is called double deflation approach followed across most of the economies globally. Thus, under PPI, each product will receive price inputs of as many as 108 different product and 15 services for calculating its input PPI. For instance, PPI input for 'construction' would be calculated by taking prices of cement – 9.3% weightage, industry wood - 5.1%, Iron, steel and its products - 30% (split into three different groups), non metallic minerals

& its products - 15.6% (split into two groups), real estate services – 7.1% and so on. In another instance, "Hotels & Restaurants" would have a weightage of 3% on input price calculation of "Air transport".

A look on the past values of PPI inflation, as given in the report, shows that PPI inflation shows lesser variance as compared to WPI inflation. During FY13-FY17, variance for WPI was 16.6 against only 10.7 for PPI. While WPI varied from 6.9% to -3.6% (range - 10.6%), PPI varied from 6.3% to -1.6% only (range - 7.8%). As mentioned earlier, this is due to double counting in WPI which accentuates the impact of any price change. However, the variance is higher in cases of primary sectors such as farming, fishing and mining which is quite perplexing. One reason could be changes in tax rates, trade margin etc because of which, WPI does not reflect the core inflation.

*****

# Understanding Rural Income Pattern

Average income level of a rural household is just about one-fifth the national per capita income as per a NSO (National Statistical Office) survey. More concerningly, the bottom 20% of the population fare much worse. The saving grace is that average debt level is just about 60% of annual income and almost 70% of it is coming from institutional sources. This is sharp turnaround from the times when local moneylenders called the shots. An attempt to look at the details of the survey.

NSO carries out a variety of surveys, called National Sample Survey (NSS), to assess the ground situation related to a specific aspect of the economy. The current survey was carried out under 77th round, which included two subjects, landholdings and indebtedness of rural agriculture households, surveyed separately until then. Information from 58,000 households were collected for the survey.

The survey classifies rural India into two categories based on the primary source of income - agricultural households (AH), those dependent upon farming as primary course of income and non-agricultural households (NAH). As per the survey, there are a total of 17.2 crore households in rural India of which, 9.3 crore or 54% are classified as AH. However, the dependency of rural economy on agriculture is higher than this because almost 50% of NAH work as casual labour, most of them, on large farms. The survey analyses the income pattern of agricultural households only.

As per the survey, average income earned by an AH is Rs 10,218 per month, increase of nearly 8% CAGR since the last survey six years ago. (While the survey doesn't give information on income of NAH, it is about 18% lower than AH as per another survey done by NABARD). With average of 4.5 members per household, per capita income works out to just about Rs 27,000 per annum, almost one-fifth that of national average per capita income of Rs 125,000. The problem is compounded by the skewed pattern of distribution. Income for households having landholding between 0.01 and 1.00 ha was only Rs 7,522, just 12.5% that of landholders with more than 10 ha of land. More concerningly, almost 20% of households earned as little as Rs 2,500 per month or Rs 560 per person per month as per another survey carried out by NABARD two years before this one.

While the households are classified as agricultural, they do not generate all of their income from agriculture, as some members could also be engaged in other trade. As per the dis-aggregation, an average household receives only about 40% of income from crop production whereas another 40% is received as wages and 16% from livestock farming. The share of crop production in total income has declined from about 50% in the last survey. This is actually a healthy trend as it points to diversification and reduces the vulnerability of households to crop failure.

An interesting aspect of the survey is that households with less than 0.01 ha landholding have higher income than those with 0.01-1.00 ha, aided by higher wages and receipt from live stocks. It appears that <0.01 ha group is spending significant amount of time in other activities which is supplementing their crop income whereas 0.01-1.00 ha group is focusing more on farming where the incremental earning is limited. Other than the poor earnings, the other unfortunate part of agricultural households is that despite being dependent upon agriculture as primary source of income, 70% of them own less than one hectare of land (equal to a plot measuring 100 meters by 100 meter). At the other end of spectrum are about 2 lakh rich households who have over 10 hectares of land, a significant share being in the state of Punjab and Haryana.

The survey also looked at the indebtedness of these households with nearly half of them being under debt. Average debt level stands at Rs 75,000. While the debt level is not huge, the problem arises because these households have very little savings and any exigency leads to significant increase in debt level. This is borne out by the fact that non-agriculture purpose such as education, medical, marriage, consumption etc accounts for more than 90% of loan taken by households with <0.01 ha land and 71% for 0.01-0.04 ha group. The silver lining is that almost 70% of debt is coming from institutional sources, saving them from usurious interest rate. Debt level ranges from Rs 27,000 for households with less than 0.01 ha to Rs 95,500 for those with 1-2 ha land, making 1-2 ha group more vulnerable.

It would be pertinent to recall some more of the findings of NABARD survey. As per that, NAH are more distressed than AH because their earnings is almost 20% lower. Another important finding of the survey was that that as much as 80% of NAH are dependent on only one person for their livelihood in contrast with only 13% in case of AH. Possibly, there is a need to prepare an independent strategy for NAH such as encouraging one member of these households to engage in livestock farming, dairying etc.

*****

# Farm Loan Waiver - Bad Politics or Good Economics?

Farm loan waiver has been a subject matter of considerable debate in the country. The mainstream media, economists from all strata and the RBI through its various reports seem to be severely critical of such moves which spoil the credit culture and lead to 'crowding out'. So, are the farm loan waivers really that bad? And does it really lead to so called 'moral hazard'? An attempt to look at the issue purely from an economic perspective without getting into the political aspects.

First thing first - As per the RBI report on state government finances, amount spent in loan waiver since 2014 is Rs 1.27 lakh crore. During the same period, banks have made provisions of close to Rs 4 lakh crore due to nonpayment of dues. Almost 90% of this is towards corporate loan accounts. This was not just a loss for the banks; central government had to infuse that much extra fund into these banks for recapitalization. This means corporate loan write-offs have caused more 'crowding out' than the loan waiver.

Second - Loans are waived only for small and marginal farmers with maximum outstanding loans being in the range of Rs 1-1.5 lakh only. In case of UP, the amount fixed was Rs 1 lakh only whereas in Andhra Pradesh, it was Rs 50,000 with loan between Rs 50,000 and Rs 1.5 lakh being waived over a period of five years. Average amount waived for each farmer in case of UP is Rs 56,000 only. This contrasts with corporate loan write-off where it is even as high as Rs 50,000 crore, enough to meet the needs of one crore farmers! (Lanco Infratech had outstanding principal amount of over Rs 44,000 crore when insolvency court directed liquidation of the company).

Third - Loans being waived are only short-term crop loan like working capital loan given to the industries. The waiver helps reduce the distress caused due to sharp drop in farm productivity and help the marginal farmer get loan to grow crop in the next season. If the loans are not waived, it may lead to even lower production, food scarcity and inflation in the subsequent years. Dr Pronab Sen, former chairman of Indian Statistical Commission, says in an article, "It is not just an ethical issue. It has economic consequence".

Loan waiver is often cited as undermining an honest credit culture, impact credit discipline and blunt incentives to repay. However, a default rate of 8% for agriculture loan against as high as 22% for corporate loan doesn't lend credence to that logic. In a damming rebuttal to this view, Dr Sen says, "Different aspects of this ominous view have been picked up by different interlocutors to create a new, frightening urban legend". Clearly urban India has not understood the dynamics of rural economy which still supports over half the country's population. It is even more important to understand this, since an average rural folk survives with an income nearly one-sixth that of urban India. Transfer of wealth in the form of Rs 50,000 per farmer carries more value for them than the write-off of Rs 50,000 crore of corporate loans.

This is not to say that loan waiver is a panacea for the ills facing rural economy. Bringing rural economy on par with the urban India, or anywhere close to it, is a challenge that the nation has been grappling with since independence. In the absence of any breakthrough, "farm loan waivers need to be viewed less ideologically and with more compassion", to quote Dr Sen.

*****

# Efficiency & Efficacy of MGNREGS

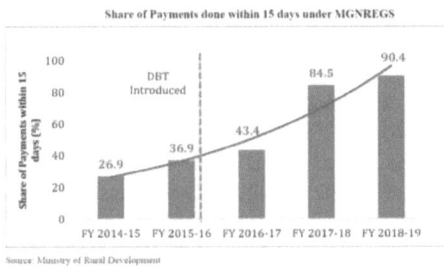

Source: Ministry of Rural Development

Among the issues covered by the Economic Survey in recent years is the gains arising out of technological intervention in MGNREGS (Mahatma Gandhi National Rural Employment Guarantee Scheme). The scheme has received even greater push with the technological interventions such as direct benefit transfer (DBT), Aadhar and more recently, Geo-tagging of assets. Even though MGNREGS has generated substantial controversies ever since its launch and continued debate on its benefits, its impact on rural economy cannot be ignored. A look at the scheme based on the economic survey report.

MGNREGS was launched in February 2006 as a measure to provide job security to rural households and reduce distress. The scheme envisages guaranteed employment of 100 days to any individual seeking the same. The scheme got an impetus with the focus on use of technology to reduce inefficiencies, much like in other government sponsored projects. These involved increasing the penetration of banking channel in rural India and deliver the benefits directly in the hands of the beneficiary. The thrust led to total banking outlets in rural India rising from around 1.15 lakh at the end of Fy14 to almost 5.7 lakh by end of FY18, as per the survey. (However, the need to bring rural India into the mainstream banking is not a new objective. Nationalization of banks, 50 years ago, was done precisely to expand banking to rural India, focused largely on urban India until then).

The expansion of banking network and opening of bank accounts was accompanied by linking the payments to Aadhar card in 2015. Other than eliminating 'ghost workers', it also helped reduce the payment cycle as central government could directly transfer funds to the bank account of the worker. This contrasted with the earlier system where funds moved from centre to state to district to block to panchayat and then, to the workers, thus leading to delays. As a result, e-payment has risen from 77% in FY15 to 99% in FY19. Out of the total 11.6 crore active workers, Aadhar data for about 88% of the workers have been seeded in MGNREGS database. (DBT has not only helped reduced leakages in this scheme but several others such as LPG and food subsidy. As per the DBT Bharat portal, central government has made estimated savings of over Rs 1.4 lakh crore on disbursement of over Rs 7.6 lakh crore through DBT so far).

Other than improving the delivery mechanism, technology is being used to verify the quality of assets being created through the scheme through geo-tagging. Geo-tagging, started in Sept'16, uses space technology to develop database of assets created under MGNREGS through mobile based photo geo-tagging and GIS based information system. As per the survey, nearly 3.6 crore projects out of 4.44 crore completed projects are already geo-tagged and available in the public domain. (However, the author was prompted to identify himself as related to MGNREGA in some capacity while searching for nearby projects through the app).

Even though the scheme was targeted to build productive capacity of the rural economy, it has lately evolved into individual beneficiary schemes (IBS); which serve the needs of individual instead of the entire community. (A significant part of Pradhan Mantri Awaas Yojana - Gramin (PMAY-G) is also being taken up through MGNREGS). The share of IBS has increased from about 21% in FY15 to over 66% in FY19. The emphasis on IBS has improved the outcome substantially with improved quality of assets as well as higher income for the beneficiaries. However, it would be premature to state whether it is a desirable trend in the longer run.

While improvement in payment efficiency or quality of assets created is welcome, what distinguishes the scheme is its ability to reduce the distress in rural households. The survey points to two studies to make this point. In the first, it segregates rural blocks into two categories - those affected by drought as indicated by the level of rainfall and others. As per the survey, while enrolment increased by 19% in the blocks that were not affected by drought during a year, it increased by an enormous 44% in the blocks that were affected by drought. In another survey, it makes a pair of two adjacent blocks and based on their consumption expenditure, identifies local distress. (If ratio of consumption expenditure is high, one of the blocks is assumed to be facing distress). The survey shows that those blocks where consumption expenditure is low relatively to its neighbor, the demand for MGNREGS is high. It also showed that after the implementation of Aadhar linked payment, the demand for work rose by as much as 76% in the distressed area (as against 18% in non-distressed area). This indicates increasing recourse to MGNREGS in cases of distress; that being the ultimate objective of the scheme.

*****

# Analyzing India's Balance of Payment - I

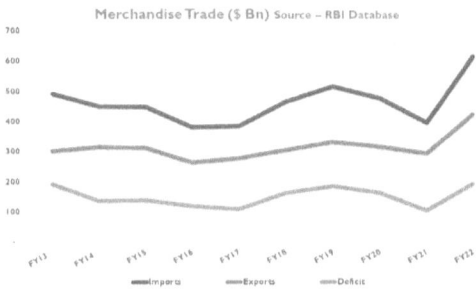

Merchandise Trade ($ Bn) Source – RBI Database

Despite having recorded significant growth in exports, India continues to record significant trade deficit. The objective of all the thrust being given to strengthen India's manufacturing capability through PLI, ease of doing business etc is to generate sufficient foreign exchange to meet our needs without creating future liability. So, what all does the foreign trade consists of and where is India spending the most. A brief attempt to delve deeper and track their performance over the years.

Foreign trade, also called balance of Payment, has a tedious multi-layered structure classified into two parts at the top level -

1. Current Account.
2. Financial or Capital Account.

Current account is further classified as -

a) Merchandise trade.
b) Invisibles.

**Merchandise Trade -**
Merchandise trade refers to trade of physical goods such as crude oil, gold, metals, electronics items etc. Among the major imports are crude oil, electronics items, machinery, gold etc. whereas major merchandise export item are refined petroleum, readymade garments, gems & jewelry.

As per RBI data, exports of merchandise goods stood at close to $429 bn in FY22. While this represents a sharp increase of 45% over FY21, increase in imports were even higher at 55%. Imports stood at $619 bn leading to deficit of $190 bn, 85% higher than last year. *Cumulative trade deficit stands at little less than $800 bn over last five years and $1.5 trillion over 10 years.* The deficit has to be financed by receipts from other sources including capital receipts or even borrowings as was being done before 1990s.

Goods traded as merchandise are classified across four levels based on their HS Code - 2-digit, 4-digit, 6-digit and 8-digit. The 2-digit level has close to 100 different items, 4-digit has about 1,000 items and 8-digit code has over 12,000 different items!

In terms of major items, crude oil (HS Code 2709, classified as petroleum oil) stands at top with imports of over $160 bn in FY22, one-fourth of total imports. However, India also exports significant amount of petroleum refined products which was valued at $67 bn during FY22. While imports of crude oil stand at $620 billion for last five years, exports stood at about $220 bn reducing the deficit on this count by that much amount. Another problem with crude oil is its high price volatility. Imports bill had crossed $160 bn in FY13 and FY14 as a result of high oil prices which came down to $82 bn in FY21 but again rose sharply in FY22. The fluctuation in oil prices put additional pressure on short-term forex management as there is no simultaneous increase in exports.

In terms of other items, electronic goods and gold stand at number two and three with import of $74 bn and $46 bn respectively. While gold imports have fluctuated between $56 bn in FY13 and $27.5 bn in FY17, electronic goods have seen a secular increase from barely $33 bn in FY13.

While imports of intermediate goods or machinery etc which add to the domestic productive capacity is desirable, imports of consumption goods such as electronic goods or non-productive items such as gold need a critical look especially as it is leading to a persistent deficit. It may be noted that India imported over $475 bn of electronic goods and $350 bn of gold in last ten years equal to over 55% of deficit during the period. In terms of exports, engineering goods have emerged at the top with exports of $122 bn, more than a quarter of total merchandise exports. This also corresponds to an increase of 45% over FY21. The other segments are petroleum refining, discussed earlier, and gems & jewelry with exports of $40 bn.

**Invisibles –**

Invisibles refer to trade in Services, Transfers (or remittances) and Income from abroad (dividends, salaries etc). Each of these segments comprise of large number of distinct sub-segments. Services comprises of Travel, Transport, Insurance, G.n.i.e. (government, not included elsewhere; An interesting category!) and miscellaneous. It is interesting to note that as per the international convention, software services and business consultancy services are not separate categories but included in miscellaneous. (The probable reason for that could be that these did not exist when the classifications were finalized). While India faces significant merchandise trade deficit, it generates a reasonable surplus as 'invisibles'.

*****

# India's Balance of Payment - II

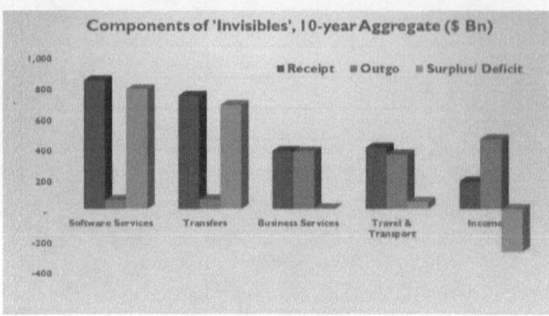

India recorded merchandise exports of $429 bn in FY22 against imports of $619 bn, leading to trade deficit of $190 bn. However, surplus on 'invisibles' account was $150 bn, reducing the current account deficit (CAD) to $40 bn.

During FY22, receipts (exports) under Invisibles stood at $370 bn, increase of 20% over previous year. This is quite impressive considering growth at 5.5% CAGR during FY16-21. Even though outgo (imports) under this head also grew at 21% reaching $219 bn, there was still a significant surplus of $150 bn. *The segment has generated surplus of nearly $650 bn in last five years, helping wipe out almost 80% of merchandise trade deficit.* Growth of IT and business services have helped considerably in improving India's balance of payment.

**Trade in Services -**

Trade in services comprises of Travel, Transport, Insurance, G.n.i.e. and miscellaneous. Most notable within this is software services (included within miscellaneous) with exports of $125 bn. The segment grew at a scorching pace of 23.5% CAGR during FY02-12 but witnessed a re-alignment during FY12-18, growing at just 3.7% CAGR. Momentum seems to be returning with 26% growth in FY22. While **business services** (also reported under Miscellaneous) also reported significant exports of about $60 bn, there is also imports outgo of $52 bn. Yet, FY22 has special significance for the segment as it generated a surplus for the first time. The segment, comprising of engineering & technical, management & consulting, trade related services etc, had grown at even faster pace than software during 2005-12 at almost 26%. The segment has a significant potential to generate forex considering India's excellence in knowledge services.

**Travel** and **Transportation** are other two services reported separately although total trade within these is not very significant. Combined receipts under the two was $50 bn in FY20 whereas outgo was $46 bn implying marginal surplus. Even though the segments, on combined basis, have recorded lower growth of 5.4% CAGR in receipts over last ten years (till FY20, before Covid) against growth in outgo of 6.4% CAGR, they continue to generate a modest surplus. However, travel faced the brunt of Covid-19 with receipts under this falling sharply to $9 bn in FY22 and $8.5 bn in FY21 from close to $30 bn in FY20. Interestingly, outgo hasn't declined so badly, down from $22 bn to $16 bn. Receipts within transportation services (primarily ocean freight) stood at $33 bn against outgo of $36 bn leading to a marginal deficit.

Transportation sector remained largely unaffected by Covid recording growth of 25% CAGR during FY20-22 in receipts and 21% in outgo.

**Transfers -**

Transfers comprises of official transfers such as donations to government agencies and private transfers such as remittances by NRIs. Total receipt under this head stands at $89 bn during the year whereas outgo is only $9 bn leaving a surplus of $80 bn. More than 90% of this is private transfers. After a decline of 1.5% CAGR during FY12-17, segment has grown at about 8% during FY17-22, possibly reflecting change in global economic environment. Private transfers have generated $675 bn of surplus over last ten years, second only to software services at $780 bn.

The third and the final category within invisibles is "**Income**". This refers to dividend, royalty, interest, profits repatriated etc by MNCs operating in India and compensation paid to expats based in India. This is the category which is servicing the capital investments (FDI, FII etc) received by India. Indian companies who have establishments abroad also earn income which is accounted as receipt. As per RBI data, payout to foreign cos and employees was $63 bn during the year whereas Indian companies and employees abroad earned income of $26 bn leading to deficit of $37 bn. Over last ten years, while income received has grown at 9.6% CAGR, outgo has grown at marginally lower rate of 7.1% CAGR. *Growth rate for the segment is significantly higher than that for other segments implying increasing global integration on capital account.* Total payments on this count stands at about $455 bn over last ten years whereas receipt is $180 bn leading to a deficit of $277 bn. The deficit is equal to almost 70% of deficit in crude oil trade. Clearly, the money received on capital account (FDI, FII) doesn't comes for free. Royalty and other payment to the global parent are regulated to manage this cost.

*****

# Capital Inflows – FDI, FII and the Rest

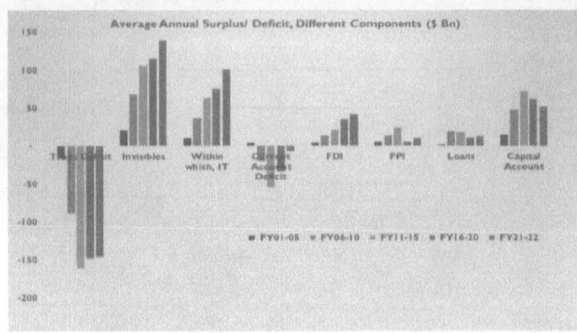

India's persistent current account deficit (CAD) is financed by the flow on capital account which forms the other part of international balance of payment. Some of the major elements of this are FDI, FPI, ECB etc. If there is a shortage on this count too, there will be a reduction in forex reserves leading to situation as seen in 1991. However, it must be understood that capital inflow is not free money and involves future obligation. A look at various component of capital flows and their flow pattern.

Capital flow comprises of following elements -

- Foreign investment.
- Loans.
- Banking Capital.
- Others.

Foreign investment is further grouped into -

a) Foreign Direct Investment (FDI)
b) Foreign Portfolio investment (FPI).

FDI is the money invested by global companies in Indian companies/ subsidiaries/ joint ventures etc. These are generally long-term investments. Portfolio investment or FPI is the money invested in the financial market, in buying shares or bonds. While there are two-way movement in case of current account trade, in case of capital account, it is four-way; investment (inflow) & repatriation (outflow) by global companies and investment (outflow) & repatriation (inflow) by Indian companies abroad. Thus, investments being done by Indian companies reduces the net FDI flow. Amount reported generally is gross FDI which is only the first. However, this consists of not just actual receipt but 'reinvested earnings' also.

During FY22, India received $84 bn of gross FDI which included $60 bn of equity inflow, $19 bn of 'reinvested earnings' and $5 bn of investment as debt. Repatriation was also quite significant at $29 bn leading to net FDI of $56 bn. This is almost the same as FY21 but higher than $78 bn in FY20. While annual growth of FDI has been erratic, ranging from -15% to 45%, average receipt during FY18-22 has been $73 bn against $46 bn during FY13-17, implying significant increase in momentum. Gross FDI over last ten years stood at about $600 bn, about 30% of which was repatriated leading to available balance of $430 bn.

In terms of global investment of Indian companies, gross outflow was $21 bn which includes $10 bn of equity investment, $3.4 bn of 'reinvested earnings' and $7.6 bn of debt investment. Repatriation was $3.4 bn leading to net outflow of $17.6 bn. Interestingly, average investment by Indian companies has come from $15.2 bn during FY13-17 to $10.2 bn during FY18-22 (unlike FDI inflow which increased). A possible reason for this could be stress on corporate balance sheet. Some important characteristics of Indian investment vis-à-vis global is higher share of debt, lower reinvested earnings (16% against 23%) and lower repatriation (16% vs 34%). Including Indian investment abroad and repatriation, total inflow stands at about $647 bn and outflow at $317 bn leading to net surplus of $330 bn over last ten years,

As compared to FDI, FPI flow is far more volatile and involves very high volume of inflow and outflow. While India recorded $386 bn of FPI inflow during FY22, the outflow was $400 bn leading to net deficit of $14 bn. The volume implies total trade of over Rs 60 lakh crore during the year! This is only the third occasion in last ten years when FPIs have been net sellers (although FY23 could be also see a net deficit). Participation by FPIs has increased significantly with inflow growing at 8.3% and outflow at 10.6% CAGR over last ten years.

Total FPI inflow over last ten years stands at staggering $2.61 trillion. However, substantial part of it has been taken out with outflow of $2.49 tr leaving net investment of only $126 bn or 4.8% of gross inflow. The figure needs careful consideration because the high volume of flow adds to the volatility of exchange rate and makes RBI's task of currency management more difficult. The role of FPIs in Indian capital markets has increased sharply over the previous decade when total inflows and outflows was only $0.8 tr and $0.7 tr.

The next item in Capital flow, Loan refers to external assistance received by the government, external commercial borrowings raised by corporate sector and short-term credit including trade credit. Banking capital refers to net forex assets of Indian banks minus net forex liabilities of foreign banks operating in India. These involves significant complexity and may be skipped at this stage. Total capital flow over last ten years stands at $5.8 trillion of inflow against $5.1 trillion of outflows leading to net inflow of $636 bn.

To sum up, India's trade deficit has increased sharply with annual average being just $16 bn during FY01-05 to $89 bn during FY06-10 and $161 bn during FY11-15. This has moderated marginally to $148 bn during FY16-20 and $146 during FY21-22. On the positive side, invisibles have steadily increased from $20 bn to $68, $106, $115 and $138 bn during the same period. Share of IT services has increased from 50% during FY01-05 to as much as 73% during FY21-22. Current account peaked at annual average of $55 bn during FY11-15 but stood at just $7 bn during FY21-22. On capital account, FDI flow has increased from $3 bn to $13, $21, $35 and $41 bn whereas FPI fluctuated, peaking at $24 bn during FY11-15 and fell sharply to $5 bn during FY16-20.

*****

# Analyzing India's External Debt Movement

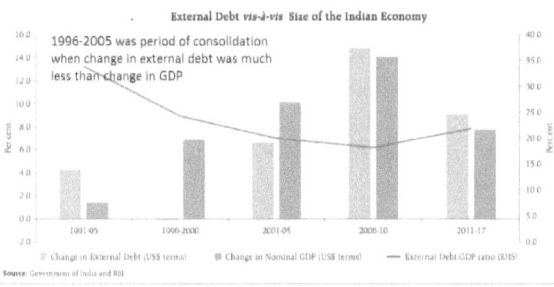

The depreciation in rupee-dollar exchange rate over last few months brings focus on India's vulnerability to sudden outflow of money. A component not looked closely is the level of India's external debt which has the potential to exacerbate the impact. While India's external debt has increased sharply over last ten years, there are several structural changes in its composition which reduces the vulnerability. A look at the details.

As per RBI data, India's total external debt stood at $620 bn at the end of March'22, up from $510 bn in Sept'18, $456 bn in Sept'14 and $113 bn in Sept'04. This corresponds to increase of 15% CAGR during 2004-14 which moderated to less than 3% during 2014-18 but has again increased to 5.7% between 2018-22. Of the total, borrowings (Loan & bonds) together account for $310 bn whereas NRI deposits accounts for $140 bn and trade credit for $120 bn. While NRI deposit would appear to be a reason for comfort, it is not exactly so since these have shorter tenure funds than other loans and comes with higher interest outgo. On the assets side, India's foreign currency reserves stood at $607 bn implying debt/reserves ratio of 102%. Debt/reserves ratio stood at 100% in 2004 which rose sharply to 150% by 2014 but has declined subsequently.

Even though the absolute level of debt has increased rapidly over recent years, its composition shows significant changes. The first, share of government debt in total debt has come down from 48% in 2000 to 20% by 2017 and remains at nearly the same level since then. This means most of the incremental debt is being raised by private sector and is backed by corporate balance sheets reducing the vulnerability. The declining share of government debt also gets reflected in declining share of concessional debt which has come down from 46% in 1991 to less than 20% by 2008 and less than 10% by 2015. Concessional debt comes with several pre-conditions and in some ways, impacts the sovereignty of the nation.

External debt causes higher vulnerability since the rupee liability associated with the debt keeps increasing with depreciation of rupee. For instance, a $100 loan raised when exchange rate was Rs 70 per dollar would require Rs 8,000 to be paid back if the rupee has depreciated to Rs 80 per dollar at the time of repayment. A mitigation measure for this is issue of rupee denomination external debt. This means instead of $100, the lender purchases rupee from domestic market and lends, let's say Rs 7,000. At the time of repayment, the borrower would not have to pay $100 but Rs 7,000. So, if the rupee has depreciated during the period (say, 80 per dollar), the lender would receive only $87.5. (Lenders make up for this by charging higher interest rate). Share of rupee denominated loan has gone up from 12% in 2000 to about 22% in 2015 and 31% by March'22. Rupee denominated loan has received a push after introduction of masala bond for corporate borrowers and rupee-based trade credit in 2015. Dollar denominated loan accounts for the highest share at 53% and is, therefore, the most tracked currency.

Yet another source of vulnerability is ratio of short-term debt to total debt. This is tracked on both original maturity as well as residual maturity basis. Based on original maturity, the ratio used to be fairly low at less than 5% till 2004 but rose to almost 24% by 2013. The same has subsequently declined to slightly less than 20% by FY22. It may be noted that short-term debt (original maturity)/forex reserves had risen to 146% in 1991 triggering the balance of payment crisis.

However, the ratio based on residual maturity is quite high at $268 bn or 43% of total debt and 44% of India's forex reserves. Trade credit at $120 bn accounts for nearly 45% of this. The ratio stood at 38% in 2008 but has risen to 42-43% level by 2015, possibly, a result of special efforts undertaken in 2013 to mobilize NRI deposits. This was done to minimize the pressure on rupee as a result of sudden outflow of dollars subsequent to 'taper tantrum'. As a percent of total reserves, short term debt (residual maturity) had gone up to 57% in 2016 due to redemption requirement of NRI deposits and came down to 53% by 2017.

The amount of short-term debt based on residual maturity implies average loan tenure of 3.4 years (total liability excluding trade credit, $500 bn/ total one year liability excluding trade credit, $148 bn). If the average tenure could be increased to 5 years, annual outgo should come down to $100 bn and total liability (including trade credit) to $220 bn. Certainly, RBI needs to encourage efforts to mobilize longer duration funds.

*****

# Finance Commission Report – The Formula for Devolution to States

The Finance Commission (FC) is an important constitutional body which determines the transfer of revenue from center to states and more importantly, fix a formula for the distribution of total pie among different states. Role of the commission is critical as most of the taxes are levied at the national level and states' own tax revenue is less than half of their expenditure. The devolution forms the bedrock of India's federal structure, giving states financial independence. A look at how the 15th Finance Commission arrived at the division and other details.

The term of the current commission was unique as it was required to submit one annual report for the year 2020-21 and another five-year report for financial year 2021-22 to 2025-26. In a departure from the past, FFC was also asked to review and consider performance-based incentives to motivate the efforts of State and/or local governments. The formula for devolution saw a marked change during 14th FC (2015-20) which raised the resource allocation to states from 32% to 42%. This was done to compensate for discontinuation of 'grants' that was made by planning commission. Abolishment of planning commission gave states access to more direct funds without any strings attached, freedom to spend as per their choices and provided greater transparency. The commission, this time, has reduced the share marginally to 41% to take care of the needs of J&K which would now be separately funded from the central kitty.

While the commission relied on past formula for 'vertical split', the bigger challenge was to devise the formula for horizontal split. The objective is to provide states sufficient resources to meet the basic needs of its population, yet, to reward overall performance of the state. Thus, six criteria have been chosen for inter-state sharing by the commission. These are population of the state, area of the state, per capital income relative to the state with highest per capita income (termed 'income distance'), forest cover, demographic performance and tax collection efforts. Weightage of these criteria are 15%, 15%, 45, 10, 12.5 and 2.5%. It may be noted while the first three criteria meet the first objective of providing resources, the other three reward performance. "Income distance" assigns highest weightage to states with lowest per capital income so that it catches up with rest of the nation. This criterion had a high weightage of 62.5% in 11th FC but has been getting reduced gradually to create space to reward progressive states.

The criteria which involve maximum deliberation is 'population' with 1971 census taken as the basis till the 13th commission. On the face of it, this does not take into consideration the increase in population thus putting more populous state with lesser resources. However, the other argument is that taking 2011 population as benchmark would put states which have controlled their population at a disadvantage. Thus, instead of getting rewarded, they get penalized. To strike a balance, 14th FC took both 1971 and 2011 population with weight of 17.5% and 10%. The 15th FC had been specifically asked to base its recommendation on 2011 census only. While the commission sticks to the mandate giving 15% weight to population as per 2011 census, it has given 10% weightage to demographic performance (measured as inverse of fertility rate). The criterion is novel as it finds a way to reward states which have controlled their population growth.

The increasing stress on ecology and environmental de-gradation led to inclusion of forest cover as a criterion in 14th FC. Continuing the same, current FC has increased the weight further to

10%. The criteria not only encourage states to preserve ecological balance but also compensates them for opportunity loss in preserving it. On final analysis, share of some of the states works out as – UP - 17.9%, Bihar - 10.1%, MP - 7.9%, WB - 7.5%.

Other than tax devolution, FC also recommends several grants. Biggest of these is revenue deficit grants, provided to states who do not have enough funds even after the devolution due to low own taxes. FC has recommended total of Rs 2.94 lakh crore of grants under this during 2021-26. It also mentions that some of these states have high expenditure on expenses such as salaries, pension and interest payments and continuation of such grants would act as 'moral hazard'. The commission has also recommended grants of over Rs 1 lakh crore for creating health infrastructure, 70% of which would go directly to local bodies. Another important recommendation of the commission is creation of a non-lapsable fund for defence needs.

Other than the centre-state and inter-state devolution, FCs are also required to allocate funds to municipal corporations including urban and rural local bodies. Delivery of social services through empowerment of local bodies has caught the attention of FCs in recent years as their involvement makes it more participatory and more effective. The commission cites experiment of Kerala in empowering primary healthcare bodies. The allocation to local bodies has gone up significantly, from Rs 97,000 crore during FC-XIII (2010-15) to Rs 2.9 lakh crore in FC-XIV and further to Rs 4.3 lakh crore by the current FC. The horizontal split, here too, involves rigorous exercise taking into account city infrastructure, air quality, water etc in case of urban bodies. The primary requirement for qualification is that the local body (both rural and urban) must submit and gets its account audited for previous years. The commission has laid stress on use of software and getting local accounts integrated with the state's accounts. Of the total funds, two-thirds, or Rs 2.9 lakh crore during the five year would go to rural area. With nearly 6 lakhs village in the country, average share of each village works out to nearly Rs 10 lakh, to be spent largely on crating assets for drinking water and sanitation.

While the recommendations are the best possible with conflicting objective of rewarding performance and providing for basic needs, it still calls for out-of-the-box thinking. For instance, assume each state as separate country with their own level of prosperity and financial strength. In such a scenario, what would a poor state do? More importantly, would a rich state let go of its resources to the poor state? An option that needs to be explored is if it possible to transfer best practices from forward states to poorer ones by linking financial devolution to it.

*****

# Indian States - Analyzing Economic & Social Performance

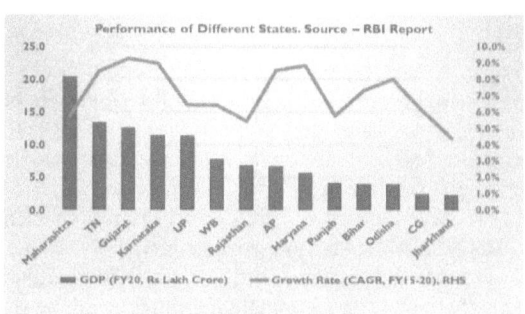

The economic performance of different states does not get the desired attention even though there is a significant disparity across them. The mass exodus of migrants, largely from Western and Southern India - the workplace, to Northern and Eastern India - the hometown was a harsh result of that. To better understand this and help policy makers and other stakeholders make more informed decision, RBI began publishing annual state level data on a variety of parameters a few years ago. Here is a brief analysis of the same based on the latest report.

From the economic perspective, the most important parameter is the size of state's economy reflected in Gross State Domestic Product (GSDP). Maharashtra is the biggest state with GSDP of Rs 18.9 lakh crore (FY21, constant price) followed by Tamil Nadu (FY22, Rs 13.4 lakh crore), Gujarat (FY21, Rs 12.5 lakh crore) and Uttar Pradesh (FY22, Rs 11.2 lakh crore). (FY22 data for some of the states are not available). In contrast, Bihar and Jharkhand at Rs 4.3 lakh crore and Rs 2.4 lakh crore have a significant low GSDP among the large states. In terms of growth rate, however, there isn't a clear trend. While some of the laggards are trying to catch up, some of the large ones appear to have reached a saturation. Among the larger ones, while Gujarat and Tamil Nadu have recorded growth rate of 9.3% and 8.5% CAGR during FY15-20 (pre-pandemic), Maharashtra has grown at only 5.8%. On the other hand, among the poorer states, while Bihar has managed growth rate of 7.3%, UP and West Bengal stand at 6.4% whereas Jharkhand managed only 4.4% growth rate.

However, GSDP, on standalone basis, has limited value. A more appropriate measure is the per capita figure. While Maharashtra, Gujarat and the Southern states are among the affluent ones with per capita net state domestic product in the range of Rs 1.3-1.7 lakh, Eastern states lag far behind with Bihar, UP and Jharkhand having the lowest income at Rs 30,800, Rs 40,400 and Rs 55,000 respectively. (Figures for FY22 or FY21). The figures for most of the states had recorded a decline in FY21 due to the pandemic but have shown some recovery in FY22. Haryana has the best per capita NSDP among the large states at Rs 1.8 lakh. This looks quite contradictory as the state also has a high unemployment rate. The reason for the dichotomy is that it also has a very high labor participation rate which leads to higher unemployment, yet higher prosperity. There is a significant variation among North-Eastern states with Sikkim being at the top with Rs 2.56 lakh and Manipur, Assam and Meghalaya at the other end with less than Rs 58,000.

An important point to note is the high share of agriculture in low per capita GSDP states. While agriculture contributes 4-7% of output in Maharashtra, Gujarat and Tamil Nadu, its shares is significantly higher at over 10% in UP, Bihar and Jharkhand. Interestingly, despite being the largest agriculture producer in the country, share of agriculture in Punjab is marginally less than 10%.

Another important parameter to understand the economic condition of states is their liabilities. Tamil Nadu and UP have the highest level of liabilities at Rs 6.6 and Rs 6.5 lakh crore at the end of FY22. This is followed by Maharashtra and West Bengal at Rs 6.1 lakh crore and Rs 5.6 lakh crore. Other than the absolute level, their growth rate gives better indication. While all these states saw their debt increase at the rate of 8-12% CAGR during 2015-20, increase was as high as 20% for Tamil Nadu. UP has managed to bring down the rate of increase from 12% during 2015-20 to 8% during 2020-22 which is noteworthy. Yet, UP has the highest liability as a percent of GSDP at 58% with TN and Punjab at little less than 50%. Gujarat and Maharashtra are better placed with the ratio at about 32%. Aggregate liabilities of all the state governments stands at Rs 69.5 lakh crore, little more than half the central government's liability of about Rs 133 lakh crore.

The state's economic performance determines its performance on social parameters, poverty rate being monitored most closely. Among the states performing poorly on this count are Chhattisgarh with poverty rate of almost 40%, Jharkhand - 37%, Bihar - 33.7%, Odisha - 32.6%, Madhya Pradesh - 31.6% and UP – 29.6%. (Figures are for 2012, latest mentioned in the report). Since all of them lie in the Eastern and Central India, the need is to make plans based on the specific characteristics of these states. States which have managed maximum reduction in poverty are Kerala with poverty rate of just 7%, Andhra Pradesh - 9.2%, Himachal Pradesh - 8% and Punjab - 8.3%. While Maharashtra and Gujarat have done very well in most economic parameters, they still have a relatively high poverty figure of 22%. These states figure put a serious question mark on the efficiency of trickle-down effect in economic development.

Another social indicator which warrants mention is birth rate, root cause of large number of other challenges. Bihar and UP, again, record the worst performance with birth rate of 2.55 and 2.51 per woman for FY20 followed by MP, Rajasthan at 2.41 and 2.35 and Chhattisgarh, Jharkhand both at 2.2. Worse, there states have not been able to achieve any significant reduction in the birth rate. While for UP and MP, it is down about 0.16 and 0.14 birth per woman, over last five years, it is down by only 0.08 in Bihar. States which have brought down the birth rate to acceptable level are Kerala, Punjab, Tamil Nadu and West Bengal, all of them having birth rate less than 1.5 against national average of 1.95.

The report can be accessed at -
https://www.rbi.org.in/Scripts/AnnualPublications.aspx?head=Handbook+of+Statistics+on+Indian+States

*****

# Analyzing Corporate Tax Exemptions

Tax exemptions for the corporate sector have become a curse considering the huge amount of tax being forfeited by the government. More so, since the large corporates are claiming more than 90% of the exemptions. As an effort to plug this, the finance minister added an important clause in the budget two years back that all customs duty exemptions would be effective for two years only. So, how much do these exemptions affect government's tax revenue. Here is a brief look.

The universe of Indian corporate sector consists of about 9.6 lakh companies which filed their financial statement for financial year 2020-21 as per the budget documents. Out of this, 4.4 lakh companies recorded profits whereas an even higher number, 4.8 lakh companies recorded losses. Total profits (before taxes, PBT) of profit-making companies stood at Rs 21.4 lakh crore or about Rs 4.8 crore per company. Despite adverse impact of Covid, profits were higher by 20% over previous year. while some of the segments were, indeed, under greater stress, higher commodity prices, higher steel prices etc helped companies in these segments compensate for losses of other segments.

Quite surprisingly, half of them reported losses and the percent has remained nearly the same over the years. It would be worthwhile to undertake closer scrutiny to check if it is a case of fudging of accounts especially for those above a threshold turnover. Total losses reported by these companies stood at Rs 8.7 lakh crore, down from Rs 11.7 lakh crore a year ago. While PBT should be the basis of tax calculation, there is another term called 'taxable income' which actually determines the tax liability. The taxable income for these companies was Rs 16.2 lakh crore which means companies claimed tax exemptions on Rs 5.2 lakh crore of their profits, almost 25% of their PBT. This implies tax loss of over Rs 75,000 crore. The effective tax rate (ER) for these companies works out to 22.2% against statutory rate of 25.5% and even lower than 22.5% in the previous year. Government introduced a new tax regime in 2019-20 whereby companies which forego exemptions are required to pay at lower tax rate of 25.2%. ER has come down sharply from 27.8% and 29.5% in the two years before the new tax regime was introduced.

While general belief is that smaller companies would be getting more exemptions, it is actually the large companies that are availing higher deductions and incentives. Companies with PBT of more than Rs 500 crore are paying taxes on only 70% of their PBT whereas companies with PBT of Rs 0-1 crore and with PBT of Rs 1-10 crore are paying taxes on 97% and 88% respectively. ER for large companies is only 19.1%, lower than 20.2% in the previous year against 24% for Rs 0-10 crore companies.

However, it is not the private sector but public sector enterprises (PSEs) that are claiming more exemptions! PSEs claim exemption on 42% of their PBT against 21% for private sector. As a result, ER for PSEs is only 17% against 23.4% for private sector. Further, there is significant difference in exemption claimed by manufacturing in contrast with non-manufacturing sector (such as banking, trading, consulting etc). While manufacturing sector companies are claiming exemption on only 14% of their PBT, the share stands at 30% for non-manufacturing companies (still better than PSEs).

So, what are these exemptions being given for? The most important ones are exemptions available in profit on exports made through SEZs, accelerated depreciation for purchase of machinery and exemptions available for power sector, the three accounting for three-fourth of total exemptions. Interestingly, while exemptions are also available for development of backward areas, high employment sectors etc, claims within these are a small part. Among the sectors claiming maximum exemptions are non-ferrous metal ore mining with effective tax rate of only 10.7%, steel products manufacturing (12.7%) and crude oil refining (16.5%). While exemptions for a nascent industry could be justified, established industries such as above claiming such huge exemption is ridiculous. The practice of claiming high tax exemptions led to imposition of MAT (minimum alternate tax) in 1980s whereby companies have to pay MAT in case exemptions lead to lower tax liability.

Apart from corporate sector, businesses are also organised as partnership firms, association of persons etc. A total of 16.2 lakh firms filed their returns with reported profits of Rs 2.7 lakh crore and taxable income of Rs 2.6 lakh crore for FY21. Despite being a Covid year, profits were higher by about 17%. The profit-making firms paid taxes on close to 96% of their declared profits against only 75% in case of corporates. Interestingly, only 3.5 lakh of these firms made losses, just about 20% against as many as fifty percent in case of corporates.

The third segment, listed out by the document, is charitable institutions who do not pay any taxes but have to report donations received. These institutions, totalling 2.32 lakh, reported total receipts of Rs 7.1 lakh crore through donations, contributions etc. The amount is lower than Rs 7.9 lakh crore received in the previous year, counter intuitive since larger section of population gave donation during the year in fight against Covid. A possible explanation could be that tighter scrutiny by government has made it tougher for people to use this as a conduit to claim exemption and evade taxes. It may be noted that the Supreme Court in a judgment recently set tougher condition for these institutions to claim tax benefits which should further help plug the loophole.

So, where does this leave us? Tax exemptions are unavoidable and probably, essential to re-balance regional and sectoral development. However, exemptions at almost one-fourth of total liability points to an inactive rather than a proactive policy. Another obvious reason the propensity of companies to inflate exemptions, monitoring which is very difficult. The minimum that can be done is shift to exemptions for fixed time period. While a beginning towards this has been made, it has to be taken up in greater earnest.

*****

# Social Sector Exchange - Understanding the Concept

The report of the committee on creation of an exchange for social sector firms is an important forward step. The exchange would help social sector firms mobilize resources by enhancing transparency and credibility through market-driven mechanism. Even though the proposal is path-breaking, bringing all the NPOs (Non-profit Organizations) on the platform would be a huge challenge. A look at some of the proposals and how SSE is expected to evolve.

SSE, much like other stock exchanges, would be a platform where all NPOs would register with the primary objective to raise funds. However, unlike other exchanges, funds won't be raised by issue of shares but primarily through bonds, mutual funds etc. The NPOs, like in case of other listed firms, would have to publish their performance reports, get the reports audited and engage with stakeholders and by virtue of their impact in meeting social goals, mobilize funds. Other than financials, they would also have to report on the social outcome achieved during each period.

Even though the functioning and scale of social sector in not much understood, they have a huge economic presence. As per the government budget documents, total donations received by charitable institutions during FY20 was as much as Rs 7.4 lakh crore. There are more than 13 lakh NPOs registered in the country implying Rs 57 lakh of donation received by each NPO on an average, not a small sum. However, lack of information available about the utilization of this fund and a general lack of transparency creates a hurdle in leveraging their network and allows unscrupulous entities to take advantage of the exemptions given to NPOs. This is the gap that the exchange can help fill.

Even though the concept and the objective is game changing, the biggest challenge for such an exchange would be to quantify the social outcome. The challenge becomes even bigger as there are different causes served by different NPOs such as children, differently abled, education, elderly, livelihoods, health, women and environment. Measuring social impact cannot be easily standardized across these different areas and would require different reporting format. To minimize this handicap, the report suggests building teams of social auditors. The lack of objective criteria to measure outcome makes the task of social auditors that much more critical.

The creation of exchange may eventually lead to mandatory registration of all NPOs to be eligible for tax exemptions and other benefits. In the longer run, this could help end the malaise of NPOs acting as a conduit for routing funds. More importantly, it could lead to enhanced Public Private Partnership (PPP) as government spends huge amount of funds but is not suitably equipped to monitor ground level progress of its programs. It may be noted that PPP concept has helped tremendously in development of infrastructure sector.

Yet, it may not be such an easy task considering the huge number of NPOs. Total number of companies listed on BSE or NSE is less than 10,000 in contrast with 13 lakh NPOs registered. Yet another challenge would be to make sure that for-profit enterprises do not grab the space available for NPOs. (The report lists out different set of requirements for NPOs and FPEs). The issue deserves attention as 67% of investors in FPEs earned a return of more than 12.5% from their investment in social cause as per the report. Similarly, large number of schools are run by NPOs which are charging significant fees and making profits. These entities qualify as commercial enterprise rather than NPO and their need for support of Social Sector exchange would have to be strictly considered.

*****

# Analysing Delays in Government Projects

Delays in government projects have always been a serious concern as it causes significant increase in cost. As per a government report, cost overrun for projects under implementation as of Dec'21 stands at close to Rs 4 lakh crore with average time overrun of 47 months. While the number is huge, it has come down over last 4-5 years. A brief attempt to analyse the entire issue.

As per the Quarterly Project Implementation Status Report (QPISR) for Dec'21 published by Infrastructure & Monitoring division of MOSPI, there are over 1,700 projects being undertaken by the central government and its agencies. While the original cost estimates for these projects was Rs 22.5 lakh crore, revised estimate stands at Rs 26.8 lakh crore implying cost overrun of Rs 4.3 lakh crore or about 20%. Further, nearly 34% of the projects are running behind schedule with delay ranging up to as much as 324 months.

Yet, project implementation seems to be gaining pace as percent completion of these projects on aggregate basis has improved from 40% in June'19 to 50% with cumulative expenditure of Rs 13.3 lakh crore by Dec'21. (*Projects completion would not always increase with time as newer projects will keep getting added and the ones with high percent completion will keep getting removed after commissioning*). 178 projects involving investment of over Rs 1.8 lakh crore have been completed in the first nine months (April'21-Dec'21) of the current year. Percent of projects facing time overruns has come down from 38% in June'19 and as high as 45% in March'15. The figure had come down to 28% by June'20 but has risen subsequently due to the pandemic.

The projects being monitored by the project management group involve minimum investment of Rs 150 crore. These are further divided into two groups: Mega – with investment of over Rs 1,000 crore and major with investment between Rs 150-1,000 crore. Out of the total, 480 projects are mega projects which account for almost 80% of total investment. Most of the projects are being undertaken in two broad segments. These are Logistics – Railways, roads, ports etc and Energy – power, coal, petroleum etc. Roads and railways account for maximum no of projects at 900 and 300 respectively. While road projects are smaller with average size being Rs 450 crore, railway projects are much bigger with average size of Rs 2,200 crore. A point to note is that average size of projects in both of these sectors has come from Rs 700 crore and Rs 2,600 crore two years back. Whether this points to any trend is difficult to say.

An analysis of the delay shows that it is the mega projects that suffer maximum cost overrun at almost 25% whereas the major projects are facing only 3% of cost overruns. This means bigger projects face greater challenge and therefore, greater focus is required towards project management for mega projects. On terms of sectors, Railways suffer the maximum with over 200 (out of nearly 300) of its projects facing cost overruns. Against initial investment of Rs 1.8 lakh crore, these projects would require over Rs 4 lakh crore implying cost overrun of over 120%. Reason for the huge slippage in railway projects is that many new rail-line projects were announced, many of them in 1990s, as a populist measure even before any feasibility study was conducted. This led to formal launch of the project but no progress beyond that. Time overrun, in case of railways, is as much as 27 years! Some of the projects completed over last 2-3 years were sanctioned way back in 1991. In view of the delays, government has taken a policy decision to complete all railways projects before approving new projects.

While the delays are dismissed as bureaucratic inefficiencies, there can be actually serious issues involved. For instance, large number of projects face land acquisition issues which are not easy to resolve even after paying significant amount of compensation. In the Indian context, problem gets accentuated due to unclear title, at times, multiple owners for the same land or land being under dispute. Another issue is inadequate due diligence by the contractor and hurried award of contract leading to under-estimation of cost, vague contractual terms, inadequate mobilization of workforce etc. The report cites several instances of delay for these reasons including some of the projects getting shelved altogether. Some of the sectors such as Power, Roads also faces considerable delays due to difficult terrain, geological, ecological issues etc. Similarly, there are projects being carried in sensitive areas such as J&K which are often suspended leading to delays. The project report may report these projects separately and focus on the ones which are manageable.

The projects, possibly, also suffer from funding issues. This is corroborated by the fact that funds allocated during FY22 was Rs 2.3 lakh crore only, less than one-tenth of the total cost. This roughly means that it would take ten years for these projects to get the entire fund needed for completion. As stated earlier, a case in point is Railways where projects were announced without adequate funds availability.

However, it is not always a case of delays. Some big-ticket projects have been completed very swiftly. For example, Nagpur Metro, approved in 2014 at a cost of Rs 8,700 crore has begun operations in a record time by March'19. Several of government initiatives are yielding results. An innovative initiative recently mooted is linking of small, localized projects with MGNREGA. This would help mobilize labour, local support and expedite the project.

*****

# GST – Journey So Far

The Goods & Service tax (GST) completed 5 years of its implementation in July'22 and despite all the hurdles, the developments are far reaching. After the initial months of excessive hassles related to filings, complains of high tax rates, inconvenience to small entities and so on, the taxation regime appears to have reduced these glitches substantially. Still, it is a work-in-progress both operationally and in terms of its potential to enable formalization of economy, widen tax base and most importantly, bring about a cultural change from tax avoidance to tax compliance. The tax information is also expected to help banks assess the credit worthiness of a business, especially small entities and make lending more efficient and less risky. This should also, going forward, help assess the economic growth in a more effective manner. A look at its progress and the changes after implementation.

Other than the technical glitches, the bigger worry was high tax rates which threatened the survival of many small businesses. The GST council acted quite proactively on this, and has received substantial praise and cut rates liberally. Almost 75% of items saw its tax rates come down from initial 28% to 18% slab in Nov'17, providing a huge relief. (The initial rate was based on the then existing effective tax rate). The committee has been pruning the list in most all of its meetings and just about 27 items remain in the top slab of 28% from original over 200 items. Items such as washing machine, small TVs, Air conditioners which cannot exactly be called common use items, have also seen the tax rates come down from 28% to 18%. Most of the items remaining in 28% slab are what are called demerit goods such as tobacco etc and luxury items. An interesting drawback with GST is that the tax rate looks very high especially in case of 28% slab even though this is less than effective tax rate of as high as 40% earlier (as in case of automobiles). Since the taxes were levied at different stages, the aggregate tax impact was not getting reflected.

The tax rate cut was followed by measures to ensure that the benefits are passed on to the consumers. GST has a unique anti-profiteering provision whereby it can levy penalty on a company if it does not pass on the gains of lower tax rate to the consumers. Even though it may not be easy to use this provision effectively, it acts as an important deterrent. The anti-profiteering agency has imposed a penalty on a leading FMCG company recently and the case is under litigation currently.

The special focus of GST council has been to ensure that the gains arising out of GST percolates to the consumers and does not get cornered by the business entities. This is evident from the modification related to taxation on restaurants. The original scheme involved 12/18% tax rate with the restaurants getting the tax credit on inputs. (This means that in a bill of say, Rs 1,500, if the cost of input was Rs 600, the restaurant would have to pay tax on Rs 900 only and not Rs 1,500). However, this benefit was not being passed on to the consumers. To ensure that restaurants do not get this undue benefit, the tax rate was reduced to 5% WITHOUT giving them the benefit of input tax credit. The measure was a smart one and shows the alacrity with which the council has been managing the transition.

Tax on under construction property is another case similar to restaurants. While the tax rate here is 12%, effective outgo would be lower as builder should pass on the tax credit received on input material. However, the builders have not passed on the benefit and therefore, the buyers prefer buying resale properties which does not attract this tax. The council is actively considering levying of flat 5% tax without any input tax benefit.

To reduce the hassles of maintaining record and filing returns for small entities in manufacturing industry, the council has increased the minimum turnover limit eligible for composition scheme. As per this scheme, a business entity does not need to maintain or file detailed entries and can just pay a fixed rate of tax, currently 2%, if its turnover is below the threshold. However, in that case, the business cannot collect tax from its buyers nor can it claim input tax credit. Current threshold stands at Rs 1.5 crore, revised up from Rs 75 lakh earlier. While the scheme is not available for suppliers, the next council meeting is expected to take up this proposal. The scheme has drawn attention as a convenient and hassle-free option and almost 20% of the registered businesses have opted for the scheme. However, from tax collection perspective, the tax rate may need to be increased as the tax mobilization through the scheme is very low. As per the data released by Press Information Bureau (PIB), GST collected through the scheme was just Rs 580 crore in April'18 against total collection of over Rs 1 lakh crore.

GST also has an arrangement called reverse charge mechanism applicable when the seller is not liable to collect tax as mentioned in case above or if he seller is not a registered entity. In that case, the buyer has to pay tax through this mechanism. To help economy get used to the taxation adequately, the tax has been postponed to Sept'19 from earlier proposed Oct'18.

Other than the operational issues, council has also taken an important decision of taking control of GSTN (GST Network). GSTN is the IT backbone which stores the data of all registered entities and through which, all tax payments and returns filing are done. GSTN was earlier registered as a private limited company with government having partial stake. The change was felt necessary considering the sensitive nature of task being handled by it.

GST has, indeed, made substantial progress towards the objective of formalization. Other than about 65 lakh businesses which migrated from earlier indirect tax regime, another nearly 50 lakh entities have registered for GST implying significant increase in formalization. While there is a  chance that these entities have registered only as a legal requirement and are not making any significant contribution to the revenue, yet it is an important development. Despite the substantial rate cuts, GST collection has moved up from an average of about Rs 90,000 crore in FY18 to over Rs 96,000 crore in the current financial year so far. The revenue collection has exceeded the projections, based on earlier collection pattern, for many of the states.

*****

# Understanding Universal Basic Income (UBI)

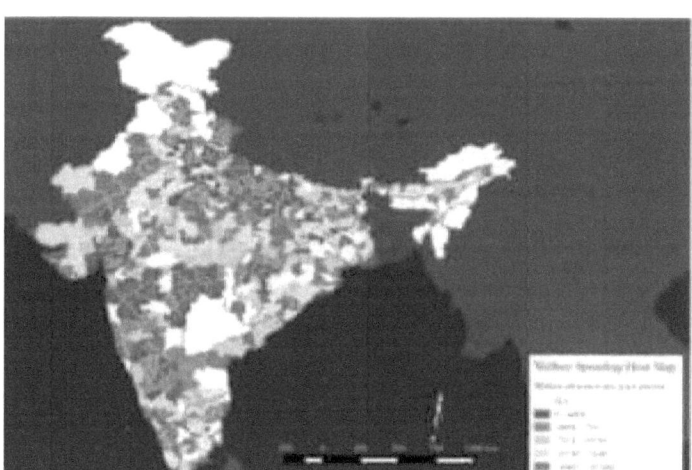

The Economic Survey floated the idea of Universal Basic Income (UBI) a few years ago which essentially means transferring a certain amount of money into the account of people rather than trying to reach out to them through the welfare schemes. As per the Survey, it is an idea whose time has come for serious discussion. A look at the rationale for the scheme and various pitfalls.

The UBI is based on two premises. First, even though the welfare scheme for poverty reduction have achieved certain degree of success, it has still not provided the poor a life of dignity and freedom from vulnerability. Second, the welfare schemes are prone to serious leakages leading to poor people remaining poor and richer/more resourceful ones cornering the benefits. So, why not shift to a scheme which involves direct transfer of money into the account of every identified individual and stop all other welfare schemes.?

To make case for the first point, survey cites a similar programme in Kenya which resulted in significant improvement in happiness, life satisfaction and reduction in stress. It cites studies to buttress the second point. For FY12, the actual benefits reaching to deserving section from two flagship schemes, MGNREGS and PDS was only about 30% with 40% going to non-poor sections and remaining 30% getting lost through system leakages. As a result, poorest 40% districts, which should receive at least 60% of the funds, receive only about 30%.

Beyond these two, there are about 950 schemes being run by government which involves significant bureaucratic costs and diversion of focus in their implementation away from more productive objectives. To make case for UBI, the survey points out that it would require annual transfer of Rs 7,600 to each individual to bring down poverty from current 22% to less than 0.5%. This would cost government nearly 5% of GDP which is equal to current government expenditure on the existing 950 schemes and would involve no additional burden. Reduction of poverty to about 6% would cost 2% of GDP. While the idea is laudable as it involves radical shift in approach towards poverty reduction, moving the goal post from feeding the poor to giving them a life of dignity. For one, by its own admission, Survey points out to significant improvement in MGNREGS aided by JAM and direct account transfer leading to reduction in leakages diluting the rationale for UBI. Secondly, closure of all schemes is virtually impossible since many of the schemes are for public good which would still need government intervention and hence, continue to put pressure on government finances. Further, whether it can replace existing schemes without causing serious disruption and whether it can prevent the vices arising out of 'free money' called 'moral hazard' needs to be considered carefully.

(Image courtesy of The Economic Survey. Highlight districts getting less funds in red).

*****

# SECTION – II
# BANKING & FINANCE

# Structure of India's Financial Sector - Part I

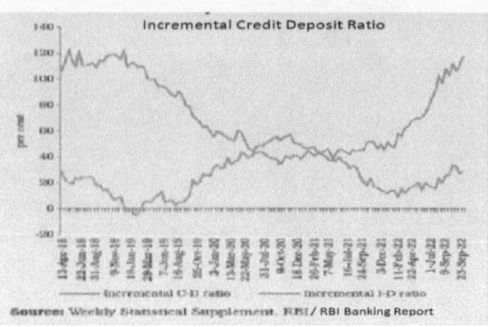

Indian financial sector withstood the shock of Covid and with resumption of economic activity, has seen significant increase in credit growth. Public sector banks (PSBs), reeling under the NPA overhang for 5-6 years, have also managed to regain. But what all constitutes Indian financial sector, their size and what is their relative positioning. And how have each constituent fared in the recent past. Here is a look at the structure of India's financial sector based on RBI's report on Trends & Progress of banking in India.

India's financial structure comprises of three main pillars - Scheduled Commercial Banks (SCBs), Non-banking financial institutions (NBFI) and Co-operative Banks (CBs). In addition to these, it also comprises of Regional Rural Banks (RRBs) and Local Area Banks (LABs). These are not grouped into any of these three categories but are considered as extension of SCBs. Clearly, the structure is too complex with large number of small banking entities which create serious challenge in terms of monitoring.

SCBs are further categorized into Public Sector banks (PSBs), private sector banks (PVBs), foreign banks (FBs) and recently formed groups, small finance banks (SFBs) and payment banks (PBs). There are a total of 78 SCBs (excluding SCBs & PBs) operating through a little over 1.2 lakh branches. Total funds managed by SCBs stood at Rs 217 lakh crore at the end of March'22, about 11 % increase over previous year. This is a significant turnaround after years of lull. Banks' assets growth had declined to less than 9% during FY14-21 after growing at as much as 18% during FY05-14.

Banks core job is financial intermediation - mobilizing funds from savers and lending to the needs segments. So, primary source of funds for banks is deposits supplemented by borrowings and reserves & surplus. Of the total, deposits accounted for Rs 172 lakh crore or nearly 80% of total liabilities whereas the other two contribute 8-9% each. Incremental deposits, closing balance minus opening balance of deposits, had reached a new high of over Rs 15 lakh crore in FY21, sharp 56% in FY21 over FY20 and remained at the same level in FY22 also. High deposits growth, despite significantly lower deposits rate, was possibly driven by higher risk aversion amidst the pandemic. Equity capital is an important requirement for banks since they have to meet regulatory norm of capital adequacy ratio (CAR). PSBs had seen sharp erosion in their equity capital because of increase in NPAs and central government had infused about Rs 3.1 lakh crore of equity between FY17-21 to help banks meet the regulatory requirement. Even now, PSB's equity is just about 6.3% of total assets against over 12% for other banks.

In terms of deployment of funds, lending, called Loans & advances in banking parlance, accounts for maximum share followed by investment in government bonds. Banks are also required to keep a part of the funds with RBI as CRR and a part is deployed in inter-bank market where banks borrow and lend to each other. While aggregate funds invested in inter-bank market is just about 5% of total assets, exposure of individual banks vary based on their risk appetite. Loans stood at Rs 122 lakh crore, increase of nearly 13% over previous year against increase of 4.8% in FY21. This is the first year of credit pickup after a long period of subdued growth. Loans & advances growth had fallen sharply from close to 22% during FY05-14 to less than 7% after that.

Within SCBs, PSBs account for the largest share managing about 60% of total funds. Even though it is the largest, their share has come down from about 70% in FY16 as a result of their efforts to consolidate their operations to bring down their NPAs. PSBs have also seen major consolidation over last 4-5 years reducing their numbers from over 25 to 12 now. In comparison, private banks totaling 21 in numbers account for 34% of business, up from 24% in FY16. (A part of this is also due to change in classification of a bank from public sector to private). Foreign banks are large in numbers, totaling 46, but have a rather small presence with less than 7% market share. SFBs and PBs are niche segments accounting for less than 1% share with total 15 such banks in operation.

Aggregate income of the banking sector during FY22 stood at Rs 15.1 lakh crore of which interest income accounted for Rs 12.7 lakh crore. Growth is marginal at 2.6%, a result of low interest rate environment. The low interest rate also helped them reduce their interest expenditure, which came down by 4% to Rs 6.7 lakh crore, less than half of total income. While the gap in interest earned and interest expended may give a perception that banking is a highly profitable business, it is not exactly so because of significantly high operating expenditure which stood at Rs 6.7 lakh crore, almost 28% of total income. More than half of this is towards staff cost. The third important cost item is provisions and contingencies at Rs 2.5 lakh crore, decline of 15% yoy. Provisions have declined over the years, peaking at Rs 3.2 lakh crore in FY18 in the midst of NPA crisis. As a percent of total income, this has come down from 25% in FY18 to 15% now. Of this, PSBs alone made provision of almost Rs 2.4 lakh crore in FY18 leading to net loss of Rs 85,000 crore. This has now come down to Rs 1.3 lakh crore helping PSBs make a respectable profit of Rs 66,500 crore. However, its share in total SCB's profits is just about 37% against share of 59% in total business.

An important ratio monitored in banking sector is incremental Credit-deposit ratio (ICD ratio) which is increase in credit upon increase in deposits during the year. ICD had declined to just 37% in FY21 but has picked up sharply to 87% in FY22. With high ICD, banks would have to increase their deposits rate to mobilize more funds, failing which they may not be left with enough money to lend. Another aspect related to bank's lending is the money borrowed by the government. Since ICD was low in FY21, high government borrowings during the year did not cause much impact on the market. However, it had to reduce its borrowing in FY22 in the face of strong credit offtake. Incremental investment in government bonds by banks came down from Rs 7.3 lakh crore in FY21 to just about Rs 3.3 lakh crore in FY22. *This is the scenario when excess government borrowings may lead to "crowding-out".* Lower credit growth in FY21 was, in a way, blessing in disguise as it helped government meet its additional needs arising out of the pandemic.

*****

# Structure of India's Financial Sector - NBFCs

NBFIs (Non-banking financial institutions) form the second pillar of financial structure further grouped into All India Finance institutions (AIFIs), Non-Banking Finance Companies (NBFCs) and Primary Dealers (PDs).

NBFCs are the second largest group after SCBs active in niche segments such as vehicle loans, gold loan, infrastructure financing etc. NBFCs are categorized into four types - deposit taking NBFCs (NBFCs-D), non-deposit taking NBFCs (NBFCs-ND), Housing Finance Companies (HFCs) and Asset Reconstruction Companies (ARCs). NBFCs-ND are further classified as systemically important (NBFCs-ND-SI) if total assets are more than Rs 500 crore and other NBFC-ND. As per the RBI report, there were 49 NBFC-D at the end of FY22, down from 82 three years back and as many as 9,467 NBFC-ND, marginally lower than 9,500 last year. Number of HFCs operating in the country stands at 95 against 100 last year. NBFCs are also classified into 11 different categories based on their activity such as NBFC-MFI (Micro-finance Institutions), NBFC-IFC (Infrastructure Finance Company) etc.

After extensive consolation, RBI introduced yet another classification in Oct'22 for NBFCs based on their size. These are NBFCs Base Layer (NBFC-BL, asset size<Rs 1,000 crore), Middle Layer (NBFC-ML, asset size>Rs 1,000 crore and all NBFCs-D), Upper Layer (NBFC-UL) and Top Layer (NBFC-TL). NBFC-UL would be populated by RBI based on certain criteria and 16 NBFCs are there in this group currently. NBFC-TL would normally remain empty but would be populated in case of substantial increase in the risk from specific NBFC. The utility of the classification become clear from the fact that NBFC-UL account for only 0.3% of share in numbers but have 26% share in total assets. On the other hand, NBFC-BL account for 94% of share in numbers but less than 5% in total assets. NBFCs in the higher layers have to maintain higher risk capital, thus, reducing the systemic risk and improving RBI's capability to monitor them.

NBFCs had aggregate assets base of Rs 38.4 lakh crore at the end of FY22, increase of about 10%. Increase is slightly lower than growth recorded by SCBs. While SCBs have a reasonably steady growth pattern, NBFCs have seen significant fluctuation. It has varied from growth of as much as 32% in FY18, before the IL&FS crisis broke out, to a decline in FY20, although marginally by 1%. Since NBFCs can't mobilize finds from depositors (except for NBFCs-D who form only 15% of total NBFCs segment), they have to depend on other market sources for the same. Major sources are Debentures at Rs 10 lakh crore, Bank borrowings, equity capital and others at Rs 9 lakh crore each. Commercial papers (CPs) and deposits account for small amount of Rs 70,000 crore each. Debentures and CPs are unsecured form of lending and led to significant loss to the lenders after the collapse of IL&FS. As a result, funds raised through these two sources have declined during FY18-22, although marginally. This was made up by bank borrowings which grew by 13% CAGR. As a result of scarcity of funds, NBFCs had to chip-in with equity capital which rose by 14% CAGR during FY20-22. Equity capital as a percent of total assets stands at 23.4% for NBFCs against only 8.8% for SCBs. HFCs had total assets base of Rs 15.3 lakh crore, increase of barely 3% over FY21. (Would be taken in another article separately).

An important structural change in the sector is increasing share of government owned NBFCs which now account for 41% share of total assets against 32% in FY18. During FY18-22, government owned NBFCs recorded assets growth of 21% CAGR against only 10% by private NBFCs. The figures were nearly the same at 13% and 11% during FY14-18. Share of government NBFCs in incremental assets growth crossed 53% during this period against only 35% in FY14-18. While the shift was driven by government's strategy to use NBFCs as the route to finance infrastructure projects, the momentum accelerated with the IL&FS debacle.

In terms of lending, NBFCs gave total loans of Rs 29.1 lakh crore or almost 76% of total assets. In comparison, loans account for only 56% of total assets for SCB since they have to meet statutory norms not applicable to NBFCs. This is an important difference between NBFCs and SCBs helping NBFCs manage their profitability. However, credit growth was muted for them at 7.6% against 13% for SCBs during the year. In terms of sector, industry accounts for 38% of lending and retail for 28%. Infrastructure projects, included within industry, account for 33% of total lending. While NBFCs are perceived to meet financing needs of MSME segment, share of MSME is total loan is less than 5%.

NBFCs recorded total income of Rs 3.8 lakh crore, increase of about 6% over FY21. As a percent of total assets, this is 9.8% against 7% for SCBs. Net profit stood at Rs 62,000 crore against Rs 1.8 lakh crore for SCBs on nearly one-sixth asset base as compared to SCBs. While NBFCs operate with higher equity capital, yet, the risk-rewards ratio appears to be skewed towards NBFCs.

AIFIs, also called development finance institutions (DFIs), refer to institutions established to meet long term financing needs of sectors such as agriculture, trade, housing and small industries. Total funds managed by AIFIs is Rs 12.2 lakh crore, increase of 14% over last year. While AIFIs raise funds from market through bonds & debentures, deposits account for maximum funds at close to 35%, reducing the cost of funds for them.

There are four AIFIs currently - National Bank for Agriculture and Rural Development (NABARD), Small Industries Development Bank of India (SIDBI), National Housing Bank (NHB) and Export Import Bank of India (EXIM Bank). (It may be noted that ICICI and IDBI were DFIs earlier, converted to banks due to unsustainability of their earlier business model). These institutions do not directly lend to consumers but provide finance to banks/other financial institutions engaged in the respective sector. AIFI played a pivotal role in providing long-term funds to sectors critical from national growth perspective although their role has diminished with expansion of banking network. Government assistance such as to agriculture or low-cost housing etc. are also routed through these agencies.

While PDs (Primary Dealers) are also included as a part of NBFIs, they are not exactly in the business of financing but assist RBI in sale of government bonds. There are 21 PDs, of which 14 are part of banks and the rest are standalone. Their role is critical since they also act as underwriters for government bond issues which means they have to purchase the bond if it does not get sold. Total auction of government bonds and treasury bills in the primary market stood at about Rs 24 lakh crore during FY22, of which, close to Rs 15 lakh crore were sold through PDs.

In the secondary market, standalone primary dealers (SPDs) play an active role. SPDs accounted for Rs 122 lakh crore out of total turnover of Rs 343 lakh crore of government securities in FY22. The turnover is achieved with balance sheet size of just about Rs 80,000 crore indicating high rotation of funds.

*****

# Structure of India's Financial Sector – Cooperative Banks

Cooperative banks form the third pillar of India's financial structure. These are further classified as urban cooperative banks (UCBs) and Rural co-operative banks (RCBs). Both urban and rural cooperatives played an important part in meeting the needs of smaller borrowers. However, their role has diminished over the years due to series of scams during different periods and technological changes helping SCBs extend its reach to these sections. With increase in central banks power to regulate them and increased focus in improving governance and efficiency, the sector should see consolidation and improved performance over the next few years.

Unlike SCBs which operate through a wide network of branches, UCBs are largely focused in a specific district/region and have limited number of branches, some even having single branch. UCBs gained prominence after 1991 with liberal licensing policy. However, a series of scams during 1990-2000 led to several restriction and cancellation of license of large number of them. The number has come down from almost 2,000 in 2004, to 1,514 now. UCBs had a total asset base of Rs 6.7 lakh crore at the end of FY22, just about 3% of assets of SCBs. Over last five years, their balance sheet has grown at just 4.4% CAGR against 8.9% for SCBs. UCBs, like banks, can raise deposits from the public which is the largest source of funds accounting for nearly 80% of total assets. This gives them an edge over NBFCs. However, almost 1,300 UCBs have deposits base of less than Rs 500 crore leading to lack of 'economy of scale'. In terms of deployment of funds, loan stands at Rs 3.1 lakh crore, 46% of total assets with the rest being used in government bonds or lies with SCBs. Loans have grown at even slower pace, just 2.3%, half of deposits growth rate. This is a classic case of 'lazy banking' when a bank does not chase borrowers but allows its money to lie idle in low return investments. It may be noted that loans account for 76% of total assets for NBFCs. Despite a low loan book, there gross NPA ratio is significantly high at 12.1% in FY21 although down to 9.7% in FY22. This is still higher than SCBs and NBFCs. Low loan base, high NPA despite low-cost deposits and higher operational cost leads to modest profits at just Rs 3,000 crore.

Rural co-operatives banks were formed to provide credit to rural areas to reduce rural indebtedness and improve agricultural productivity. RCBs have a very complex structure, classified into two groups - short term lending institutions and long-term lending institutions. The short-term institutions primarily provide crop loan/ working capital loan through a three-tier structure - State co-op banks (StCBs, 34 in numbers), district co-op (DCCB, 351) and primary agriculture co-op societies (PACs, 1,02,600 in numbers). StCBs operate through over 2,000 branches or about 60 branches per StCB. DCCB has network of about 14,000 branches which works out to 40 per DCCB. Other than direct lending, StCBs also lend to DCCB which, in turn, lends to PACs and also to borrowers directly. PACs are largely single branch entity with average asset size of about Rs 3.3 crore. They are owned by local village people and lend to members only. The long-term lending institutions comprise of 13 state co-op agriculture & rural development banks (SCARDBs) and 600 primary co-op agriculture & rural development banks (PCARDBs). Despite being reasonably large in number, share of long-term institutions in total assets is only 4%.

Total assets managed by these five rural cooperative banks is Rs 13.6 lakh crore. While this is nearly double the size of UCBs, there would be some double-counting as PACs receive funds from DCCB which, in turn, gets it from StCBs. The figure is for FY21, latest provided in the report. Assets have grown at about 7% CAGR during FY17-21, lower than SCBs but better than UCBs. Deposits account for only 60% of their funds against 80% for UCBs. This is an important characteristic to note since rural population has lesser surplus money to park in the bank. Rest of the money is mobilized as borrowings, primarily through NABARD. RCBs are doing better than UCBs in terms of loans given with 58% of total assets or Rs 7.8 lakh crore given out as loans.

However, RCBs profitability is much worse with profits of just Rs 3,500 crore, not much higher than UCBs despite double the assets base. A part of this is due to higher cost structure (due to higher borrowings) and presence in segment with high NPAs. For PACs, accounting for one-fourth of total, gross NPA is as high as 33%. Almost half of PACs are making losses although the amount is quite negligible at just about Rs 1,500 crore.

Cooperative banks are facing increasing pressure with digital banking and banking correspondent model adopted by SCBs. The share of SCBs is total loans given to agriculture sector has gone up to 75% in FY22 whereas RCBs share stands at just 13%, down from about 17% in FY16. Cooperative banks also suffered due to dual reporting structure, both to the concerned state government and RBI. The banking act amendment in 2020 giving RBI more power to regulate them should improve the efficiency of these banks. The objective should be to reduce the multiple layer and merge the smaller ones with bigger ones to bring about economies of scale. An example is the amalgamation of as many as 13 DCCBs with the State Cooperative bank in Kerala in FY20.

**Recap -**

- SCBs have total asset base of Rs 217 lakh crore against Rs 38.4 lakh crore for NBFCs and about Rs 20 lakh crore for Cooperative banks (Urban plus rural).
- Against this, profits made by the three segment stands at Rs 1.8 lakh crore, Rs 60,000 crore and Rs 6,500 crore respectively indicating sharp difference in their operational efficiency.
- GNPA ratio for the three segment is 5.8%, 5.8% and 15.3%.
- Other than NBFCs, NBFIs also include AIFIs and HFCs which handled Rs 12.2 and Rs 15.3 lakh crore respectively.
- RCBs had total assets of Rs 13 lakh crore through a three-tier structure of StCB, DCCB and PAC.
- There are over 1 lakh PAC with total assets of Rs 3.34 lakh crore or just about Rs 3.3 crore per PAC.

*****

# Analysing RBI's Balance Sheet

RBI's balance sheet for the year 2021-22 (FY22) has expanded by 8.4% as per its annual report released last week. While this is moderately higher than expansion of 7% in the previous year, it is significantly lower than 30% recorded in FY20. So, what has helped RBI manage its balance sheet expansion? Or for that matter, is balance sheet expansion a bad sign? Here is an attempt to analyze RBI's balance sheet and answer these questions.

RBI's balance sheet stood at Rs 61.9 lakh crore at the end of FY22 against Rs 57.1 lakh crore last year. Its balance sheet consists of three major items on the liabilities side and two on assets side. The liabilities are equity capital & deposits, liabilities against notes issued and risk provisions. On the assets side are assets of currency issue department (ID) and assets of banking department (BD). Thus, only ID appears on both assets and liabilities side and all other liabilities are backed by assets of BD.

ID issues currency, which gets recorded in the balance sheet as liability and is bought by banks by payment of foreign currency which they receive from their operations. Thus, all the foreign currency that flows into the country are absorbed by the central bank. These dollars are invested back in international bonds/securities or deposited with IMF. RBI need not necessarily issue notes but can also give cash from its reserves, if it has, in exchange. The currency was lent to the government also in lieu of bonds called 'deficit financing' but was discontinued in 1997. For FY22, liabilities of ID dept increased from Rs 28.3 lakh crore to Rs 31.1 lakh crore, up by about 10%. This liability is backed by Rs 29.9 lakh crore of foreign bonds and Rs 1.2 lakh crore of gold.

The second item in the liabilities side is deposits, largely funds parked by banks as part of CRR or through other monetary instruments such as reverse repo. Total liabilities under this head rose from Rs 14.9 lakh crore to Rs 17.3 lakh crore, up 16%. This is on account of increase in CRR from 3.5% to 4% under which, banks are required to deposit funds with RBI. Of the total, deposits under reverse repo stands at Rs 7.8 lakh crore. Deposits under this head has risen sharply over last three years, from Rs 2.1 lakh crore at the end of FY19 as a result of surplus liquidity and low credit off-take.

The third item, risk provisions, is a unique feature of central bank's balance sheet and requires considerable explanation. Two main items under this are revaluation reserves and contingency fund (CF). Revaluation reserve further comprises of currency and gold revaluation account (CGRA), Investment Revaluation Account-Foreign Securities (IRA-FS) and Investment Revaluation Account–Rupee Securities (IRA-RS). CGRA is an interesting concept used to manage gains/losses arising out of change in price of gold and change in exchange rate. An example would better illustrate this. Assume RBI had absorbed \$100 bn when exchange rate was Rs 50 per dollar. The value of this investment would stand at Rs 75*100 bn in FY22, implying an unrealized gain of Rs 25*100 bn. As per the practice, RBI would have to show assets of Rs 75*100 in its account books (and not Rs 50*100). The impact of rise in gold prices is also the same. So, 100 tons of gold purchased at Rs 20,000 per 10 gms would imply an unrealized gain of Rs 100*(500-200) crore. As per the Annual report, RBI holds 760 tons of gold, a good part of which was purchased when gold prices were less than Rs 20,000 per 10 gms.

However, it cannot take these gains to income statement as these are unrealized and can get eroded if rupee appreciates or gold prices come down. To balance its balance-sheet, it creates a corresponding liability as CGRA. Similarly, any increase in price of foreign or domestic bonds (as a result of decline in yield) leads to gain in value of these investments which are recorded as IRA-FS & IRA-RS. All the three items 9and a few more smaller ones) are clubbed under revaluation reserves. There is yet another fund called contingency fund (CF), an emergency fund mandated by RBI Act and receives funds from RBI's profit & loss account.

For FY22, CGRA rose from Rs 8.6 lakh crore to Rs 9.1 lakh crore due to increase in gold prices and rupee depreciation. It may be noted that CGRA balance had declined in FY21 due to drop in gold prices and rupee appreciation. IRS-FS reserves have seen interesting movement over last few years. It rose from 16,000 crore at the end of FY19 to Rs 54,000 crore in FY20 due to global monetary policy easing which brought down yields and led to increase in bond prices. However, bond prices have again increased over last two years with monetary tightening. As a result, reserves have declined from Rs 53,000 crore at the end of FY20 to Rs 8,800 crore in FY21 and to negative Rs 94,000 crore now. Since the reserve can't be negative, it is adjusted by transfer of funds from CF reserves. To make up for this decline in CF and to meet statutory requirement, RBI transferred Rs 1.15 lakh crore from its profit & loss account, up sharply from only Rs 20,000 crore in FY21. As a result, surplus available with RBI to be transferred to central government declined from Rs 99,000 crore in FY21 to Rs 30,000 crore in FY22.

*Endnote - RBI earned income of Rs 81,600 crore from its overseas investment implying an interest rate of 2.11%. Earnings had moved from a low of 1.1% in FY18 to 2.65% in FY19.*

| RBI Balance Sheet - Major Components (Rs Lakh Crore) | | | | | | | |
|---|---|---|---|---|---|---|---|
| **Liabilities** | | | | | **Assets** | | |
| | | | FY21 | FY22 | **Issue Deptt** | FY21 | FY22 |
| 1 | Notes issued | | 28.3 | 31.1 | Investment-Foreign | 27.2 | 29.8 |
| | | | | | Gold (against notes issued) | 1.0 | 1.2 |
| | | | | | **Banking Deptt** | | |
| 2 | Deposits | | 14.9 | 17.3 | Investments-Foreign | 12.3 | 11.4 |
| 2.1 | | Reverse repo | 7.3 | 7.2 | Investments-Domestic | 13.3 | 14.9 |
| 3 | Other Liabilities | | 13.9 | 13.5 | Gold | 1.4 | 2.0 |
| 3.1 | | Contingency Fund | 2.8 | 3.1 | Bank loans | 1.4 | 2.1 |
| 3.2 | | CGRA | 8.6 | 9.1 | | | |
| 3.3 | | IRA-(FS+RS) | 0.7 | 0.2 | | | |
| | Total Liability | | 57.1 | 61.9 | Total Assets | 57.1 | 61.9 |
| | *Source – RBI Annual Report. Smaller items not shown* | | | | | | |

\*\*\*\*\*

# Banks' NPA – Taking Stock

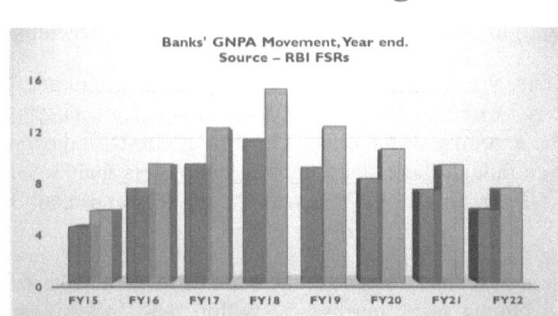

Much to the relief of RBI and the government, Banking sector's Non-Performing Assets (NPA) has come down to seven years low for the year ended March'22. This is a huge achievement, a result of proactive management by all stakeholders including the regulator whose relief measures gave borrowers enough time to recover from the Covid shock. The improvement deserves greater attention because RBI's Financial stability report (FSR) in June'21 has projected that banks' GNPA may increase to 9.8% by March'22. Here is a look at the aggregate NPA level, sectoral and other trends.

As per RBI's latest FSR, Gross NPA (GNPA) of banks stood at 5.9% at the end of March'22. The ratio had peaked at 11.6% in March'18 and came down to 8.4% in March'20, just before the Covid. With aggregate loans & advances of Rs 119 lakh crore, this corresponds to Rs 7 lakh crore of GNPAs, down from Rs 9 lakh crore in March'18. Generation of NPA (fresh slippage), which was over 12% during FY18, has declined to 2.8% by March'22. Interestingly, slippages for PSBs during FY22 is less than that for private banks implying lesser impact of Covid induced shock on PSBs. While private sector and foreign banks were reasonably well placed even earlier with GNPA of less than 4%, Public Sector Banks (PSBs) have recorded significant improvement with the ratio coming down from over 15% in March'18 to 7.6% now.

The clean-up has come with a price as banks had to make huge provisions against these NPAs. As per the government, banks wrote-off a total of Rs 9.9 lakh crore in five years till FY22, of which, PSBs share was Rs 7.2 lakh crore. On the other hand, banks managed to recover about Rs 4.8 lakh crore from its pool of NPAs during the same period, including Rs 1 lakh crore from the written-off accounts. (Writing-off a loan means bank has assigned zero value to the loan in its accounts and reduced its profit or equity by same amount. However, the bank continues its effort to recover the loan and adds it back to the accounts as income in case of recovery).

A figure closely related to NPA is PCR or provisions coverage ratio. This is equal to amount kept aside by the banks (not shown as assets in the balance sheet) to be adjusted against write-offs for NPAs. Higher PCR implies lower possibility of unusual write-offs and in turn, greater ability of banks to absorb shocks. For instance, in the worst case, if a bank with PCR of 70% recovers only 20% from all its NPAs, it would have to reduce its equity capital by only 10% as 70% of the money would be adjusted from the amount kept aside as PCR. With PCR of just 40% for PSBs in March'17, the situation was quite alarming. The same has improved to over 70%, aided by recapitalization of close to Rs 3 lakh crore by the government and improving profitability. The recapitalization has also helped PSBs improve their CRAR (equity capital to risk weighted assets ratio) to 14.6%, sufficiently better than global benchmark of 8%.

Of the four broad sectors, viz, Industry, Services, Retail and Agriculture, Industry continues to account for maximum NPA with GNPA ratio of 8.4% GNPA for Industry stood at over 20% in March'18 reflecting the enormity of the crisis. On absolute basis, Industry segment account for 44% of total NPAs even though there share in total loan is less than 30%. Other than industry, agriculture sector has NPA ratio of 9.4% whereas for services and retail, it stands at just 6.3% and 1.8%.

Apart from concentration in Industry segment, the other distinct characteristic of India's NPAs is that it is concentrated among large borrowers (Within both Industry and services segment. Borrowings of more than Rs 5 crore). While share of total loan given to this segment is 48%, they account for 62% of total NPA. This is still a significant improvement from March'18 when their share in GNPA stood at as much as 85% with loan share of 53%. A focussed approach by the banks to reduce their exposure to this segment and efforts at recovery, including through NCLT, helped them clean up some of the mess. Interestingly, the GNPA share of top 100 large borrowers has come down from 21.2% to 6.9% during the period while their share in total loan has increased from 16% to 17.1% implying the stress has shifted to large borrowers excluding top 100.

Within Industry, there are 15 sub-sectors. Out of these, construction and gems & jewelry have highest GNPA ratio of 19.4% and 18.4% respectively, although down from 25% four year back. Sub-sectors which have seen sharpest turnaround are Basic metals and Engineering with GNPA ratio of 35% and 28% in March'18 which has down to 6.5% and 13% now.

Other than the NPAs of banks, the RBI report also looks at the performance of NBFCs and UCBs (urban co-operative banks). GNPA for NBFCs stands at 6.2%, marginally higher than that for banks but almost the same as a year ago. The ratio had spiked to 6.8% in Sept'21. For UCBs, GNPA rose from about 12% in March'21 to 16% by Sept'21 and has declined to 9.6% by March'22. While the report attributes the sudden spike to Covid-19, it would be important to make sure that UCBs are not resorting to 'ever-greening' of loans.

*****

# Curious Case of Bond Market Movement!

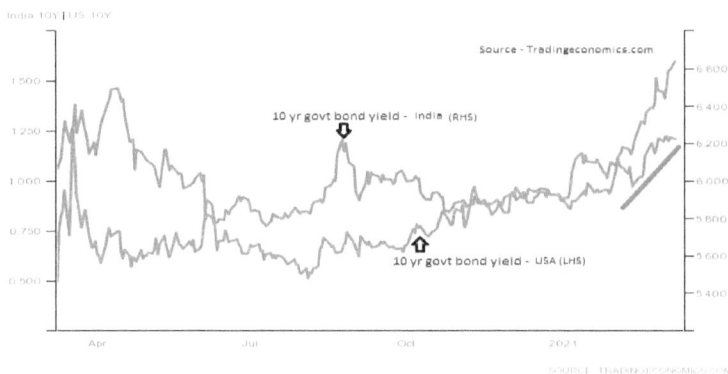

Bond markets have moved up sharply since the beginning of 2021. Not only India, even globally, bond markets are behaving much the same. As a side-effect of this, equity markets witnessed huge sell-off when US government bond yields rose sharply. So, why are bond markets behaving like this and why is it worrying for the central banks? An attempt to understand the dynamics and issues involved.

Bond yield and bond prices are inversely related expressed by the equation, $P = F/(1+r/100)^n$ where P - market price of bond, F - face value or amount the investor gets on maturity, r – yield/rate of return/interest rate and n – maturity period. (The simplest form of equation). Increase in bond yield means buyers would be paying less to buy the bond and in turn, earn higher interest rate.

The yields are increasing primarily for two reasons. The first, simple demand-supply dynamics. Huge borrowings by the government, about Rs 12 lakh crore in FY22 on top of the same amount in FY21, meant that market would be flush with bonds during the next 12 months. Naturally, higher bond supply would bring down its price and thus, increase the yield. The second reason for spike tightening of money supply by increasing interest rate as the economy gains momentum. Higher interest rate leads to bond yields going up. The bond market movement is not unreasonable as MPC faces the tough task of normalizing the policy rates. As per RBI bulletin, liquidity in the market was as high as Rs 8.4 lakh crore in Oct-Nov'21, up from Rs 5.95 lakh crore in Jan'21, a potential source of speculative and inflationary movement as the economy picks-up.

Interestingly, RBI has taken a dim view with one of its monthly bulletins calling the yield movement, "adventurism by some bond traders!". RBI governor called bond yield as "public good" and its orderly evolution as its priority. So, why is RBI spooked? A reason for the same is that a spike in yield at this moment may discourage borrowers and derail the growth momentum. However, more plausible reason appears that as debt manager to the government, it is trying to mobilize funds for the government at the cheapest rate.

Despite all its efforts, RBI has not been able to have its way, affecting government borrowings. This is done by RBI through auction for sale of bonds through Open Market Operations (OMO).

Much to RBI's chagrin, yields being quoted in the bids are higher than RBI's cut-off leading to rejection of bids. RBI conducted an auction on 5th March'21 for sale (re-issue) of Rs 12,000 crore of government bonds maturing in 2030. Even though it received bids worth over Rs 25,000 crore, only two bids worth Rs 1,100 crore were within the cut-off limit of 6.2225% reflecting the disconnect between bond market and RBI. Interestingly, RBI had kept the cut-off limit for the same bond at 6.0596%, almost 0.16% lower, during the auction held just two weeks before this one. Even on that day, it received bid worth only Rs 100 crore within this cut-off in contrast with total bids worth over Rs 15,000 crore. The dynamics of market is evolving so fast that despite increasing the cut-off from about 6.06% to 6.22% in just two weeks, bids falling within the cut-off increased from Rs 100 crore to only Rs 1,100 crore. (What would have been the result had it kept the cut-off at 6.2225% on 18th Feb'21?). The auction result seems to reflect the sentiment of entire market and it is difficult to believe that only some bond traders are playing with the market.

A fall-out of the tussle between RBI and bond market is the "devolution" of large number of bonds. Bond auction is backed by primary dealers (PDs) as under-writers. If bids received are higher that the cut-off and if RBI rejects these bids, PDs have to buy those bonds, the process being called devolution. This, of course, comes with a price as PDs demand higher commission to act as under-writers in such high-risk auction. Additional commission paid to PDs for the devolvement was Rs 0.49 per Rs 100 worth of bond or as much as 0.49%. (Normal commission is less than 0.1%). RBI is, thus, paying significantly higher additional commission to defend the yield. While it is too simplistic, the additional commission added to the cut-off yield of 6.06% may be closer to actual level of bond yield. RBI has also been conducting simultaneous sale and purchase of bonds, called 'operation twist' whereby it purchases long-term bonds (reducing its supply thereby, increase its price and reduce yield) and sells short-term bonds. However, it has not been able to achieve the desired outcome.

So, have the market players become too greedy? Have they become opportunistic? While RBI has been doing a great job, its communication in monthly bulletin appears an attempt to browbeat the market players. The efforts to bend the market is certainly not something that looks defendable, howsoever honest, the intentions may be.

*****

# Revisiting History – Banks' Nationalization

Nationalization of 14 banks in 1969 has been termed as the most defining economic event by RBI; even bigger than the reforms of 1991. The event, although, had political developments of that time as trigger, did lead to complete re-orientation of Indian Banking. Here is a look at the background and the changes that the decision achieved.

India's banking sector witnessed an upheaval in July 1969 when 14 large banks (out of over 90 commercial banks, then) above a threshold size (having deposits not less than Rs 50 crore) were nationalized. While this is popularly known as nationalization of banks, this was not the first decision towards that. Nationalization had actually started in 1955 when the then largest bank, Imperial Bank, was taken over by the government and renamed State Bank of India (SBI). This was followed by nationalization of banks owned by princely states in 1959 which were made subsidiaries of SBI (hence the name State Bank of Patiala etc).

The decision also has a political connotation notably, to establish the position of the then Prime Minister, Late Mrs Indira Gandhi. This is also echoed by the fact that it was carried out through an ordinance (and was ratified by the Parliament only afterwards). Yet, that was, at best, a secondary objective. The exercise was repeated in 1980, after Mrs Gandhi came back to power, nationalizing six more banks meeting the cut-off criteria. However, banks alone were not under the radar of the government. Even large insurance as well as coal-mining companies were nationalized in 1970s. Indeed, the nation took a 'Socialist' turn during the decade and the word "Socialist" was added to the preamble in 1976.

The backdrop of the event was the fact that privately owned commercial banks had failed in the core objective of banking i.e. financial intermediation – mobilizing resources from the savers and lending it to the sectors aligned with national objectives. Some figures lend credence to the rationale. As per RBI database, gross domestic savings as a percent of GDP stood at 12% in 1968-69, just before the nationalization, which rose to 21% by 1978-79. (The next wave of growth in domestic savings and investment started around 2005).

Low savings rate had its genesis in low banking penetration. As per the RBI document titled 'History of RBI', out of 6,00,000 villages in India at that time, only about 5,000 had banks. Not only villages, even coverage of towns was low at about 25% only. The other side of the coin was the skewed nature of credit distribution. As per RBI's history, metropolitan cities got the maximum benefits with credit received by them being 106% of their deposits against less than 40% for rural area. The ratio changed to 84% and 59% by 1981.

So, who was gaining from this? A committee of economists' set-up then made some insightful observations. The report stated that credit was being appropriated by few large industrial houses leading to growth of monopolies and concentration of economic powers. And this was being done through direct/indirect influence of the industrial houses on banks' operations. As per the report, close to 200 directors of 20 leading banks held directorship in 1,100 other operating companies, a clear case of 'conflict of interest'. Close analysis of five leading banks showed directors of these banks were connected to over 600 manufacturing, trading and other companies. (The policy separating banking from other businesses, imitated around then, has become more stringent over the years). However, this alone was not the reason for the momentous step. A bigger reason was enabling credit to agriculture sector and kick-starting India's green revolution which had witnessed two famines around this time. As a result of nationalization, share of scheduled commercial banks in total loan extended to agriculture sector rose from barely 14% in 1971-72 to 41% ten years later and further to 58% by 1990-91. (RBI, possibly, did not maintain separate data for loan to agriculture before nationalization). SCBs continue to be the dominant force in rural financing even now accounting for over 72% of rural financing. Share of banking (together with insurance) in GDP has risen from 1.7% in 1969-70 to 3% in ten years and now stands close to 6%.

A pertinent question that comes up is, did nationalization help meet national objectives? No doubt, as figures mentioned above show the decision changed the entire landscape leading to 'inclusive' banking. While this also, possibly, led to inefficiency, it was certainly a lesser evil than what the nation grappled with before nationalization.

*****

# The 'Bad Bank' – Understanding the Structure

The formation of government backed National Asset Reconstruction Company Ltd (NARCL) or the 'Bad Bank' is a novel experiment which should help take a focused view to resolve NPAs while freeing bank management to devote their energy on core banking. A look at the bad bank and how it is expected to operate.

NARCL is an asset reconstruction company (ARC) set up by domestic banks, both public and private, with public sector banks having 51% share. As an ARC, it would buy bad debts from banks, to be sold to a buyer/investor at a suitable price or liquidated in case it is unable to find one. While there are quite a number of ARCs present in the market, none of them is of the size proposed for NARCL because of inherent risk of the business. While there is no figure available for total loan being managed by private ARC, it could be close to half of proposed size of NARCL.

The need for such a company, owned and operated by banks themselves, arises as most of these loans are given by groups of banks. The resolution, therefore, becomes difficult due to different rules & procedure, multiple levels of co-ordination and inadequate expertise available with banking officials to manage the resolution process. Still the most important factor is fear of questions being raised on taking a decision which may be prudent business wise but on the face of it, involves loss. (For instance, selling a business with loan of Rs 500 crore for Rs 120 crore since the assets have become junk). The arrangement would also free bank management from overseeing the recovery process and focus on their core banking function.

So, how will the arrangement work. Banks will sell the bad loans to NARCL at 18% of loan value and would get 15% of the price in cash whereas the rest would be in the form of security receipts (SRs). SRs would be encashed when NARCL recovers money from that particular loan account. *The differentiating factor between NARCL and other private ARCs is that central government has provided guarantee for these receipts for five years.* It means that if, on resolution, bad bank receives less than amount assured through SRs, government would pay the difference. For instance, assume a loan account worth Rs 10,000 crore which has turned bad. NARCL will buy this at 18%, or Rs 1,800 crore. Of this, it would pay Rs 270 crore upfront as cash and issue SRs worth Rs 1,530 crore. If NARCL recovers only Rs 1,200 crore by selling the business, government would pay the remaining Rs 330 crore to the bank which had originally sold the bad debt. However, in most likelihood, NARCL should be able to recover close to 25% from these assets.

In such a case, the surplus would be passed on the originating bank after deducting a fee. NARCL is projected to take over loans worth Rs 2 lakh crore. At 18%, its total liability works out to Rs 36,000 crore. Of this, Rs 5,400 crore would be paid upfront and SRs worth Rs 30,600 crore would be issued, the amount guaranteed by the government. The NARCL will pick up bad loans above Rs 500 crore only.

The assets purchased will not be managed by NARCL itself but will be entrusted to India Debt Resolution Company Ltd (IDRCL), another company with expertise in asset management and resolution. IDRCL is also owned by banks consortium but with public sector banks having stake of 49%. This would allow IDRCL to function more independently, free from variety of procedural requirements that PSBs are bound by. However, the decision on sale value of the asset would be taken by NARCL and not IDRCL.

Another important development aiding the formation of NARCL was permission granted by RBI to transfer even those accounts which have tuned bad due to fraud by promoters, a reversal from its stated position six months back. The task of managing all related legal issues, filing of cases, managing court proceedings etc would also get transferred to NARCL/IDRCL. It may be noted that many loans have turned bad because of frauds and the very purpose of setting up NARCL would have defeated if RBI had not allowed this. (This, however, does not close cases against bank officials of collusion, if any).

In the first phase, NARCL will take over loans totalling Rs 90,000 crore for which banks have made full provision. (When a borrower defaults on loan payment, the loan account is classified as NPA and banks have to keep aside a part of its profit (or equity) as provision. As a result, outstanding loan amount gets reduced in bank's balance sheet. Full provisioning means bank has set aside entire value of the loan from its profit and outstanding amount has become zero. However, banks record this under another head and continue to take measures for recovery). Since its value is zero on their balance sheet, cash receipt as well as SRs from NARCL would show up as profit in their account. Apart from this, the sale would also clean up their balance sheet as these bad debts would no longer appear in its account books.

*****

# NBFCs – A Liquidity Crisis or An Insolvency Crisis?

The NBFC segment has seen significant churning after the IL&FS implosion. While one set faced severe liquidity crisis, the better ones managed to maintain their growth momentum. The analysis, despite being little dated, give very useful insights. A look at the details.

A finance ministry report released towards the beginning of 2020 disaggregates the NBFCs figures into two sets – the good ones numbering 211, accounting for 82% of the market share and not-so-good ones numbering 145. The good ones have not only cornered all the incremental lending but have also pocketed the loan paid back by the rest. As a result, assets of first set have risen by much higher 20% while the second set has seen its borrowings decline by nearly Rs 90,000 crore, close to 16%.

The same disaggregation has been done for Housing Finance Companies (HFCs) also, with the first set of 76 HFCs controlling 81% of market share and second set of 18 HFCs. The first set has seen 38% growth in their borrowings from banks (plus NHB) against decline of 11% for the rest. In terms of market borrowings (through instruments such as commercial paper, certificate of deposits which are purchased by MFs, Insurance companies etc), while the first set managed growth of 14%, second set suffered a significant decline of 27%. Total decline (bank plus market borrowings) of Rs 68,000 crore in funding of second set is less than gain of Rs 1.44 lakh crore for the first set giving a picture of growth on aggregate basis.

RBI's Financial Stability Report (FSR) gives another insight on divergence in performance of two different groups within the financial firms. Very large firms (debt>Rs 5,000 crore), accounting for 40% of total loan share, recorded credit growth of 48% during FY19, up from 22% in FY18. (Growth figures of only very large firms and not the entire sector). While this would look unreliable considering the general state of the financial sector, a disaggregation between government owned and private sector firms reveals the true picture. Against growth of as much as 93% recorded by public sector firms, private sector companies managed growth of only 40%. The growth difference was subdued in FY8 at 46% and 19%. (The divergence in performance is also visible in manufacturing sector. Borrowings of PSUs in the manufacturing sector recorded growth of 58% and 44% during FY18 and FY19 against decline of 10% and 0.5% for private sector firms).

And this is not all. The market is also rewarding the best at the expense of the rest. This is borne out by the difference in interest rate (called spread or risk premium) charged by the two sets, against detailed in RBI FSR. The difference in rates between the top 25% NBFCs (the top quartile) and the third quartile which was just about 30 basis points in Sept'18, before the IL&FS crisis broke out, shot up to about 150 basis points in Nov'19. (The figure had been fluctuating between 50-100 during Jan-June'19 and moved up again to 150 bps in Aug-Sept'19).

The spread has gone up not just because of higher rates for not-so-good ones but also because the good ones are getting loan at rates better than earlier. And this becomes clear from spread between government bonds, which are risk-free, and the top NBFCs. The spread between three-month government bonds and top quartile NBFCs has come down from about 80 bps before the ILFS crisis to just about 30 bps by Aug'19. (An explanation for this could be decline in avenues for funds deployment for funds surplus firms as many of the NBFCs, the fund seekers, get driven out of the market).

So, what would or what should the not-so-good ones do? They would probably have to get into the fold of the better ones – a merger, an alliance or some such arrangement with them. But certainly, they can't blame the market for their current woes.

To sum up –

•       The better NBFCs and HFCs are receiving all the funds even though the rest are fund starved.

•       The divergence is also visible between public sector and private firms with PSUs getting favourable treatment.

•       The risk premium for not-so-good ones, over the good ones, has gone up.

•       The risk premium for the good ones, over the government bonds, has come down.

*****

# What ails NBFCs

The default by IL&FS created a storm in the market like not seen for a long time. Despite the swift and proactive decision by the government to take over the management of IL&FS, the issue became a systemic crisis not only affecting the NFBC sector but to an extent, the entire financial sector. The stakes are high for the sector with aggregate balance sheet of nearly Rs 30 lakh crore at the end of FY19. The current crisis revolves around inability of NBFCs to meet the immediate cash needs even though the balance sheet may have sufficient assets. However, it is essential to understand the identity crisis that sector grapples with for almost 20 years, not captured by any of the mainstream media. Going forward, more serious challenge for the sector would be to sustain itself as RBI is certain to come up with more stringent guidelines after the dust settles. A look at the background and issues being faced by the NBFC sector.

NBFCs (Non-Banking Finance Company) are another category of financial institutions primarily engaged in meeting the financing needs of the segment not adequately covered by banks. These institutions were very popular till around 2000 due to the inability of banking sector to reach to all the nook and corner of the country. However, advancement of technology, innovations such as Banking Correspondent and several other factors helped banks extend their reach substantially. This is corroborated by RBI data which shows that the share of personal loans in total bank credit has increased sharply from 8.3% in 1993 to 22.3% in 2007 and stands at about 25% at the end of FY18. (Banks' retail lending is not restricted to housing loan alone. Half of the retail portfolio comprises of non-housing loan).

The overlap of operations between banks and NBFCs compelled NBFCs to look for ways to maintain profitability including other avenues for lending. This was also the period when infrastructure financing through development financing institutions (DFI) lost appeal. This resulted in winding up of DFIs with ICICI being merged with ICICI bank (2002) and IDBI getting converted into a bank (2004). DFIs were set up in post-independence period with special status and certain privileges to finance long gestation, critical developmental projects but perhaps, had outlived their purpose by then.

This created a vacuum for infrastructure financing which emerged as an attractive proposition for NBFCs. So much so, that infrastructure now accounts for almost half of the loan portfolio of NFBCs sector. However, there is a crucial difference between the cash flow generated from infrastructure and retail sector loan, something probably not adequately factored-in by NBFCs. Even though retail loan also has higher duration, it starts servicing itself almost immediately. Further, it is easy to detect default early on. Not so, in case of infrastructure loans. However, there was an even bigger challenge the sector had to grapple with, bigger reason for the current crisis.

While there was a crisis building up in terms of finding a borrower, there was also a crisis in terms of finding whom to borrow from! And probably this is a bigger reason for the current crisis then the first. The sector was marred by several frauds involving swindling of depositors' funds during 1990s and early 2000s. This compelled regulators to put severe restriction on their deposit taking activities. Between 1998 and 2008, number of deposit-taking NBFCs came down sharply from 1,420 to 336 whereas total deposit held by them came down from over Rs 13,000 crore to just Rs 2,000 crore. While the deposit taking saw a revival after that (with fewer, better regulated firms), the fund mobilization was still very small due to variety of restriction and stipulations in comparison to the space available for NBFCs to grow. This is reflected in the fact that balance sheet size of NBFC-D is just about 15% of total NBFC sector showing the huge market captured by non-deposit taking NBFCs. Clearly, deposit mobilization was not a winning strategy for them.

This brings us to the current crisis. In the absence of public deposits, NBFCs have to rely on banks, money market and promoters' equity for funds. (This is not to say that NBFCs should have been allowed to mobilize funds from public. In fact, restricting that was a far reaching and prudent approach from the perspective of depositors). Higher cost of funds from banks (whom they have to compete with, for loan disbursal) compelled them to increase their exposure to money market through instruments such as commercial papers. RBI data shows that during 2013-17, NBFCs' borrowings through commercial paper rose by 28% CAGR against just about 6% for bank borrowings. This was also the period when banks were preoccupied with the NPA crisis and had reduced lending, throwing open vast ground for them to grow their business.

While there is no harm in borrowing though an instrument which is cheaper, the problem with commercial paper is that it is a short-term instrument, intended to serve as a 'stop-gap' source of funding. However, due to pressure on margins (as described in Part I), NBFCs have increasingly resorted to this method of financing to meet even their longer-term lending needs. This is what is referred to as asset-liability mismatch. For IL&FS, current liability (maturing within 12 months) was Rs 37,000 crore at the end of FY18 against current assets of barely Rs 32,000 crore, a sure recipe for disaster. (How rating agencies failed to see this certainly needs to be investigated).

In their quest to make the most of short-term arbitrage opportunity, some of the NBFCs are also operating in the near-term market alone. While cost of short-term funds in the money market is lower, short term retail lending rate is higher than long term rates as these are generally taken to meet some exigencies. For a stock exchange listed NBFC, current portion of liability stands at over 80% of total liability! While this is backed by assets of similar maturity, a sustainable business model stipulates that current portion of liability should be restricted to 30-40%.

So, what is it that NBFCs can do to sustain themselves? Promoter's equity as a source of funds offers hope. A look at the NFBCs, who are doing well, shows that majority of them are backed by a strong promoter group/company. Even though return on equity for the sector is about 8-9%, for these promoter groups, NBFC is a part of strategy to provide support to their core business. So, it acts as financer for an automobile or a tractor manufacturing company or even someone selling consumer durables.

So, what is the road ahead for NBFCs? Winston Churchill said, "Never waste a good crisis". The IL&FS crisis could do to NBFC sector what NPA crisis did to Public Sector Banks. Like mentioned in Part I, the inevitable change in guidelines and greater vigilance from regulatory bodies would make their operations more difficult and may even bring out some more skeleton from the closet. This may lead to shrinking of their business and some consolidation even. Over the medium term, it would not be surprising if there are very few stand-alone NFBCs left in the market.

*****

# Housing Finance Companies (HFCs) – A Crisis of Identity

Housing finance companies (HFCs) are facing increasing attention and tightening of regulations, fallout of NBFCs crisis. A turning point has been the default by DHFL, a leading HFC. The crisis being faced by the industry is unprecedented and can lead to fundamental change in their business model because of their inherent disadvantage vis-à-vis banks. But what are HFCs, how big is the industry and how are they different from NBFCs and banks? A look at the same.

HFCs are specialized financing companies providing credit to housing sector. These were regulated by National Housing Bank (NHB) and brought under the regulation of RBI in Aug'19. Even though they are non-finance companies, they are different from NBFCs as they are mandated to focus on housing finance only. As per RBI, there are a total of 100 registered housing finance companies (HFCs) at the end of March'21. The largest of the HFCs are HDFC Ltd with balance sheet size of over Rs 3 lakh crore, now merged with HDFC Bank and LIC housing finance with balance sheet of close to Rs 2 lakh crore. The top 5 HFCs account for close to 80% of the market. This gives a reason to deliberate on whether it is prudent to give license to smaller entities as they pose higher risk of regulatory oversight.

As per the RBI data, HFCs had a total balance sheet size of close to Rs 14.8 lakh crore at the end of FY21. This is less than half the balance sheet of NBFCs at Rs 35 lakh crore and less than one-tenth that of over Rs 196 lakh for the banking sector. However, since they are concentrated in a specific segment, they have an important role to play. Against this balance sheet, HFC have a total loan portfolio of about Rs 12.8 lakh crore, increase of 8% over previous year. Almost 75% of the loan goes towards housing loan whereas non-housing loan such as loan against property, project loan etc. account for the rest. These loans have seen their share increase over a period and are at the heart of the asset-liability mismatch and insolvency crisis.

While HFCs are credited with increasing the total size of housing market with innovative products and customer service, they ceded the leadership to banks by 2003. Digitization and adoption of best practices helped banks increase their share from about 32% in FY98 to 70% by FY07. A fight back by HFCs and diversion of banks' attention to corporate loan subsequently led to decline in banks' share to 57%. Banks also have higher exposure to affordable housing segment with loan under Rs 25 lakh accounting for 54.3% of total portfolio. For HFCs, this accounts for only 44%. In fact, the share of this segment has increased for banks whereas it has come down for HFCs over last five years.

A reason for ceding the leadership position by HFCs is higher cost of funds which reduces their competitive advantage and possibly, leading to disbursement of riskier loans. The irony of the situation lies in the fact that they compete with banks with one-fourth of their borrowings coming from banks only. A testimony of this irony is that HFCs which are doing well are either deposit taking or promoted by another financial agency, either banks or insurance company like LIC. Increasing regulatory tightening and elimination of avenues to earn higher returns is making their survival even more difficult. It would not be surprising if many of these cease to exist five years from now.

*****

# Understanding the Dynamics of Money Market

Money market has been witnessing increased volatility with tightening of interest rate by RBI. With average turnover of over Rs 6 Lakh crore daily, any uncertainly in the market is a cause of great concern for RBI which has been pumping in money to keep the market stable. But what exactly is money market and how does it function. A brief look.

Money market refers to various platforms where financial instruments with short term maturity are traded. The duration of the instruments is less than one year. It is further classified into three segments - Overnight market where the transaction is for one working day only, notice money market with duration of 2 to 14 days and Term money market. The transactions in the term market are carried out for 15 days to one year.

Unlike capital market where the instruments available are only bond and equity, money market operates through a variety of instruments. These are called call money, repos, Commercial Paper, Certificate of Deposit and Collateralized Borrowing & Lending Obligations (CBLO) etc. Besides, there are instruments exclusively used by government to raise funds from the money market. These are called treasury bills (T-bills) and cash management bills.

Call money are unsecured lending instrument used only for overnight operations and restricted to scheduled commercial banks and primary dealers only. It is a stop-gap arrangement not exactly to meet any financing needs but to help banks meet their statutory requirements of maintaining CRR etc. While these are popular instrument among the bankers, it has limited depth due to significant restriction in participants. As per RBI data, average daily turnover in this segment was only about Rs 12,000 crore during June'22 against as much as Rs 3.4 lakh crore in CBLO.

CBLO or Collateralized Borrowing and Lending Obligation has a much wider participants including insurance companies, mutual funds, provident funds and even select corporate, other than the above-mentioned groups. CBLOs allow members to borrow against the collateral of eligible securities mostly central or state government papers. It is a popular instrument where most of the MFs park their excess cash with banks being the lead borrower. As stated earlier, the instrument recorded average daily turnover of about 3.4 lakh crore.

Commercial Paper (CP) is an unsecured money market instrument, open to large number of participants and probably at the heart of the current crisis. Companies, including NBFCs and AIFIs, Cooperative societies, trusts, limited liability partnerships and corporate having net worth of at least Rs 100 crore are eligible to issue commercial papers. However, these entities cannot invest in CPs issued by related parties. CPs have become highly popular replacing the short-term bank credit due to lower funding costs.

However, unsecured form of lending makes CP among the riskiest instrument. As per IL&FS annual report, it had outstanding CPs of Rs 5,750 crore at the end of FY18, up from Rs 3,200 crore a year ago. As per RBI annual report, leasing and finance companies account for more than half of the total issuances. These are the papers most vulnerable and cause of worry for those who have invested in it. As per RBI data, total issuance during July'22 has been Rs 1.2 lakh crore. This has come down from as much as Rs 2.6 lakh crore in July'18, a fallout of IL&FS crisis. Total CP

outstanding had come down from Rs 6.4 lakh crore in Sept'18 to Rs 3.4 lakh crore by March'20 but has risen marginally to 3.7 lakh crore by June'22.

Repo or ready forward contact is an instrument for borrowing funds by selling securities with an agreement to repurchase the said securities within a year. While the securities are normally government securities, some corporate debt with 'AA' rating are also eligible to be used as securities. Another instrument in the money market is Certificate of Deposit (CD), generally issued by banks or other eligible financial institutions. Banks can issue CDs for maturities from 7 days to one year whereas eligible FIs can issue for maturities from 1 year to 3 years. However, banks have to pay higher rate of interest to sell these as compared to CBLO, CPs etc.

*****

# Derivatives Market in India - An Overview

Derivates market in India has grown in leaps and bounds after being introduced in the year 2000. Total turnover has reached a level of Rs 165 lakh crore (notional value) in FY18 from just about Rs 1 lakh crore in FY02, the first full year after it was introduced. The turnover has increased over four times in last five years itself. While derivatives serve an important function as hedging instrument, a sharp increase like this could be a sign of speculation. However, before debating on the speculative nature of trade and other ills, here is an attempt to understand the market.

"Derivatives" is a type of security, also called contract, which derives its value from another asset. This means that it doesn't have an independent value like say, a stock whose price is dependent upon the company's performance or say, any commodity, whose price is determined by the demand-supply dynamics of the commodity. The price of the "derivative" is driven by the price of the asset that it is representing. That other asset could be stock of a company, gold, currency or any such product whose value is readily available in the market. (So, if the aggregate salaries of the CEOs of companies are actively available in the market, you can create a "derivative" product which tracks the aggregate salary and you can buy/sell the same depending upon your expectation of their future salaries. Or, a CEO can hedge his salary by taking a counter position). In the equity derivative market, underlying assets are either individual stocks or the indices such as Sensex, Nifty 50 etc.

Derivates are further classified into "futures" and "options". Futures contracts are binding contract to buy/sell the underlying asset at a specified price on a specified date. A simple example would help understand the concept. Assume an investor is apprehensive that the price of a stock he holds, currently trading at Rs 100, can crash due to market volatility. However, he doesn't want to sell the stock, so he sells the stock "futures" at the specified price of Rs 102. If the price actually falls, he will deliver the stock to the counter party at Rs 102 and save himself from the loss. And if the price doesn't fall, he can still purchase the stock from the market at nearly the same price and sell to the counter party. In practice, actual delivery rarely happens and the parties concerned only pay/receive the difference between market and contract price.

Options contract are where the buyer gets the right but not the obligation to buy/sell the specified asset at the specified price. The buyer has to pay a premium for acquiring this right which is usually in the range of 0.1-0.2% of the contract value. However, the premium may go up depending upon the volatility in the market or movement in the price of the underlying stock. Options are more popular product accounting for over 80% of derivatives contract.

Before understanding the market further, let's have a look at some of the statistics. Equity derivatives market traded nearly 200 crore contracts with turnover of over Rs 165 lakh crore during FY18 (not sure if you can visualize that amount!). However, it must be understood that the amount is notional and not the money that is actually transacted. In case of options, actual transacted value is largely, the premium paid and in case of futures, the difference between stock price and contract price. This is illustrated by the fact that against the above mentioned turnover, actual settlement was only about Rs 1.2 lakh crore.

Unlike equity market where one can buy/sell even one stock, derivatives are traded on minimum lot size basis with Rs 5 lakh as the minimum notional value. For example, in case of NIFTY futures, the current index of about 10,500 represents the notional value of one unit. With one lot comprising of 75 units, minimum exposure in NIFTY futures works out to about Rs 7.9 lakh. However, the trader only needs to put-in the margin money, roughly around Rs 90,000 and not the entire amount.

The other differentiator in comparison to the cash segment is that the derivative contracts expire on the last trading day of the month and cannot be settled before that. So, even if the trader anticipates adverse movement, he cannot settle the contract but can take another contrary position to neutralize the impact of the movement. While this would reduce his losses, he will need additional margin money for this. In case of options, the buyer has to pay an upfront premium calculated through complex models but normally less than 0.5% of notional value of the contract.

Despite the huge trade in derivatives, they have become high risk and speculative instruments, far more than even the equity cash trade. That is so because speculators have over-numbered the hedgers undermining the original objective of acting as a hedging instrument to the owners of the underlying assets. As per a SEBI report, ratio of equity derivatives trading to equity cash trading has gone up sharply from 3.2 in FY10 to over 23 times in FY18. This ratio is in the range of 1.1-7.2 times for all other exchanges except one mentioned in the report. The report also shows that one out of six individual trades in derivatives even though they don't trade in cash segment, defying the very objective of derivatives.

Other than traders' speculative tendencies, derivatives trade across global exchanges has also probably added to the speculation. Indian equity derivatives are traded across ten global exchanges of which, Singapore Exchange (SGX) is the most popular. SGX accounts for over half of turnover in futures although its share in options trading is negligible. To counter the increasing dominance of SGX in Indian derivatives market, NSE recently discontinued its agreement with SGX which allowed SGX to trade in NIFTY indices.

To counter the speculative tendency, SEBI increased the margin requirement in June this year. The upfront margin required to be deposited has been increased from about 7% to over 10% of the notional trade value now. It has also proposed gradual move to physical settlement from the current system of cash settlement whereby the traders pay/received the money and don't have to sell/purchase stocks for settlement.

However, it would be virtually impossible to alter the fundamental nature of equity trade which is speculative. What is more important is to reduce information asymmetry, being perpetuated through insider information.

*****

# IDBI Bank Turnaround – A Brief Case Study

IDBI Bank has been in the news due to government's plan to divest its holding. This follows bank's revival after being under RBI's PCA for an extended period of time. At one point of time, banks Gross NPA ratio had crossed 30% with GNPA for corporate loan crossing 50%! So, what all the bank went through and where does it stand now. Here is a look at the same.

IDBI Bank is majority owned by LIC with 49.2% stake and government with 45.5% stake. It is classified as a private bank since LIC is running it as promoter. The bank had balance sheet size of Rs 3 lakh crore at the end of FY22, marginally higher than FY21 but lower than Rs 3.5 lakh crore in FY18. (Entire analysis based on its annual reports sourced from BSE). This comprises of Rs 2.3 lakh crore or over 75% of deposits and Rs 42,500 crore of shareholders' funds. In terms of deployment, Rs 1.45 lakh crore or less than 50% has been given as loan recorded as 'advances' in banking parlance. Investments, primarily in government securities, stands at Rs 83,500 crore whereas the rest is parked with RBI and in inter-bank market. Advances grew at 14% during FY22, higher than industry average of about 9%. Advances have accelerated for the first time since FY18 with improvement in financial strength. Banks advances had declined by more than 25% between FY18 and FY21 when it was put PCA watch (Prompt Corrective Action) by RBI. A bank is put under PCA if its financial parameters such as capital adequacy, NPAs etc do not meet the prescribed norms whereby its lending and other activities are restricted. At the end of FY18, bank's gross NPA stood at Rs 56,000 crore or 32% of total advances. For 'Industries', NPA was Rs 43,500 crore accounting for almost 80% of total NPA. Gross NPA to advance ratio for 'industries' stood at an unbelievable 54% in FY19.

NPA discourse centers on the amount of loan given, total amount of loan under default or gross NPA, provision made, write-offs and recovery or the amount from this loan portfolio which comes back to the bank. (The last is important as a number of defaulting loans start paying up if the economic conditions improve). The bank had a reasonably low GNPA of Rs 13,000 crore at the end of FY15 but added Rs 43,000 crore of NPAs between FY16 and FY18 (On net basis i.e., additions minus reductions). From FY19, NPAs started declining totaling Rs 19,000 crore, less than half, during FY19-21. As a result, GNPA, which had reached Rs 56,000 crore at the end of FY18 came down to Rs 34,000 crore by FY22.

As mandated by RBI, bank had to make higher provisioning for these NPAs. Provisioning refers to the amount bank has kept aside as reserve to make up for potential non-recovery/ under-recovery from its loan portfolio. It is made from bank's operating profit and if the profits are not sufficient, by reducing its equity capital. Total provisions made by the bank at the end of FY16 was only Rs 10,000 crore. Additional provisions made during the next three years (FY17-19) stood at Rs 73,000 crore, more than four time its operating profit during the period! (Total provisions are higher than increase in NPA because bank had to make provisions for old NPAs also). Since profit was not sufficient, provisions resulted in losses leading to decline in equity capital. Provisions came down to Rs 16,000 crore during FY20-22, less than one-fourth in the previous period and less than the operating profit. As a result of provisioning, bank's PCR (Provisions Coverage ratio) improved from 55% in FY17 to acceptable 83% in FY19 and 94% by FY20. PCR of 94% means bank needs to recover only 6% from its pool of NPAs to maintain profitability and any recovery more than this would get added to its income.

The next item in the NPA discussion is 'technical write-off', the loan which bank removes from its balance sheet on the assets side and reduces the provision reserves by the same amount on the liabilities side. (Despite the write-off, bank continues its efforts to recover money from the borrower). Write-offs stood at just Rs 3,000 crore in FY17 but rose sharply by Rs 12,000 crore and Rs 14,000 crore in the next two years (FY18-19). While provisioning was four times the operating profit, write-offs were also almost 70% of operating profit, further adding to the financial stress. Write-offs came down to less than Rs 4,000 crore on an average in the next three years. Total pool of written-off loans which stood at Rs 11,000 crore at the end of FY17, rose to Rs 36,000 crore at the end of FY19 and Rs 44,000 crore by FY22. (Numbers do not add up because of another number called recoveries, explained later).

There is yet another important parameter in the NPA discourse and that is – recoveries. This can also be classified into two – recovery from a loan account not 'written-off' and from a written-off account. So, if a bank made a provision of Rs 80 crore against a loan of Rs 100 crore (not written-off) and gets back Rs 40 crore from the borrower, it would lead to write-back of Rs 20 crore. (Provisions minus loss incurred, 80-(100-40)). Bank has made total recoveries of Rs 28,000 crore in five years between FY18 and FY22, just about 20% of the loan amount. While it is a huge price to pay for its indiscriminate lending to corporate sector, what is left of the bank is worth the price. including alleged mala fide lending practices. It may be noted that investigations are going on regarding its lending to high profile corporate which have defaulted. There is still a GNPA pool of about Rs 34,000 crore which can yield Rs 7,000 crore at this rate (or even more).

From the written-off' loan accounts (Rs 44,000 crore in FY22), if the bank is able to make any recovery, it is added to bank's income for the year. Aggregate recovery made from these accounts was only Rs 5,150 crore during four years (FY19-FY22). The amount is almost negligible, yet the recovery is pursued vigorously to avoid future 'moral hazard'.

So, where does the bank stand now? As per the latest financials for nine month ended Dec'22 (FY23), GNPA has further come down to Rs 23,500 crore and GNPA at 13.8%. Bank's provisioning has further improved to 98%. This means any recovery more than 2% would add to the bottom-line. Net profit for nine months has further risen to Rs 2,500 crore, 44% higher than previous year. Bank's provisioning has further improved to 98%. This means any recovery more than 2% would add to the bottom-line. Bank has also realigned its business strategy and has shifted focus from high-risk corporate to retail. Share of corporate loan in total loan has come down to 37% from about 55% five years ago. Net profit for nine months has further risen to Rs 2,500 crore, 44% higher than previous year. However, it had accumulated losses of over Rs 43,000 crore at the end of FY22. It would need to wipe this out before it can be truly out of the woods.

*****

# Urban Co-operative Banks – Analyzing the Crisis

Urban cooperative banks have gained prominence over last few years with failure of a few prominent ones, issues related to governance and misappropriation of funds and changes in regulations. A look at the issues affecting urban cooperative banks and forward path.

Cooperative banks form the third pillar of financial intermediation after scheduled commercial banks and NBFCs. Cooperative banks are further classified as rural or urban, the focus here being on urban cooperative banks (UCB). UCBs are largely localized banks owned and operated by its members who are also its customers. (A person desirous of availing loan from a UCB must become its member first). As per RBI, there are a total of 1,534 UCBs in the country with total assets of Rs 6.6 lakh crore at the end of March'21. This is less than 5% of the total assets of the financial sector implying a rather insignificant role for them. UCBs gained prominence from 1993 with a liberal licensing policy by RBI in view of their ability to connect well with the local population. However, several scams during 2000-05, most notably, the Madhavpura scam, led to a rethink on their operating framework which continues even till now.

The board of PMC bank was suspended by RBI in 2019 primarily because the board granted loan to a particular group far in excess of what is prescribed by RBI and non-reporting of default. The allegations of the chairman being linked to the concerned company raises even greater concern. However, this is not the first case of a UCB entering into fraudulent practice. In another high-profile case, Bombay High Court had directed the concerned authority to file a case against Maharashtra state cooperative bank and its board of directors for sanctioning loan worth thousands of crores to several factories which defaulted subsequently. RBI's website lists nearly 25 instances of restriction being put or extended on UCB. UCB were also accused of being a conduit for converting large sums of unaccounted money into white after demonetization.

The dual reporting structure lies at the core of the governance crisis being faced by UCB. UCBs are formed as cooperatives and shareholders elect the board of directors (BoD). (A recent RBI paper proposes that UCBs would have to constitute another board of management, different from BoD). However, the election process has largely degenerated with the state political leaders or local businessmen/ industrialists retaining their hold on the operations. This has led to serious conflict of interest as many of these banks have acted as easy source of money for them. While RBI has the power to remove the chairman of a commercial bank, it doesn't have such power in case of UCB. (RBI has the power to suspend the board but that is an extreme step).

However, it is not only about governance. UCBs are also constrained by their size which limits their profitability and therefore, commercial viability. Average assets of UCBs are close to Rs 400 crore only against over Rs 1 lakh crore for a commercial bank. Almost 60% of UCBs have deposit base of less than Rs 100 crore with large number of them being single branch bank. This puts a strain on their profitability because of high overhead costs. Only 5% of them have a deposit base of over Rs 1,000 crore giving them sufficient 'economies of scale'. While the reported NPA is just about 7%, the development at PMC bank puts a question mark over the credibility of their reporting. The multiplicity of UCBs and their size makes them 'too small to govern' and it would not be surprising if actual NPAs for more of them are worse than this.

While UCBs played an important part in meeting the needs of smaller borrowers till late 90s, the 'raison d'être' for their existence has largely disappeared now. This is because commercial banks have largely reached the farthest corner of the nation with IT based solutions, innovations such as banking correspondent and aggressive banking. The fact that they pose disproportionate risk to the financial sector and can cause severe erosion of confidence warrants a proactive rather than reactive stance. An appropriate path going ahead could be merger of smaller ones with the bigger ones or bunching together of all cooperatives within a state or a region into a special purpose vehicle. This could be taken over as a subsidiary by a commercial bank with suitable incentives. If the government can bite the bullet of large-scale mergers of public sector banks, this is a smaller nut to crack.

*****

# Bimal Jalan Committee Report – A critical Analysis

The Bimal Jalan committee was formed to determine RBI's surplus reserves. While the report helped RBI transfer some surplus to the government, there was still lot of money left with RBI. So, what are the recommendations of the committee and how does RBI's balance sheet look like. A brief look at the same.

The Bimal Jalan committee, formed in 2018, was tasked to review the existing economic capital framework (ECF) of RBI. While economic capital sounds fancy, in simple terms, it is nothing but the equity capital available with RBI. ECF refers to the policy determining how much equity capital it maintains and how much it transfers to the government. This could be loosely compared to the policy in case of any listed company, where management is expected to maintain equity capital required to run the company and transfer excess as dividend to the shareholders.

Before looking at the surplus, it is imperative to look at various component of RBI's balance sheet. The major elements are 'notes in circulation' at Rs 21.7 lakh crore at the end of June'19, deposits of Rs 7.6 lakh crore and other liabilities & provisions of Rs 11.6 lakh crore. Provisions would be close to Rs 10.7 lakh crore within the third component. (These are FY19 figures although the report uses FY18 figures in its report). This, essentially, is the surplus and subject of deliberation on how much of this is required to manage risks faced by RBI.

Provision consists of Rs 2.3 lakh crore of contingency risk buffer (CRB) and Rs 6.6 lakh crore of revaluation reserves. CRB is profit retained by RBI over the years whereas revaluation reserve is 'unrealized' equity. It may be noted that RBI generates significant amount of income even though its expenses are quite low. For instance, during FY19, it earned a total income of Rs 1.9 lakh crore against expenditure of Rs 17,000 crore only. (However, FY19 was an exceptional year due to forex accounting changes and its income is generally half of this). This excess of income over expenditure, after transferring a part of it to the government as dividend, adds to its balance-sheet. CRB needs to be maintained to address any financial stability risk which refers to the risk of a bank failure. RBI needs to have sufficient reserves as it may have to pump-in the money as lender of last resort.

The second component, the revaluation reserve, refers to excess of current price over purchase price of foreign currency and gold held by RBI. For instance, assume RBI had bought 100 ton of gold when the prices was Rs 20,000 per 10 gram. At the current rate, this would be valued at close to Rs 40 crore against purchase price of Rs 20 crore. However, since it is not sold by RBI, it remains as 'unrealized' gain on the balance sheet. The same applies to its foreign currency reserves where it may have brought some part of the reserve even at Rs 40 per dollar and imply unrealized gain of as much as Rs 30 per dollar. Even though some part of its reserves may be held in the form of other currencies, rupee is largely depreciating because of higher inflation rate against all the major economies. (Considering the total size of revaluation reserves, average purchase price of dollar could be close to Rs 50).

This brings us to the report of the Committee. The two major recommendation of the committee is to main CRB in the range of 5.5-6.5% of its balance sheet and keep revaluation reserve as it is. Based on FY19 balance sheet, CRB would correspond to Rs 2.3-2.7 lakh crore. Since RBI was maintaining higher surplus than the lower end figure, it has transferred the excess to the government.

While the committee's conservative approach to not touch the revaluation reserves may have its merit, a critical examination of the issue may be in order. The biggest risk that revaluation reserve is required to face is risk of flight of foreign capital. Assuming such a scenario does occur, RBI would have to sell huge amount of dollars to keep the market running. Since the rupee would depreciate in such a case, it would receive more from selling the dollar than what it would have paid for purchasing it. As a result, flight of capital would not dent the revaluation reserve. While this would reduce its total dollar reserve, that is a different risk not addressable by revaluation reserve. The revaluation reserve would decline only if the price of dollar falls which would happen if there is excess supply of dollars. This would signify strengthening economy which is not a risk. A figure buttressing this point is the fact that revaluation reserves accounted for only 38% of RBI's economic capital in 1997-98 against as much as 73% in FY18. Releasing even 13% and bringing it down revaluation reserves down to 60% would free up over Rs 3 lakh crore from its surplus.

Even CRB should be benchmarked against the total balance sheet size of banking sector, which it intends to protect. While report does make indirect reference to that, the benchmarking should explicitly link CRB to the total balance sheet of the banking sector rather than to that of RBI.

*****

# RBI's 12th Feb Circular - Understanding Supreme Court's Ruling

In an important ruling, the Supreme Court quashed RBI's circular dealing with loan default and initiation of insolvency process. The ruling had received widespread attention as it dealt with a very important and complex issue related to running of businesses. It came as a big relief not just to specific sectors but to businesses, in general. So, what was that circular and why SC rejected it? An attempt to understand.

The RBI circular, issues on 12th Feb'19 called 12th Feb circular rather infamously, said that banks would have to treat the loan as default if there is a delay of even one day on loan repayment. The bank would then have to initiate resolution process to recover the loan amount. However, this is still not the controversial element. The critical part starts after this as the circular stipulates that *bank would have to file case against the defaulter in insolvency court* if they are not able to recover the amount in 180 days. RBI guidelines so far stipulated that bank would have to classify a loan as special mention account (SMA) if there is a delay in loan payment but not compulsorily initiation of insolvency. (SMA-0 for delay between 1-30 days, SMA-1 for 31-60 days and SMA-2 for 61-90 days). If the loan remains unpaid beyond the period of 90 days, then only, it is to be classified as 'default'.

After the promulgation of Insolvency & Bankruptcy Code (IBC), government had inserted a clause, 35AA, in banking regulations Act. As per the clause, *"government may authorize RBI"* to direct banks to initiate insolvency process against a defaulting company. This power has been used twice before the circular was issued, when RBI directed banks to start insolvency process against defaulting companies totaling 12 in numbers in the first list and 26 in the second list.

As per its ruling, the Supreme Court stated that RBI's powers are limited to government's order, that too, in specific cases of default only. The circular, thus, fails to meet two stipulations. It needs an authorization from government. Second, it can be invoked only against specific defaulters and cannot be invoked as a blanket order. The ruling means that hypothetically speaking, if the government had authorized RBI to issue such a blanket order, it would have been against the law. The ruling re-affirms the fact that the discretion to drag a defaulting company to insolvency court rests solely with banks. This is important as it allows banks to explore ways to recover loans while keeping the company afloat as witnessed in case of Jet Airways.

The circular, issued during the tenure of Mr Urjit Patel, had generated lot of heat as RBI had taken a rigid stand on this. In the face of intransigence, despite several representations from the banks, the matter was taken to the Supreme Court which had stayed its implementation in Sept'18. This was also among the issues of differences between the government and RBI ultimately leading to resignation of the governor.

So, what next? The ruling saves many companies which are under default. However, a number of these companies are going through resolution process outside IBC and have a chance to salvage value. So, while these NPAs still need to be resolved, the ruling allows them a breather and the sword hanging over their head has been moved away.

*****

# Operation Twist! – RBI's Latest Instrument

In an interesting move, RBI conducted simultaneous sale and purchase of government bonds in late Dec'19. Even though it is normal practice to either sell or purchase bonds to manage liquidity in the market, doing both simultaneous was possibly the first time in India. So, what is the reason for this and what are its implications. An attempt to understand.

RBI had announced that it would sell bonds with maturity of 3-months to 1-year worth a total of Rs 10,000 crore and purchase 10-year bonds for the same amount. The objective was to increase short-term yield and reduce the longer-term yield and is called 'operation twist'! So, how does that happen? When RBI sells bonds, the supply of the bond of that particular maturity goes up in the market and thus, reduces its price. This means the holder of the bond would pay lesser for the amount it would receive on maturation of the bond. This reduces the denominator in the yield equation, thus, increasing the yield. Similarly, purchase of the bond from the market reduces its supply, increases the price, thereby, reducing the yield. An increase in short-term yield and decrease in long-term yield would 'flatten' the yield curve. (The yield curve under normal circumstance is upward sloping due to higher risk premium for bonds with higher maturity). The current gap in yields between the two tenure is nearly 100 basis points (1 percentage point).

The exercise broadens RBI's job of managing money supply through monetary policy, liquidity management and now, yield management through operation twist! But why is RBI doing this. A reduction in longer-term rate is aimed at inducing investment and high value purchases such as housing as these are dependent upon on longer term yields. A similar exercise was first carried out in USA to spur investment without affecting the overall supply of money. However, increasing the short-term rate looks somewhat contrary to the current policy stance. This may give a signal that RBI may not be interested to bring down rates further in the near term.

But can a transaction of Rs 10,000 crore affect the yield curve considering the fact that total government bonds outstanding is over Rs 60 lakh crore? While the total outstanding is huge, bonds in the specific maturity bracket is relatively small. As per RBI database, total of Rs 2.68 lakh crore of government bonds are maturing during April-Dec'20. Auction of Rs 10,000 crore implies 3.7% of the outstanding stock which is not insignificant. For 10-year bonds auction, the share is even higher at 5.6% with Rs 1.79 lakh crore of bonds maturing during April-Dec'29. And the auction conducted today has indeed made an impact. Yield for 10-year bond has come down to 6.58% against 6.77% just a fortnight ago. Similarly, the yield for 1-year bond has risen from 5.26% for the fortnight ended 20th Dec'19 to a range of 5.47%-5.58% now.

Yet, the story doesn't end here. While the transactions between RBI and financial institutions are highly efficient, there is a  huge gap in its transmission to the economy for a variety of reasons. Whether this will have any impact in the real economy is still uncertain. And if RBI does more of such operations, it would not be surprising.

Endnote – Of all the government bonds still outstanding, costliest bond was issued in Dec'2000 with coupon rate of 11.6%.

*****

# Regional Rural Banks – An Overview

Regional Rural Banks (RRBs) are also witnessing a wave of government pushed amalgamation, like other segments of banking sector. Even though RRBs are healthier and less politically influenced than co-operative banks, the reason for their establishment itself doesn't seem to hold good now. While amalgamation is one way forward, the real benefit would be if they are merged with the sponsoring bank. A look at RRBs, a brief historical perspective and current status.

RRBs were established in 1976 after passage of RRB Act with the primary objective to meet the financing needs of rural India. It may be noted that 1970 witnessed considerable action to take banking to rural India and reduce the menace posed by usurious money lenders Almost all private banks were nationalized in two phases during this decade. RRBs are a joint venture between central government, the respective state government and a sponsoring bank which looks after its operations. The initial expansion phase led to its number rising to 196 in just about a decade and helped in its objective to increase rural lending. The share of institutional credit rose from 32% in 1971 to 66% by 1991. (Most of the rest coming from moneylenders).

However, like in case of many government-led initiatives, the model began to show signs of stress with many of these banks starting to make losses. The first phase of consolidation, started around 2005, leading to its number coming down to 82 by 2010. The period of consolidation partially coincided with the period when NBFC segment also recorded significant churning, a result of increased regulatory scrutiny. Number of deposit-taking NBFCs during 1998-2008 came down sharply from 1,420 to 336. The RRBs are going through another phase of amalgamation with their numbers coming down to 43 as on 1st April'20.

A look at their financials shows total balance sheet size of Rs 6.2 lakh crore in FY21 as per the RBI data. This corresponds to just about 3% of the size of commercial banks and half of rural co-operative banks. Despite the inefficiency, RRB's mobilize almost 80% of its funds in the form of low cost 'deposits', reflecting the faith of depositors due to its localized operations. However, they do not seem to have been very active in loan disbursal with disbursal being Rs 3.3 lakh crore. This corresponds to share of just about 12% of total credit flow to rural India. Total loan outstanding is less than half of total funds available, the rest of the funds being invested in government securities.

FY21 was a productive year for RRBs as they turned profitable after a gap of three years. Aggregate profit stood at Rs 1,682 crore against loss of Rs 2,200 crore in FY20 and Rs 650 crore in FY19. Number of RRBs making losses stood at 13, against 19 in FY20. Gross NPAs for RRBs has improved to 9.4% from 10.4% in FY20.

Despite the thrust provided to RRBs, their share in rural lending did not really record any significant jump. From initial share of 9%, its share has stabilized at close to 12%. Close to 75% of the credit to rural India is provided by the commercial banks. This raises the question as to whether there is any real reason to keep RRBs as separate entity other than practical issues related to merger. It would possibly be more appropriate to amalgamate them with the sponsoring bank or even, carving out an altogether separate entity, a subsidiary within each commercial bank to meet the needs of rural India more proactively.

*****

# Money Supply – Understanding the Different Forms

The term 'Money supply' is often used in business and policy conversation and is an important tool to steer the economy. How is that so and what are the characteristics and significance of different types of money supply. A look at the same.

The first form of money is Mo also called reserve money and is equal to currency in circulation (CIC) plus banks' deposits (required as reserves) with RBI. CIC is currency printed by RBI and injected into the economy through purchase of foreign currency, gold or government bonds. Thus, RBI's liability is not limited to the currency it has actually printed. So, hypothetically, if banks are freed of keeping a reserve with RBI and demand all their money, RBI will have to print that much additional currency to meet its liability. As per RBI data, CIC was Rs 28.5 lakh crore whereas M0 was Rs 35.5 lakh crore at the end of FY21 (31$^{st}$ March'21), increase of 16% and 14% CAGR during FY18-21.

The second group is M1 also called narrow money and is equal to currency with public (CIC minus cash with banks) plus banks' demand liability. Thus, it includes the liability of RBI and partial liability of banking sector. The demand liability is a primary source of risk for banks since it would not be able to meet its obligation in case of a scramble for cash withdrawal. To mitigate this risk, banks are required to keep a part of their deposits with RBI. At the end of FY21, M1 was Rs 47.5 lakh crore arising out of nearly Rs 14 lakh crore of demand deposit with banks.

M3 or broad money forms the third group of money and includes time liability of the banking system. It is the total liability of RBI plus the banking system. Since it is time liability, it does not cause significant risk to the bank unless there is a significant asset-liability mismatch. While M0 and M1 remain linked to CIC, M3 keeps increasing faster as the economy grows. With time deposits of over Rs 140 lakh crore, M3 stands at much high figure of Rs 188 lakh crore. Even though this figure is too large, it is backed by productive assets created in the economy by government/private sector and generates sufficient cashflow to meet the liability. The ratio of M3 to M0 is called money multiplier and currently stands at more than 5 times, up from close to 3 times in 1990s.

*****

# Banks' Credit Growth – Changing Dynamics

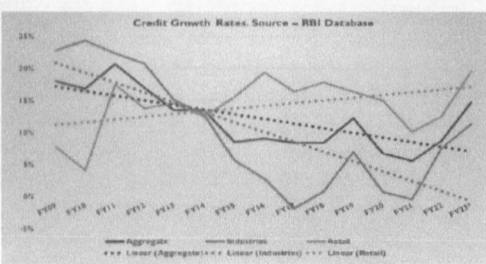

Indian economy appears to be gaining momentum as evident from banks' credit growth which has reached almost 18% till the first week of Oct (Oct'22 over Oct'21). The figure stood at less than 7% CAGR during FY19-22. While this gives RBI and the government some relief, there is a significant change in the drivers of loan growth also. Here is a look at the same.

Credit or loans are classified into four broad categories - Industries, Services, Personal (or retail) & Agriculture. As per RBI database, total loan extended by the banking sector stood at Rs 124 lakh crore at the end of Aug'22 (details available till Aug'22). Retail loan at Rs 36.5 lakh crore has become the largest segment surpassing 'industries' segment in FY21. It is also is the biggest driver for the current year (FY23) with growth rate of 19.5% accounting for half of the incremental credit. The segment has gained prominence over last few years with re-alignment of banks' lending strategy, particularly public sector banks following significant increase in corporate default. It may be noted that GNPA ratio for industries had reached as much as 20% In FY18 whereas retail GNPA remains at less than 2%. Within retail, while housing loan accounts for about Rs 18 lakh crore, other personal loan (non-vehicle, non-credit card, non-education) accounts for over Rs 9.5 lakh crore. While there is no clarity on what this money is being used for, possibly, it is meeting the financing needs of small, family-owned businesses.

'Industries' is the second largest segment with total loan book of Rs 32 lakh crore, or about 26%. The segment has seen significant change in its performance over last one and half decades. While the credit grew by as much as 20% during FY08-14, it fell to barely 2.8% during FY14-19 and further to 0.5% during FY19-21. The shift was due to sharp increase in NPA forcing banks to reduce lending and corporates to undertake 'balance sheet repair' through divestment etc. With some belt tightening and improvement in profitability, the segment seems to be regaining the momentum. Credit growth improved to 7.5% in FY22 and has risen to 11.4% for FY23 so far. There is a re-alignment within industries also with MSME recording credit growth of almost 30% against about 6% for large industries.

The third category, 'Services' accounts for Rs 31.6 lakh crore, marginally lower than Industries. Unlike industries, services comprise of heterogenous group of sub-segments such as wholesale & retail trade, real estate, transport etc. NBFCs and HFCs (Housing finance company), which are lending institutions, are also a part of this segment. The lending institutions, together, accounting for Rs 16 lakh crore of loan, more than half of total services segment loan. The two sub-segments (lending and other services) display quite different dynamics. While other services managed growth of only 4.8% during FY19-22, lending institutions grew at a substantial 13.6%.

Their growth rate has now jumped to as much as 28% in FY23 so far against just about 8% for other services. The high growth rate for lending firms looks quite surprising especially in view of failures such as IL&FS, DHFL and increasing regulatory glare. The growth is, possibly, driven by government-owned NBFCs even as the weaker ones remain under stress.

Within 'other services', trade recorded significant growth of 13% during FY19-22 and further to 17% for FY23, driven by increasing needs during Covid. The sector had seen a sharp decline from 17% during FY08-14 to 10% during FY14-19. However, real estate continues to remain under stress, growing at 4.8% in the current year. The sector had seen sharper meltdown, with growth falling from 16% during FY08-14 to less than 6% during FY14-19. The fourth category is agriculture & allied activities which accounts for just Rs 15.4 lakh crore loan. The segment had recorded a reasonable growth rate of 9.5% during FY19-22 which has further accelerated to 13.4% during the current year.

*****

# Analyzing India's Financial Sector Interconnectedness

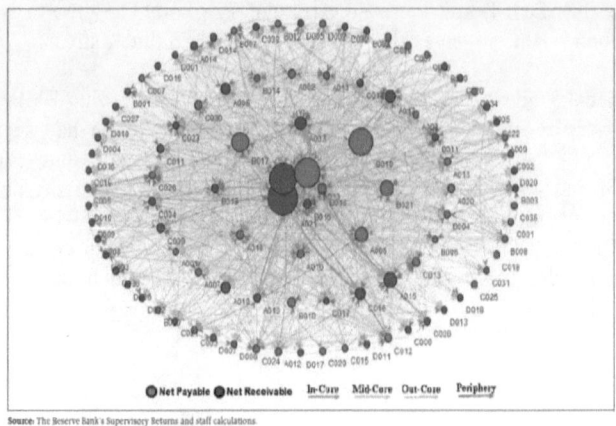

Source: The Reserve Bank's Supervisory Returns and staff calculations.

Financial system is a network of institutions such as Banks, NBFCs, HFCs, insurance companies, mutual funds and so on, connected with each other as lenders or borrowers. While the interconnectedness helps channelize savings into investments, it can also trigger risk events as seen during the global financial crisis in 2008. Indian financial system also saw failures of some financial institutions in the recent past such as IL&FS, Yes Bank, PMC, Reliance Capital etc. These failures did not lead to cascading effect or systemic failure because interconnectedness of Indian financial entities was within its risk absorbing capacity. Here is a brief look at the same based on RBI's latest financial stability report.

The term interconnectedness in simple terms means dependency of financial institutions (FIs) on one another for funds. The dependency arises as segments such as insurance industry or mutual funds receive large sum of money but do not have sufficient avenues for deployment. Hence, they lend it to other financial institutions such as banks, NBFCs or HFCs (Housing Finance Companies) who may be lending to private borrowers. Interconnectedness is an important parameter monitored by the regulator as it helps them identify 'systemically' important financial institutions, failure of which can trigger failure of more entities.

As per the report, total bilateral exposure across different entities (including exposure within the same group) stood at Rs 53 lakh crore, up 21% from a year ago. As a percent of total assets managed by these entities, this works out to around 13%. While the figure is not too large, there could be higher dependence of individual entities and RBI needs to keep constant watch on the same. The biggest lender group is mutual funds industry having lent Rs 10.6 lakh crore (net) to other FIs at the end of Sept'22. This corresponds to an increase of 11% from a year ago, sharply lower than 36% recorded in Sept'21. A reason for this could be lower fund mobilization with sharp increase in stock market volatility. The lent amount constituted over 30% of their total corpus and the rest is deployed in equity market, government securities etc. In terms of their borrowers, SCBs (scheduled commercial banks) are the largest accounting for 55% of lending whereas NBFCs accounted for 19%. Interestingly, the share of NBFCs has come down from 26% a year ago, a result of increasing risk aversion among MFs.

Insurance industry is the other funds surplus segment providing Rs 7.4 lakh crore, about 14% increase over last year. Here too, SCBs (scheduled commercial banks) are the largest borrowers with 42% share and NBFCs with 30%. A differentiation between insurance industry and MF is that the former has deployed close to 55% of their funds on long term basis against 16% by MFs. This is so because cash outflow for insurance industry is longer term in nature unlike MFs which are exposed to short term redemption possibilities. Share of LT debt for MFs has come down sharply from 36% in Sept'20. It may be noted that MFs had faced severe redemption pressure in March/April'20 at the onset of Covid-19 when RBI provided them the much-needed liquidity. MFs, wiser after that experience, have reduced their exposure to longer term instrument even though that gives better return. A point that comes to mind is – is it possibly to give license to insurance industry to enter into lending business to reduce the cost of intermediation?

On the other side of transaction, NBFCs are the largest borrowers with maximum borrowings of Rs 11.3 lakh crore, up 8% from a year ago. SCBs are the largest lender accounting for 59% of NBFC's total borrowings, up from 53% in Sept'21 and barely 40% in Sept'17. It is important to note that MFs and insurance industry are lending less to NBFCs and more to SCBs (as stated in previous paragraphs) which, in turn, is lending to NBFCs. This is helping them transfer their risk to SCBs which have huge balance sheet size and therefore, higher risk capacity. SCBs have borrowed about Rs 8.9 lakh crore from MFs and insurance industry out of which, it has lent Rs 6.7 lakh crore to NBFCs. (SCBs do not figure in the list here since its net exposure to other FIs is small). Composition of NBFCs' borrowings has also changed significantly. Share of commercial papers (CP), an unsecured from of lending, has fallen from 13.1% of total borrowings in Sept'18 to 7.7% by Sept'19 and only 3.4% by Sept'22.

HFCs is the other largest group, borrowing Rs 7.1 lakh crore, up just about 5%. This accounts for almost half of total assets for HFCs indicating their huge dependency on other segments. Even for HFC, SCBs share in total lending stands at 48%. However, share of insurance has increased from 18% to 21% whereas MF's share has declined from 22% to 17%. This implies higher dependence on longer-term funds and helps reduce risk. Share of CP for HFCs also has come down from 18.4% in June'18 to 10.4% by Sept'19 and 6% now.

Apart from dealings with other FIs, banks also lend/borrow among themselves in inter-bank market. Total exposure in the inter-bank market stood at Rs 6.8 lakh crore in Sept'22, up from Rs 5.8 lakh crore a year ago. Almost 75% of this exposure is short-term in nature indicating that these are used to meet short-term mismatch in asset-liability. PSBs are primarily the lenders whereas private banks are net borrowers. Private sector banks borrowings have increased sharply to Rs 6.5 lakh crore, up nearly 70% over last two years. While foreign banks (FBs) have a net zero position in the inter-bank market, there share in total market is 14.5% with less than 7% share in total assets. This means one set of FBs is cash surplus and lending whereas another set is cash deficit and borrowing quite heavily.

As a percent of total banking assets, inter-bank market size has declined from 9.5% in March'13 to 6.2% in March'17 and 3.3%. This means lesser scramble for short-term funds, better asset-liability mismatch and more responsible banking. It may be noted that global inter-bank exposure had crossed 20% in 2007 as per an IMF paper before the global financial crisis erupted. Sudden freezing of funds in the inter-bank market was among the causes of collapse of several banks that time.

Degree of interconnectedness within banking sector is also measured by specific indicators such as cluster coefficient and connectivity ratio. For Indian banking industry, cluster coefficient stands at 41.3%, marginally up from 40.5% a year ago. The coefficient has been largely constant in the range of 40-42% over last five years. The connectivity ratio stands at 18.3%, marginally up from 17.7% a year ago but down from about 25% in March'15. This roughly means, out of a group of five banks, only one bank has borrowed that too, from only one bank. As per the IMF paper, connectivity ratio across global banks had gone up to as high as 79% before 2008 crisis which means banks were borrowing not for its own need by for onward lending to gain from interest rate arbitrage.

*****

# 'Bank'ing on Consolidation

The amalgamation of Bank of Baroda, Vijaya Bank and Dena Bank happened just about a year after the successful merger of SBI and its subsidiaries. It clubs two PSBs having less than 2% market share with a mid-sized bank to create the country's third largest bank. However, there are still around ten PSBs with less than 2% market share. This means many more steps would be required to make any meaningful change in the banking industry landscape. A look at the details of amalgamation and what it achieves.

In terms of size, Bank of Baroda is the largest of the three with total deposits of Rs 5.9 lakh crore (FY18) followed by Vijaya Bank at Rs 1.6 lakh crore and Dena Bank at Rs 1.1 lakh crore. More than the size, banks' financial performance and NPA level differ substantially. While Dena Bank has gross NPA of 22% (up from 16.3% in March'17), BoB's NPA stands at 12.3%. In comparison, Vijaya Bank is much better placed with NPA of just 6.3%. The difference gets reflected in the profit figures also with BoB and Dena Bank reporting loss of Rs 2,400 crore and Rs 2,000 crore respectively whereas Vijaya Bank recorded profits of Rs 720 crore. Hopefully, the share swap arrangement gives shareholders of Vijaya Bank sufficient reason to cheer.

An important aspect of the decision to amalgamate is geographical continuity. While BoB is Gujarat based, Dena Bank is Mumbai based and Vijaya Bank, Bengaluru based. As a result, the new entity would extend from West to South and would have the resources to extend its reach to Central and Northern India. (If say, Dena Bank was replaced with a bank based in North India, it may have made the combination somewhat disoriented).

In terms of operational factors, one key difference in the performance is the business handled per branch. While for BoB, it is close to Rs 200 crore, it is Rs 130 crore for Vijaya Bank and further lower for Dena bank at Rs 100 crore. This may put some pressure for Dena Bank's branch rationalization especially in areas overlapping with BoB.

While the fragmented nature of banking sector is being talked about since 1990s, sustained efforts to achieve consolidation are being taken only recently. The fragmentized nature of the industry is reflected in the Herfindahl Hirschman Index (HHI). HHI for Indian banking industry stood at 6.2% in 2017 which went up to 7.3% after the merger of SBI and will go up to 8.0% after this amalgamation. (The calculation is based on RBI data for FY17 gross deposits). An HHI of 18% is considered ideal for a market which implies sustainable market with adequate competitiveness.

The biggest hurdle for any merger move is the resistance from employees due to fear of job loss, relocation, downgrade etc. However, the terms of employee engagement has evolved substantially over last 10-15 years from confrontation and non-cooperation to productive engagement and greater flexibility from Corporate HR. SBI merger is a case in point where six different entities were merged with the seventh. While the merged entity has to sacrifice the excess non-monetary perks and facilities it may have got used to, the less privileged ones become eligible for better facilities actually boosting the morale. This was demonstrated from the merger of SBI associates.

Trivia – At the time of merger, some of the SBI associates had NPA level as high as 25%!

*****

# SECTION - III
# POLICY & REGULATIONS

# Has Inflation Targeting Delivered?

The Monetary Policy Committee (MPC) completed five years of existence in Sept'2021. The committee was mandated to maintain CPI inflation within band of 4%+-2%, called Flexible Inflation Targeting (FIT). Before its formation, while RBI was required to manage inflation, there was no specific inflation target assigned. So, did FIT help India rein-in inflation? While figures do suggest that, it was also, possibly, aided by factors unrelated to monetary policy actions. An analysis of the same based on an RBI paper.

As per the paper, a part of RBI's report on Currency & Finance, average inflation came down from 7.3% during April'12-Sept'16, when FIT was adopted, to 3.9% during Oct'16-March'20. While inflation had started declining even before FIT, it still averaged 5.4% in the two years before FIT. Other than the decline in CPI, inflation was closer to the target of 4% even across sub-groups, as opposed to wide variations earlier. Food inflation fell from 8.7% to 3.3% whereas fuel & light declined from 6.7% to 4.1%.

However, it is not simply because of FIT but structural issues also helped bring down the inflation. For instance, food inflation came down with record food grains and horticulture production which reduced imports and minimised the impact of high global food inflation on domestic economy. Food inflation management was also aided by improvements in road network, tele-density, market penetration etc which helped reduce traders' margin at different stages of the food supply chain. It may be noted that breakdown of this supply chain network since the beginning of the pandemic has again contributed to high food prices. Food inflation, however, remains vulnerable to shocks due to monsoon and unique characteristics of Indian agriculture such as sharp increase in prices before harvesting and price crash on stock arrival.

Even though food and fuel recorded lower increase, their price volatility (measured as standard deviation of monthly y-o-y inflation figures) remained high. (Inflation of 5% for three successive months is better than 3%, 7% and 5% because volatility is high in second case). For fuel, in fact, volatility went up from 2.3 to 2.9 whereas it remained nearly same at 3.3 vs 3.4 for food. (Volatility of global crude oil price was as high as 27.0 in the first period against only 9.9 during FIT. However, its impact on domestic inflation was reduced by adjustment in tax rates keeping the prices reasonably stable). The volatility impacts the core inflation through increased costs (during upswing) as well as affecting the inflation expectations. This is where monetary policy comes into play. Even though it cannot control the volatility, it plays an important role in avoiding the generalisation of inflationary pressures by anchoring expectations and providing greater level of certainty. The inflation expectations have an important role to play as households and businesses make spending and investment decisions based on the expected level of inflation.

The impact of MPC's decisions gets reflected in the decline in volatility of core inflation which came down sharply from 1.8 to 0.7. Core inflation is obtained by excluding food and fuel prices from the headline inflation. The decline in volatility of aggregate inflation was less significant; from 2.4 to 1.4 because of, as mentioned earlier, higher volatility of food & fuel prices. Similarly, median inflation expectations of urban households over a one-year ahead horizon moderated to an average of 8.7% from 12.5% during the pre-FIT period.

An interesting point mentioned by the report is the linkage between increase in wages in rural India and inflation, both feeding each other. Agricultural labour wages came down from average of over 6% till July'17 to less 4% after that. This moderation in the growth of wages played a role in containing food price inflation. Lower food inflation, in turn, helped maintain wage growth at lower level.

The paper also looks at two other dimensions of inflation – skewness which tells how often monthly inflation was above average and Kurtosis which tells proportion of monthly inflation figures that are far away from average. Skewness improved from 0.1 to 0.9 with adoption of FIT which means over most of this period, inflation was lower than the average. Similarly, kurtosis improved from -1.5 to 0.9 implying that there were very few instances of large deviations from the mean.

*****

# Inflation - A Monetary Phenomenon or More Than That?

The finance minister, Nirmala Sitaraman, at the peak of the inflation, said that monetary policy alone cannot manage inflation as several exercise required to manage it are beyond its control. This goes against conventional wisdom which says inflation is invariably a monetary phenomenon. So, which of these views is correct? An attempt to understand that.

First, a brief attempt to understand what drives inflation. Primarily, inflation is either cost push which means prices of inputs are rising rapidly or demand pull which means output is not sufficient to meet all the needs. Both of these could be linked to adage, "Too much money chasing too few goods". These can be influenced by appropriate monetary policy, essentially raising interest rate prevailing in the economy. Higher interest rate reduces demand by making loan-based purchases costly and by increasing the propensity to save by virtue of higher interest rate. This brings greater alignment between production and consumption and cools the economy.

However, while monetary policy work reasonably well in case of what is called 'core inflation', it has limited impact in case of food & fuel inflation. More so because demand for both of these do not decline much even with an increase in price, more so in case of food (low price elasticity). On the other hand, higher food inflation leaves households with lower disposable income and reduces demand for other segments. Monetary tightening in such a case would further affect the demand for other sectors and throttle growth.

Fuel inflation is also not influenced by the monetary policy since it is a globalized commodity. Further, it is not exactly a market-driven commodity but prices are manipulated by the oil cartel, OPEC and now OPEC+. So, if the demand is projected to decline, the cartel cuts production and prevent the prices from going down. Monetary tightening reduces the demand for products & services which consume high amount of oil and thus, bring down fuel demand, called 'second order impact'. But it also affects other segments and thus, comes at a price of lower growth. These abnormalities are understood very well and central banks across the world focus primarily on core inflation, excluding food and fuel.

However, there is yet another way prices may rise - inflation due to disruption in supply chain, the biggest cause since the pandemic began. Manufacturing sector has faced huge shortage of products such as semiconductor chips, iron ore, metals even shipping containers and so on. These were in short supply for varying periods as a result of lock-downs across regions during the pandemic and more recently, due to Russia-Ukraine war. While a tighter monetary policy cannot influence these, measures that can reduce the impact on domestic economy are quantitative restrictions on exports, increasing export duties, reducing imports duties etc. on products in shorts-supply. While these are not exactly desirable, these have to be resorted to considering the extraordinary circumstances. These are the measures taken by the government in May'22 for manufacturing sector and more recently, for agricultural products.

So, does it mean the reduction in interest rate undertaken since the pandemic began and the resultant increase in money supply did not have any impact on inflation? While it may have had some impact on inflation, especially in interest rate sensitive sectors, it needs to be noted that large part of surplus money is coming back to RBI. As per RBI data, at its peak, banks parked over Rs 8 lakh crore with RBI, up from just about Rs 2.5 lakh crore before the pandemic as factories are running with low capacity utilization (CU) and credit demand is low. Improving economic outlook, rising credit demand and second order inflation getting more entrenched prompted MPC to increase rates since May'22. As a result, money supply has come down to Rs 7.4 lakh crore in April'22, Rs 5.5 lakh crore in May and Rs 3.8 lakh crore during June-July.

So, where does this leave us? As mentioned earlier, monetary policy for inflation targeting is an effective tool but has limited impact in case of inflation caused due to food, fuel or supply chain disruption. Monetary policy can help bring down demand pull or cost push inflation. However, if it is driven by supply side factors or by food and fuel prices, it is essential to take measures which the finance minister has talked about.

*****

# Monetary Policy Normalization – A Tough, Balancing Act

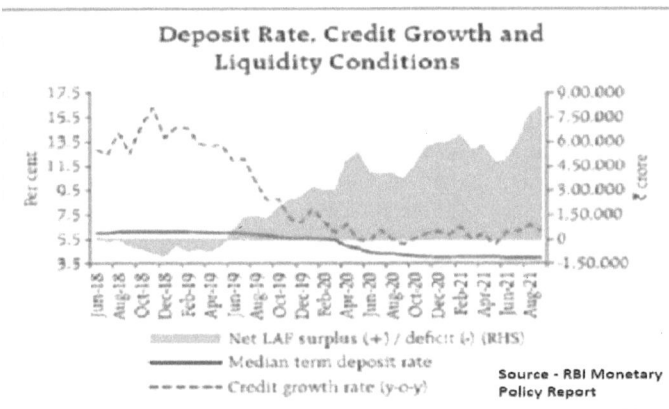

Deposit Rate, Credit Growth and Liquidity Conditions

Net LAF surplus (+) / deficit (-) (RHS)
Median term deposit rate
Credit growth rate (y-o-y)

Source - RBI Monetary Policy Report

Central banks across the world adopted ultra-loose monetary policy in response to the pandemic to spur consumption and keep the engines of economy moving. The year 2021 was unusual as the central banks faced the tough task of balancing interest with fading impact of Covid-19 and inflation becoming persistent. A look at steps taken by RBI during the year to manage the transition.

Monetary policy is tasked with setting the interest rate and liquidity condition in the market. When the demand in the economy is higher than supplies, interest rates are increased which acts as a brake so that economy doesn't over-heat and inflation does not rise beyond the target level. On the other hand, when there is lack of demand, rates are brought down and liquidity is pumped into the market to help spur consumption and/or investments. To manage the crisis arising out of Covid-19, RBI brought down the repo rate to 4% by May'20 from a level of 5.4% in Aug'19 with assurance of ample liquidity. The reverse repo - interest that banks receive when they park excess funds with RBI - was also brought down to 3.35%. Lower reverse repo means banks have lower incentives to park money with RBI and therefore, push lending. Other than reducing rates, RBI also injects liquidity in the market through purchase of government bonds, the Indian version of quantitative easing. (The mode is very popular in developed economies because of lower level of inflation).

The measures led to significant increase in system liquidity. As per RBI, surplus liquidity in the banking system was Rs 7 lakh crore per day in June-Aug'21 which rose further to Rs 9.0 lakh crore in Sept'21 and even further to Rs 9.5 lakh crore in the first week of October. This is in contrast with the situation till May'19 when RBI had to inject money to meet the shortfall. (The surplus liquidity is estimated by the amount absorbed by RBI through various methods such as reverse repo, liquidity adjustment facility and so on). As per RBI, potential liquidity overhang amounts to more than Rs 13 lakh crore.

It would be pertinent to note that the liquidity push doesn't really lead to higher lending as there was not enough demand. Non-food credit given by banks had risen by only 5.5% for year ending

March'21, against 6.1% for March'20 and 15.2% for March'19. The credit appears to be picking up, being up by 6.8% y-o-y for fortnight ending 24th Sept'21.

The improving pace of economic activity and possibly, a 'nudge' by one of the monetary policy committee members prompted RBI to start reducing the liquidity overhang by mid-2021 so that it remains ahead of the inflation curve. RBI announced in August that it would absorb up to Rs 2 lakh crore through 14-day variable reverse repo rate (VRRR) auction every fortnight. Until then, liquidity absorption was done through fixed reverse repo only. Unlike fixed reverse repo where interest rate is fixed, banks bid a rate at which they would park money with RBI and thus, helps in 'price discovery'. RBI has increased the amount by Rs 50,000 crore every fortnight.

The increasing amount of VRRR has also led to higher yield (or interest rate) bid by banks in the auction. As per RBI data, the yield on VRRR auction has moved up from 3.38% to 3.99% between 7th and 28th Sept. (As yields increase, banks would be willing to deposit more money with RBI). The increasing yield in VRRR also affects the interest rate prevailing in the market, reflected by the 10-year government bond yield. The yield has moved up from the low of 6.12% in September to 6.36% in October.

Another measure taken by RBI to normalize liquidity is announcement that it will discontinue purchase of government bonds. As per RBI, it had injected Rs 2.4 lakh crore through this mode during six months of FY21 against nearly the same amount last year. (While liquidity condition doesn't call for any more purchase of government bonds, RBI may still do so for a specific purpose called 'operation twist')

The trajectory of India's monetary policy is also guided by the US monetary policy since that determines the flow of capital. US recorded inflation of 4.2% in April'21, where it generally remains lower than 2%, and has stayed above 5% since then. US Fed in its last meeting, decided to reduce its asset purchase program, the quantitative easing, by $10-15 billion from Nov'21, from a peak of $120 bn in preceding months. The US 10-year govt bond yield has been reflecting the changed condition, having moved to almost 1.6%, up from less than 1.3% in the beginning of August. The US Fed action has important implication for exchange rate also. Rupee has depreciated to 75.30 per dollar in October, a 15-month low, from 73.70 just about a month back. The comfortable part is, RBI is sitting on a huge reserve of dollars and can intervene in case of sharp movement in exchange rate.

So, what lies ahead? RBI has started the exercise to normalize in right earnest. However, it faces a fine balancing act going forward. The risk of not raising rates pre-emptively, like in the 2009-10 period, leading to high inflation is as high as the risk of raising rates too early which could adversely impact the GDP. The government also has a critical task at hand. If it reduces taxes on fuel prices and manages food supply chain well, that could help bring down inflation and provide RBI some more time to wait before raising rates.

*****

# Towards Better Corporate Governance – Strengthening Audit Framework

The decision by two of the top audit firms not to take non-audit work for their audit clients, is the culmination of regulatory efforts to improve the standard of corporate governance. However, the immediate trigger is a discussion paper, floated by MCA (Ministry of Corporate Affairs), which proposes a variety of measures to make audit procedures more independent. A look at the issues raised and proposals suggested by the paper.

Audit and other corporate facing services have been going through intense scrutiny after surfacing of frauds at IL&FS, DHFL, HDIL etc. The failure of auditing agencies in these cases led to the remark by a regulator, "While the audit procedure is not expected to find needle in the haystack, if it not able to detect the 'elephant in the room', something is seriously wrong". The instances of collusion are not new. Corporate India was rocked by the Satyam scandal over a decade ago, where the auditors were found to be hand-in-glove with the promotors.

The discussion paper is quite blunt in its elabouration and begins with a basic fallacy – though auditors are appointed by shareholders to safeguard their interest, the effective power of appointment and dismissal lies with management. This has even greater implication as not only shareholders but other stakeholders such as lenders, regulatory agencies, government and public, in general, also look up to their reports to get a true picture of the company.

The paper touches upon five threats that auditors face and measures to remedy these. These are self-interest threat, self-review threat, advocacy threat, familiarity threat and possibly, the most important, intimidation threat. Self-interest threat arises as the auditor is dependent on the auditee for fees and other non-audit assignments. The auditor doesn't have much recourse if the management stops such assignment in case the auditor's review is not to their liking. Self-review refers to a situation where the auditor audits the financial statement of a company which has been prepared by another team from the same firm. It is highly likely that the auditor would accept the statement and not raise objections even if he finds any. The Advocacy threat arises when the audit firm promotes the interest of the client, for its own benefit.

While some firms may maintain sufficient degree of independence on these counts, it is difficult on the last two. A report on global financial crisis alluded to partner of an audit firm playing golf with the CEO of the auditee, a case of 'familiarity threat'. A study of corporate frauds would reveal how years of working together brings-in a certain sense of complacency and reluctance on the part of auditors to raise red flags. The last, 'intimidation threat', has a much serious connotation as it is not restricted to dismissal or discontinuation of other assignments. There have been instances when clients with clout in corridors of power have used threat of litigation, even jail to suppress irregularities.

The paper suggests several measures as remedies. The first is prohibiting non-audit services entirely (against a negative list currently existing), mandating a minimum fee so that there is no cut-throat competition to win an audit and subsequent compromise in quality of audit etc. Another suggestion worth mentioning is appointment of auditors by external agencies like CAG.

However, some of the suggestions appear unusual and unimplementable such as prohibition/ restriction of personal relationship.

Other than these threats, the discussion paper also makes note of issues affecting the quality of audit, one of which is dominance of 'big four' firms. While the paper notes that 70% of audit work of listed firms in India is done directly or indirectly by the big four, it doesn't have any firm proposal to reduce this. Some of the ways to do this could be mandating joint audit with a smaller firm for say, at least half of the audit assignments, building a corpus to provide financial support to new firms for initial years etc.

Two other important measures suggested by the paper is – initiation of concurrent audit and submission of quarterly returns of unlisted subsidiaries if the parent company is listed. Concurrent audit refers to involvement of lenders to check proper utilization of funds lent. While MCA looks set to mandate this, the discussion revolves around the threshold to make it compulsory and scope of such audit. The other issue is also far reaching as unlisted firm offers an easy way and have often been used to hide irregularities for promoters with ulterior motive.

The discussion paper is far reaching, although harsh in some ways, and provides a way forward to make auditors, a watchdog again. Audit firms also appear to be waking up to the new reality as evident by series of resignations citing non-cooperation, non-sharing of information etc. Yet, controlling the ways of an ingenious and sinister mind is an everlasting challenge and if India Inc is hit by audit failures again, a decade from now, it won't really be surprising. It would be pertinent to mention what a leading, well-respected industrialist once wrote, "I would rather hire a person with high integrity and low intellect than a person with high intellect and low integrity. The damage, the later can cause, is much higher".

*****

# PLI (Production Linked Incentives) Scheme – Case of Electronic Goods Sector

Government's PLI (Production Linked Incentive) scheme received great attention as global mobile manufacturers controlling 60% of the market applied and received approval under the scheme. These companies have, together, projected production of mobile phones worth over Rs 10 lakh crore cumulatively over next five years. About 60% of this would be for exports market. Here is a look at the scheme for mobile manufacturing companies.

As per the PLI scheme, announced on 1st April 2020, companies engaged in mobile phones and electronic components would be eligible to receive incentive of 4-6% if they achieve incremental sales of specified amount over the base year. Incentives imply that government would pay back these companies an amount equal to 6% of sales, going down to 4% in the fifth year. Incremental sales required to be achieved by global manufactures is Rs 4,000 crore in the first year, i.e. 2020-21, going up to Rs 25,000 crore in the fifth year. For domestic players, the requirement is much lower - Rs 500 crore in first year, going up to Rs 5,000 crore in the fifth year. For specified electronic component such as SMT components, semiconductors, PCBs etc., requirement is only Rs 600 crore by fifth year. However, this looks quite liberal and the scheme could have set more ambitious targets with higher rewards for this segment.

A smart clause in the proposal that mobiles phone manufactured by global companies should be of minimum Rs 15,000 price (~$200). Despite having larger share in terms of volume, under Rs 15,000 phones contribute only about one-fourth to total sales value. The clause would free-up the lower end market for domestic manufacturers who could eventually, move up the value curve. The scheme is also expected to enable increase in domestic value-addition from current 15-20% to 35-40%. To meet its part of obligation, government has projected about Rs 41,000 crore of outgo. However, this could go beyond Rs 50,000 crore, looking at the projections made by the companies. Still, this could actually be a revenue neutral exercise as higher production and higher value addition would also increase government's tax revenue from the sector.

Electronic goods sector, particularly mobile phones, has seen rapid growth over last 4-5 years and is projected to grow rapidly, that being the reason for government's decision to introduce the scheme. As per RBI data, India's imports of electronic goods have almost doubled from Rs 1.96 lakh crore to Rs 3.9 lakh core during FY15-19. While India has also managed to increase its exports, that is still only about 20% of imports.

While government keeps devising scheme for exports promotion, indeed almost all governments across the world do so, this scheme looks more promising as MNCs which have applied control almost 60% of global market. Global exports of mobile phones stand at over $250 bn (~Rs 20 lakh crore) with China controlling almost half the market. The scheme came at the right time as large number of MNCs operating out of China have been looking at reducing their dependency on China, a fall-out of pandemic which originated there. Meeting the sales target would involve shifting of production from one country to another rather than finding an altogether new market. More so, as three of the companies are contract manufacturers and do not have to worry about finding the market. As per government's release, these companies have committed to achieve incremental production of Rs 9 lakh crore cumulatively over next five years (annual value after that would be about Rs 2 lakh crore). Even at 60%, exports would only be 6% of global trade, not an impossible target. Domestic companies have projected incremental production worth Rs 1.25 lakh crore.

The scheme is unique in the sense that it seeks applications and gives approval upfront, minimizing the potential of bogus exports and inflated claims. The scheme has succeeded in getting global players to set-up/ expand facilities in India to serve the global market. Encouraged by the response, the scheme was soon extended to a variety of sector. Among the major sectors covered under PLI scheme are automobile and auto components, advanced chemistry cell batteries, specialty steel, telecom products, solar panels and most important of all, semiconductor chip and display board manufacturing approved in Dec'21 involving incentives of Rs 76,000 crore. Total incentives to be given stands at close to Rs 2.3 lakh crore across all schemes over five-year period.

\*\*\*\*\*

# Enhancing India's Exports - Devising A Strategy

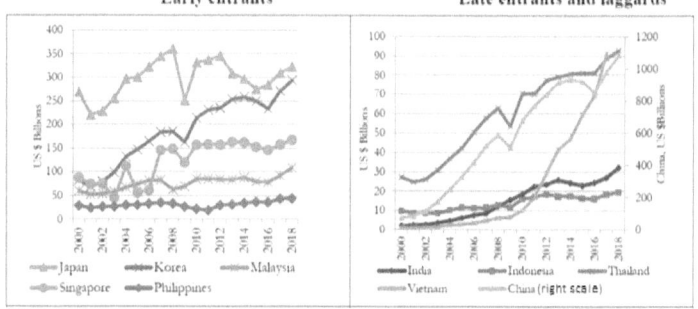

Exports of NP by Asian Countries, USD Billions, 2000 to 2018

Source: The Economic Survey (based on UN Comtrade database)

The disruption in China's exports and in turn, global supply chain, as a result of COVID-19 calls for a re-orientation of global supply chains entailing China plus One strategy. As a matter of fact, the rapid spread of the pandemic from China to rest of the world got aggravated due to over-dependence of global economy on China. This opens a door for nation such as India to push itself as a reliable alternative. A look at how China succeeded and what India needs to do based on the Economic Survey.

The first wave of exports growth till about 2000 was driven by leveraging advantage arising out of low-cost unskilled labour. As per the Survey, China successfully benefitted from this with its share in China's export basket increasing from 28% in 1980 to 46% in 1990. However, India could not leverage its capacities and the figure remained constant at around 30% during 1980-2000. More unfortunately, it suffered a premature decline after that to just about 16% in 2018 (non-oil exports).

The second wave of exports is driven by new age Network Products (NP) which refer to production chain of items such as computers, electronic & electrical equipment, telecommunication equipment etc. These products are manufactured by Multi-National Enterprises (MNEs) through their global production networks called global value chain (GVC). The survey raises a question as to whether it is in our interest participate in GVCs (Global Value Chains) or rely on local value chain to boost exports.

The importance of NPs is evident from the fact that these accounted for nearly 30% of world exports. Even as India's export of NPs increased from about $2 billion in 2000 to $32 billion in 2018, its share is just 10% in India's export basket. In contrast, these products account for about half of total exports of China, Japan and Korea. Furthermore, India is among the few developing countries who run a trade deficit in NP with imports of $68 billion. The paradox of India's manufacturing policy is that even though MNEs have set up production base for these industries here, they have been largely catering to domestic market only. (Does a policy like mandatory sourcing from domestic MSMEs etc also play a role in this?)

Higher level of participation in GVCs implies that exports of these goods would have higher import content than other exports where inputs are sourced locally. This would imply lower net value addition; yet, because of scale of selling in the world market, would lead to higher gain on absolute basis. For instance, China's share of value add in some NPs is only 3%. As per survey's estimates, increase of 10% in value of imported inputs leads to 18% increase in total exports implying net additional exports of 8%.

Not only does the low participation in NPs affect the exports, it also implies lower share of markets of traditional rich country. The high-income OECD markets accounted for half of China's exports in 2018 while the corresponding figure for India was 40%. Countries with low level of participation in GVCs, especially a developing nation, find it difficult to export capital intensive products to the quality/brand conscious markets in richer countries. This is borne by the fact that OECD countries accounted for only 22% of Indian exports of passenger vehicles in 2015 with the rest being exported to low- & middle-income countries. On the other hand, labour-intensive product such as apparel derived as much as 64% of exports from OECD countries. The survey quotes a regression analysis of Veeramani, Aerath and Gupta to analyse the impact of this. As per the analysis, China's exports exceeded that of India by about 743% per year during the period 2000-2015 which reduces to just 37% if the difference in exports to OECD countries are removed.

So, where does this bring us to? First, India's needs to become a part of GVC for new age NPs. Second, India needs to increase its share of total OECD market for traditional, unskilled, labour-intensive industries also such as textiles, clothing, footwear and toys by integrating with its GVC even if it involves some sacrifice in terms of playing second fiddle. GVCs for these industries are controlled by firms based in developed countries but actual production is carried out through sub-contracting arrangements. While India's FDI and manufacturing policies also need to differentiate between export-oriented units and those catering to domestic market, it has failed in this so far. Whether this can be achieved in future would be a tough call.

*****

# Strengthening Manufacturing – Case of Apparel and Leather Industries

The push to Indian Manufacturing sector and 'Make in India' campaign can receive a boost from some key sectors whose growth has preceded the growth of the economy across the world in recent times. These are Apparel and Footwear offering significant opportunity to accelerate employment generation and boost growth. A look at the dynamics of these sectors.

The stress on the sectors is backed by an interesting set of data pointed out by a recent Economic Survey. A group of seven East-Asian countries reported average growth rate of as much as 35% and 38% CAGR for Apparel and Footwear industry for the twenty-year period after their economy took off. While it is difficult to assign a specific reason, this could be because these are low capital intensive but high employment leading to spur in consumption demand. As per the Annual Survey of Industries, Apparel and footwear account for only about 1.2% of invested capital across industries but employ almost 10% of workforce. For example, number of jobs created per crore of investment in apparel is 24 times that in Steel industry, whereas footwear generates nearly ten times more employment than Steel. Further, these two are also the sectors requiring least skilled workers and hence, can employ the lowest strata of the society. Further, the low level of skill also comes with lower cost of labour adding to the comparative advantage of the sector. The average salaries for the sectors is only 70% of the average salary across industries and half of the salary across metals and automobile sector.

Other than the importance of these sectors in generating employment and boosting growth, the need to focus on these sectors stems from another reason also – the decreasing low cost labour advantage of China which provides opportunity to countries like India. China's share in global exports which moved up from less than 25% to 40% in about a decade has come down marginally over last few years and looks difficult to pick up again. As per the Economic Survey, the labour cost in some of the states in India is now generating sectors and could be almost one-third that in China.

Despite these compelling reasons, the sectors have not been able to follow the growth trajectory as shown across East-Asian countries for a variety of reasons. Paradoxically, labour, despite offering a competitive advantage, has acted as a drag due to plethora of regulations and restrictions related to wages, overtime, employment conditions etc. The most glaring reflection of the labour market problems is small sizes of factories in India restricting the gains arising out of economies of scale and reducing market reach. Nearly 80% of firms in India employ less than 50 workers against only 15% in case of China.

The government does appear to have realised these impediments resulting in a revamped textile policy announced in June last year. However, the policy for footwear industry is still awaited.

*****

# Shell Companies – the Menace & the Modus Operandi

The central government de-registered over 3 lakh shell companies from the Ministry of Corporate Affairs (MCA) register and disqualified over 3 lakh directors after demonetization. Over 1.2 lakh of them are facing further scrutiny. So, what are shell companies and how they operate? A look.

Shell companies are entities, mostly registered as financial services firms, but usually not engaged in any regular business activities. The entity would register another company as its subsidiary and so on, thus creating a multi-layer structure. This would make it difficult to trace the fund flow and detect for instance, that company at layer 1 owns the company at layer 5. Shell companies came under government's radar soon after demonetization as large amount of unaccounted cash was deposited in their accounts during that period. Many of these have closed down after subsequent funds withdrawal. Since their ownership structure is obscure, it has been difficult to trace the ultimate beneficiary, prompting government to crack down on them.

The multi-layer structure is created to undertake unlawful transactions, most common being generating fake invoices. The company at layer 5, issues an invoice without actual delivery of goods or service. The company at layer 1 pays the money thus managing to reduce its profits in its books. The more sinister ones show losses in their books and swindle bank loans, many times, in collusion with bank officials. The black money then gets absorbed through another set of shell companies who accept white money from individuals and companies who need to pay in black for transactions such as property purchase and give them cash, in return.

The operator in the above arrangement can keep the money white also through sales of shares of layer 1 company at inflated price to layer 5 company. Since these are unlisted firms, it is virtually impossible to prove the illegality of transaction. Many of these companies are formed with fake addresses and other details for siphoning of funds and close down after completing the transaction

Shell companies also serve as a front for under-invoicing/over-invoicing in cases of foreign transactions. For instance, an exporter would declare lower value of goods (under-invoice) and the rest of the money would be paid by the buyer to the shell company as consultancy or any such charges. T.his would then be transferred to the intended party as salary, sitting fees etc. In the same manner, an importer over-invoices and get the excess, after deducting a commission, transferred to an overseas shell company. The practice is even more prevalent in cases of transaction with countries where tax rates are lower, those where legal enforcement is weak or those with which India does not have a treaty. Shell companies are actually present across the globe. As per the leaked Panama Papers last year, many of the shell companies identified their directors by numbers rather than names.to hide their identity

An interesting fact about shell companies is that a large number of them are registered at the same address. For instance, 114 companies were found to be running from a single room in Hyderabad in a ROC's raid! In its continued effort to choke them, government is considering making geo-tagging mandatory for the companies.

However, a shell company, in itself, is not illegal. There are variety of legal purposes a shell company serves such as a company holding shares of a group of individuals in other listed companies. Such a structure helps the individuals to brings together dividend income etc from all the sources and distribute subsequently. Or an individual/company can transfer the ownership of its brands or trademarks to a shell company.

*****

# Understanding GAAR (General Anti-Avoidance Rules)

Consider a situation where a foreign entity provides loan to an Indian company and receives interest which is not fixed but linked to profits. Or consider a treaty between India and country X whereby sale of shares in an Indian company held by an investor from country X shall be taxed only if the shares sold are more than 10%. The investor floats two subsidiaries and sells 9.9% shares through each of them. Are these tax mitigation, tax evasion or tax avoidance??

Modern system of taxation started with fairly simple rules. However, the rule books keep getting fatter with the cat-and-mouse game played between tax authorities and taxable entities, primarily corporate entities. However, the response, so far, had largely been through amendments to deal with specific instances of tax avoidance.

In simple terms, GAAR is a set of rules incorporated into the Income Tax Act (to be implemented from 1st April this year) which seeks to address all cases of tax avoidance. The rules state that if some entities have entered into an arrangement whose main objective is to obtain tax benefits and which doesn't serve any other commercial purpose, then it is a case of tax avoidance. As a result, the entity would not receive the intended tax benefits even though other provisions of the Act entitle him to that. For instance, in the first example, the deal is clearly an equity deal since the lender's gain is linked to profits. However, to take advantage of tax savings on interest paid, it is shown as a lending and borrowing arrangement.

Maximum impact of GAAR would be on cross border tax avoidance since these cases provide maximum opportunity for manipulation. However, it would apply only if it meets certain criteria such as whether the deal has been done on an arm's length basis or not, whether it results in abuse or misuse of some laws or if it has been carried out in an manner which suggest lack of bona fide purpose. Since these criteria are quite complicated and even subjective, an approval panel headed by a judge has been set up which would determine whether a case is fit for applying GAAR or not. GAAR also recognises genuine arrangement for tax mitigation. For instance, if a company shifts its production base to an SEZ to avail tax benefits, it is perfectly legal and GAAR cannot be invoked. (However, if it shows production from other units as coming from SEZ, it is no more legal.!)

*****

# The Insolvency and Bankruptcy Code – Analyzing the Performance

Bankruptcy process under IBC (insolvency & bankruptcy code) is facing another challenge with resurgence of the pandemic and call for suspension of IBC. The code had been suspended in March'20 to protect the companies who were facing issues due to the pandemic. The code has faced several challenges after being introduced close to five years ago even though it has been a game changer in giving lenders a control over corporate promoters. Nevertheless, A look at how IBC has fared so far and other characteristics of bankruptcy resolution.

Bankruptcy resolution essentially refers to the process of transfer of ownership of a company which has failed to pay its dues to the lenders or other creditors. As per IBBI's (Insolvency & Bankruptcy Board of India) news bulletin, over 5,200 cases have been filed for bankruptcy resolution till March'22. Of this, about 800 cases were filed in FY22. This is a significant decline after a record filing of almost 2,000 cases in FY20 indicating improving health of corporate sector. While this looks paradoxical as companies faced greater stress during Covid-19, the efforts of various policy making bodies and rigorous scrutiny helped these companies manage their finances better. In terms of sectors, construction & real estate account for the largest number of cases at nearly 1,500 whereas trade (wholesale & retail together) account for another 600 cases.

In terms of resolution, decision has been reached in about 65% of cases, or nearly 3,400, significant improvement from 54% two years ago. While the number is still not very encouraging, it would be unfair to call it inefficient especially considering the complexity of India's legal system. It may be noted that a corporate case filed in civil court takes on an average as many as four years for resolution. An important development is lenders and debtors reaching an agreement to withdraw or settle the case after it is filed for IBC. This process got a fillip with the amendment of IBC in 2018, called section 12A, which allows companies to come out of IBC if it can arrive at a settlement with the creditors subject to certain conditions. This has even greater implication since out of about 600 cases withdrawn under section 12A, over 75% cases involved less than Rs 10 crore and were primarily adding to the burden of IBC system without much economic gain. About 1,300 cases, almost 40%, have been settled among the parties or withdrawn including section 12A cases.

However, the real concern is high percent of cases, 47% or close to 1,600, being settled through liquidation as there are no buyer. While the number is large, it must be noted that 1,200 of the companies being liquidated had been transferred to IBC from earlier regulations and were non-functioning even before being transferred. Average value of the assets for these companies was only 8% of the claims at the time of admission. Number of cases which have gone through the entire bankruptcy process and received approval of their resolution plan is about 480.

A look at the amount involved gives an idea of the magnitude of task at hand for IBC. These 480 companies involved claims totaling over Rs 6.8 lakh crore out of which, creditors received about Rs 2.2 lakh crore implying recovery rate of 33%. While this looks low, it is still not too bad considering the nascency of the process. Among the companies, with low recovery rate is Reliance Infratel which had debt of over Rs 41,000 crore but fetched only about Rs 4,200 crore from its resolution.

Liquidation means the bankrupt company received no bids (or the bids were rejected) and its assets would have to be sold-off. The amount realized in these cases is negligible. For a set of close to 200 companies where final report is submitted, liquidation has yielded Rs 1,900 crore against total claims of over Rs 49,000 crore implying recovery rate of less than 4%. What is more colossal is that financial claims stands at Rs 7.5 lakh crore for other 1,400 companies under liquidation, of which, they would be able to salvage very little. It may be noted that banks have written-off Rs 10 lakh crore of loans over last four years till FY22. Hopefully, the system would function more efficiently after the mess created over last 10-12 years gets cleared. Two large companies being liquidated, Lanco Infratech and ABG Shipyard had outstanding loan of over Rs 50,000 crore and Rs 16,000 crore. The fate of these companies is an important lesson and hopefully, banks would act more proactively in initiating bankruptcy against large corporate.

An interesting, yet, possibly, an unhealthy, trend is invocation of insolvency process by operational creditors (supplier of raw material, transporter etc.). Over half of the cases have been filed by operational creditors. While the law gives them power to fight for their dues, exercise of this power calls for caution and prudence. This is so because their dues, in general, is much less that of financial creditors and invocation of insolvency puts financial creditors also at risk as insolvency invariably leads to loss of value. That the IBC route is being used as pressure tactics is evident from the fact over half of the cases filed by OCs have been closed or withdrawn by the concerned parties. Further, over 70% of cases which have been withdrawn were filed by OCs.

Another outcome of IBC is 'voluntary liquidation' where the promoters of a company can opt for this if the company is shut or is making losses. This is again an important provision as the concerned promoter gets an exit route and does not have to keep incurring routine cost such as security, utility etc. The company in such cases, however, *should not be having any debt* or the debt level should be less than liquidation value. Over 1,200 such cases have been put before the insolvency court, half of which have been closed. It is interesting to note that the closed cases realized over Rs 3,300 against debt of only Rs 22 crore. It is difficult to visualize as to why there is no buyer in the market for such companies and what leads these reasonably healthy company to opt for liquidation.

Even if the numbers do not give much to cheer, insolvency courts have done some wonderful work against considerable odds. Passage of the Act when the economy is going through a tough phase has led to higher 'supply' and lower 'demand' of stressed assets affecting the resolution. Yet, there are gaps, especially in the process especially in the resolution of large accounts (Over Rs 5,000 crore) in case the company faces liquidation. This could involve greater deliberation and include time extension, exploring options for 'operating lease', sale as parts which may attract more bidders etc.

*****

# Fertilizer units Revival – A transformational initiative!

The revival of three closed fertilizer units at Sindri (Jharkhand), Gorakhpur (Easter U.P.) and Barauni (Bihar) is a landmark development, having been under consideration for almost a decade. In terms of value, the cash amount involved is not too much. The complex decision has involved all the six M's, typical of any corporate decision-making process – Man, Machine, Material, Market, Money and Management.

Of the Six M's, Money was and will always remain the most critical factor and the revival involved about Rs 10,000 crore of loan and interest waver dues to Central Government other than the fresh investment to be done by the new SPV. The second M – Management was tweaked by roping in three cash-rich PSU majors operating in equally complex line of business, NTPC, Coal India and IOC. The three would form a SPV (Special Purpose Vehicle) which shall take over the assets of these fertilizers unit. The parent company, Fertilizer Corporation and Hindustan Fertilizer, would also remain as minority partner to provide continuity and operational support.

The most important reason for these units to close was high cost and unavailability of raw material, the third M. To mitigate this risk, the government has allocated natural gas to these plants through gas pooling mechanism ensuring relatively cheaper source of gas. Simultaneously, GAIL will lay a pipeline from North to East India which will provide gas to all the three plants, apart from meeting other industrial requirement in the Eastern region. Regarding the next M – Market, it may be noted that for fertilizers, Eastern India is completely dependent on imports or dispatches from other regions involving significant cost of transportation as it is a bulk commodity. Further, on aggregate basis also, India is about 25% dependent on imports. With the revival, not only will there be savings in freight cost but also its dependence on imports would come down to about 10% on current needs basis.

That leaves us with last two M's – Man and Machine, the two critical factors favoring a revival. Even though the machines of old units would be mostly obsolete, it should still be partially usable specially the auxiliary units and support infrastructure providing savings not only in terms of money but also time and convenience. It may be noted that while the SPV would put in about Rs 6,000 crore in each of these units, yet the estimated investment required is only about half of what is required for setting up a new plant. While the revival would make use of part of the manpower still available at the site, the new management should also be able to hire fresh talent due to large number of employees retired in the course of last fifteen years since the closure of the plant.

The decision, as mentioned by the finance minister, is truly transformational achieving the best of both worlds in terms of preserving the blocked wealth and minimal fresh investment to provide a fillip to the region's economy. The decision should be the beginning and spur many more such decisions to unlock huge value blocked in closed public sector units.

*****

# Government e-Marketplace – A Gem Indeed!

Government e-Marketplace (GeM), the platform to route all government procurement has helped not only improve efficiency but also bringing about greater transparency. The enormity of the project lies in the fact that it facilitates transaction of goods & services worth, may be over one lakh crore!

GeM is the online platform for sourcing of all government routine needs such as computers, office equipment, stationery etc where all the sellers would be registered with their products, pricing and other specifications. Government departments including PSUs would simply log in and place order just like an ordinary folk would do on the portal of e-commerce firms. However, for purchase above Rs 50,000, the buyer will have to call for e-bids to discover best price. The portal also enables demand aggregation from all the dept and bulk ordering to drive better bargain. What is interesting is that it has been enabled for engaging taxi services also! It would not be surprising if hotel bookings are also done through GeM in future, an important element of expenditure for government.

The implication of the shift cannot be underestimated and it certainly revolutionizes government procurement. The gains from the project are immense including bringing transparency and significant reduction in costs. A rough comparison between online and offline price of products in these categories indicates that government stands to achieve cost reduction of 20-25% or up to Rs 25,000 crore! Most importantly, it is a body blow to the people who have built a fortune from their access to the corridors of power. The platform enables every seller to register and get direct access to all government purchases. The platform can be a big business opportunity to firms like Flipkart which has been going through a tough phase. It also helps government get rid of time consuming and repetitive tendering process and thus cuts down on administrative costs.

The platform is initially limited to select goods and is only available for offices located in NCR. However, it would be expanded in its scope and reach once the test phase glitches are rectified. The only issue that needs serious attention is training of government employees as the whole procurement process would involve a large number of people and it is not easy to get people out of old habits. Other than that, there is nothing that appears with the potential to derail the train.

\*\*\*\*\*

# Towards Energy Security – India's Strategic Oil Reserve

India and UAE reached an agreement some years ago to facilitate filling of crude oil strategic reserve. The agreement is diplomatic coup of sorts, for India as it gets a commodity so precious to the nation and so much in abundance with UAE. The agreement goes a long way in building India's strategic reserves in a cost-effective manner since there would be not outgo of money in the current exercise. A look at the concept of strategic oil reserves and India's preparedness.

The concept of strategic oil reserve was mooted after the Oil crisis of 1973-74 when US decided to build non-commercial oil storage reserves as hedge against supply disruptions. OPEC nations had stopped supplies of oil in 1973-74 in retaliation against US' arms supply to Israel. US has a large reserve of almost 100 mn tons, equal to 70 days of oil imports. According to EIA, more than 500 mn tons of oil is stored across the world as strategic reserve, primarily in oil importing countries. Not only does the reserve serve as buffer against supply disruption, it can also help cool down price by increasing market supplies, like release of dollars by RBI to bring stability in forex market.

Although India has been quite late in building its reserves, its criticality is undeniable. The significance of the reserve is only marginally less than holding of food grains reserves to meet any exigencies in case of crop failure. India's vulnerability to oil shocks is even greater since nearly 80% of the requirement is met through imports, primarily from Middle East countries.

In the first phase, India has built reserves at three places on the east and west coast for easier sourcing of crude oil. The reserves have total capacity of 5 mn tons, nearly half of which has been filled so far. These reserves are built in underground rock caverns to save the cost of building huge storage tanks. It may be noted that reserves of this magnitude would require nearly 25,000 tanks of 50 meter radius and same height. Yet, the current reserves capacity can meet just about 10 days of imports and does not provide much hedge. The second phase of expanding storage capacity is still at a preliminary stage.

The second challenge after building the reserve is filling it, which would require approximately Rs 14,000 crore in all. This is where the agreement with UAE comes in handy. The two countries have reached an agreement whereby UAE could fill half of the capacity (0.75 mn tons) at one of the sites. While India would be free to use two-thirds of this (0.5 mn tons), the remaining third would serve as storage for UAE to meet its trading needs. Further, India would hold the first right over the UAE's storage also in case of any emergency. While gains for India is undeniable as it gets almost Rs 1,400 crore of oil for free, UAE gets to keep its oil close to East Asian consumption center and gain trading advantage.

*****

# SECTION - IV
# INDUSTRY

# Survey of Indian Industries

The provisional data of Annual Survey of Indian Industries for the year FY20 (pre-Covid) shows a remarkable change in terms of engagement, with profits declining but wages increasing. Furthermore, even though profits fell sharply, total fixed capital increased which points to a continued strong outlook. The survey conducted by the Ministry of Statistics, Planning and Implementation (MOSPI) comes with a time lag as it is based on actual field-based survey. This covers nearly 80,000 factories, almost one-third of all factories and involves extensive data collection and compilation exercise. Although the report is not widely covered, it is the most comprehensive dataset for all policy matters related to industry and must be looked more closely. Here is a look at the key findings.

As per the survey, there are a total of 2.46 lakh factories in operation in the country. The decadal growth rate (2010-20) of factories stands at 4.5%, against 2% during the previous two decades and 0.3% during 1980s. The survey only covers factories and not services which may look like factory operations such as Oil depots, railway workshops, computer services, restaurants, hotels, café etc. Further, it only includes factories employing at least 10 persons. (So, figures for entire set of industries would be significant higher).

These factories operate with total invested capital of Rs 49.7 lakh crore. The figure is important as an unusually high amount of invested capital may make the operations unsustainable. This is corroborated by the fact that invested capital grew by as high as 20% CAGR during 2006-13. The decline in profits with decline in demand and inability of companies to meet their payment obligations led to sharp rise in bad debts till 2016. Growth figure for invested capital fell sharply subsequently and stands at less than 7% since then. Furthermore, increase in borrowings has come down from 17.3% to 3.1%.

Total outstanding loan for the sector stands at Rs 13.3 lakh crore, not much higher than Rs 12.2 lakh crore in FY14. Debt has fallen in three out of last six years, a process called 'deleveraging'. Debt/equity ratio for the set has come down from 1.1:1 in FY15 to 0.58:1 in FY20. It is important to note that improvement in debt profile helped industries tide over the demand slump and cost increase due to supply chain disruption caused due to Covid.

The next figure that needs to be analyzed is profits. Profits for the set stood at Rs 4.7 lakh crore. Surprisingly, profits have fallen sharply by 16% during the year even though Gross Value Added (GVA) has declined only marginally. This is so because wages have risen impressively. (GVA is derived by subtracting cost items such as raw material, electricity & fuel, interest cost etc. from revenue. Essentially, GVA comprises of wages, profits, taxes and depreciation. From economy's perspective, increase in GVA is more important than any of these individual items). While profits grew by only 1% during 2014-20, wages have grown significantly by 10%. Wages-profits dynamics was similar during 2008-14 also, when wages grew by 16% while profits rose only 7%. This is in sharp contrast to 2002-08, the peak of economic boom, when wages grew only 11% even as profits had grown by 43%. *This points to shift of surplus from the provider of capital to provider of labour, a very important shift.* It may be noted that the above figure is only for blue collared workers. For while collared employees, change is not so pronounced. However, a number missing in the survey is the number of units making profits which would help take a micro view of the sector.

While it is difficult to ascertain as to what has helped achieve this. Possibly MGNREGA, which provided another avenue for labour, coupled with an uptick in industrial activity increasing the demand for labour, helped achieve this. For 1981-82 to 2019-20, the correlation between increase in no of employment and increase in wages is very strong at 80%.

With regard to total employment, these factories employ a total of 1.66 crore people, blue collared workers being nearly 80%. As stated in the previous para, while employment has grown in the recent decades over previous decades, it is still not inadequate to absorb India's huge population looking for work. The forty-year labour market trend shows impact of industrial cyclicity and Indian economy's increasing resilience to handle it. While total employment declined at 1% CAGR during FY82-FY87, it increased by 3.1% during FY87-FY96. The next recession caused a decline of sharp 2.8% during FY96-FY04, recovering to 6.2% CAGR till FY12. With the next down-cycle, while labour growth came down to 2.8% till FY20, it still remained positive. It may be noted that the total number of employees had actually declined by over 15 lakhs during FY96-FY04.

In terms of sectoral distribution, Food products industry account for maximum 18.4 lakh persons. However, Textiles taken together with Apparel employ much larger, 28.8 lakh persons, almost 20% of the total workforce and is therefore on the top of the government agenda. Total emolument per person stands at Rs 2.15 lakh per annum, an impressive increase of 16% annually over last two years and 11% over last seven years.

However, more important figure to look at for India is employment intensity or number of persons engaged per unit of capital invested. The most important sector on this count is Apparel generating maximum employment of 19.1 workers per crore of investment. This contrasts with only 0.26 persons employed in the petroleum refining industry. The high employment intensity of apparel sector means a person can start an apparel factory employing ten persons with just Rs 50 lakh of investment, equivalent to cost of a flat even in a tier II city. Sector's value addition per unit of capital invested is also the highest at 0.57 against average of 0.24 across all industries.

For a country like India, most suitable industries would be those which employ greater number of people and add more value per unit of capital to minimize capital needs. Regarding GVA/capital, Apparel, other transport equipment and Pharma are among the sectors with high productivity of about 0.6. It implies that for every crore of investment, these sectors generate Rs 60 lakh of value. Among the sectors with low GVA/capital are Oil refining and Metals at 0.08 and 0.17. (Incidentally, these are also the sectors with highest amount of invested capital at Rs 5.9 lakh crore and Rs 8.8 lakh crore). Even food processing industry has a relatively low GVA of 0.27 which could be the key reason for inadequate investment in food processing industry. However, the sector's growth is important because it employs largest number of people and is critical to improve the earnings of rural India. An interesting aspect of the discussion is that Tobacco products is the most productive sector on both count adding 1.54 crore of gross value per crore of investment and employing as many as 37.1 workers per crore of investment! Yet, as a result of its adverse impact, the sector has seen its share come down over the years.

In terms of size or what is called economies of scale, petroleum refining and allied industry are biggest with average investment of Rs 360 crore per factory. In contrast, wood products, leather, apparel etc deploy less than Rs 6 crore per factory making them most suited for small entrepreneurs. However, the data needs to be considered with caution as the smaller sectors also generate significant amount of effluent and factories may not be adequately equipped to control the ill-effects of these effluents. Government's subsidy towards providing centralized waste treatment facilities etc would help the growth of these industries in a more sustainable manner.

One interesting result that comes out from the analysis is that sectors with higher capital investment also pay higher wages to its employees. Average wages for workers in top three capital intensive sector is Rs 4.1 lakh against wages of Rs 1.73 lakh in lowest five sectors. A reason could be that capital intensive sectors would have greater degree of automation requiring more precision and higher level of skill and therefore, better paid jobs.

Another insight worth considering is the distribution of factories across rural and urban areas. While rural India accounts for 42% of the factories, the share in total invested capital in significantly higher at 59%. This implies bigger size of factories in rural India with investment of Rs 28 per factory against Rs 14 crore in urban center. While the result may be contrary to perception, the reason is not hard to seek. A large number of factories come up away from urban centers, say at a distance of 50-60 km in areas classified as rural. Primary reason for the same is availability of cheap and large tracts of land in these areas and more stringent regulations in urban areas. A number to corroborate this is rent paid - as a percent of total output, it is 0.04% in rural area against 0.07% in urban area. (The figure includes only rent paid for land or mines royalty and not real estate rent which is included elsewhere). Ironically, average household income in rural area (including all households) is just about one-fifth of urban household income despite accounting for higher proportion of factories.

In terms of States, Gujarat and Maharashtra account for highest amount of invested capital at Rs 9.6 and Rs 6.2 lakh crore. However, Tamil Nadu accounts for highest number of persons engaged at 26.6 lakhs, almost 30% more than Gujarat, with an investment of Rs 4.5 lakh crore. For a country like India, probably Tamil Nadu would offer more clues to engage large skilled force more usefully. While most progressive states have seen capital invested increase by about 20% during 2017-20, Bihar, Jharkhand and Orissa have seen a decline of 2-4%. UP has been an outlier, recording increase of 19%, quite contrary to its impression of being a laggard.

An information not given in this year's report but very pertinent relates to contribution of factories with respect to their size (irrespective of the industry). For FY16, while factories employing up to 50 people accounted for just 8% of total invested capital, its share in number of persons employed was almost double at 14.5%. In contrast, mega factories employing more than 5,000 persons account for 22% of invested capital but engaged only 9% of people. Further, productivity (GVA/Invested Capital) of smaller factories is 50% more than that of mega factories. While mega factories have an important role to play, it is equally essential to push MSME sector to find income generating avenues for India's vast population.

*****

# Deciphering Core Sectors

Core sectors recorded growth of 8.4% for the month of April'22 as per the ministry of commerce data highest in last six months. For FY22, index grew by 10.4% and is 3.4% higher than pre-pandemic value. Five out of the eight have recorded increase of more than 8% in April'22 and more than 6% during FY22 over their FY20 level. Performance of core sectors is of greater significance as most of the these are not consumed directly but cater to other industrial segments. So, the increase in their production indicates significant momentum in industrial activity. Here is a brief look at the composition of eight core industries and their performance.

The eight core sectors comprise of coal, fertilizers, cement, electricity, crude oil, natural gas, petroleum refining and Steel. Out of these, petroleum refining has the highest weight of 28% whereas cement and fertilizer has the lowest weight of 5% and 3% respectively. Core sector, together, command a weight of 40% in IIP and impact the performance of IIP both directly and indirectly.

Out of these eight, cement and electricity are almost completely produced and consumed domestically and its performance indicates changes in domestic demand. Cement has recorded growth of as much as 21% during FY22 driven by significant increase in construction activity. The figure is 7.8% higher FY20 and much above the average growth of 4.9% during FY13-20. Electricity sector has also recorded impressive growth at 10.7% in April'22 and 8% during FY22. FY22 growth is 7.4% higher than FY20, higher than 6% during FY13-20. However, electricity generation is actually lagging behind the demand over last two months, possibly, a result of lack of demand planning. While coal was also largely a domestic industry, sharp increase in capacity addition in power generation without similar increase in mining capacity has led to demand-supply mismatch and sharp increase in imports. Coal mining has risen by 8.5% during FY22 which is 6.5% higher than FY20. The growth is significantly higher than average growth of 3.7% during 2013-20. With sharp increase in electricity and subsequently coal demand, coal mining industries put-in some extra effort resulting in sharp increase of 29% during the month of April'22.

Steel is an interesting sector which has recorded marginal decline of 0.7% in April'22 but grew by 17% in FY22. Over FY20, growth rate is 6.9%, better than average 5.5% till FY20. The sector had a bumper year with significant global demand and limited production capacity leading to sharp increase in prices and profits. The excessive profits, affecting other consuming industries, compelled government to impose 15% duty on steel exports in May'22 which should cool down the prices.

Out of the remaining four, production of Oil and Natural gas is impeded by lack of domestic reserves and more than 85% of oil and about 60% of gas needs is met through imports. Oil production has been declining consistently over last several years with decline in FY22 being 7.7% over FY20. Since FY12, production has declined by as much as 22%. In case of natural gas, FY22 was a good year with production increasing by 19.2% over FY21 and 9.5% over FY20. However, likelihood of its production increase maintaining this pace is low. Even though the production of oil has decline, it does not indicate lack of demand. It only means the country is importing more.

Fertilizers is an important sector where imports were significant peaking at $7 bn in 2012 but with increase in domestic production capacity, the same has come down to $1.4 bn in 2020. The sector grew by 8.7% in April'22 on top of growth of 15.2% in March'22. However, these were unusual months and its FY22 growth is only 2.4% over FY20. Yet, this is better than average growth of 1.2% during FY13-20. Even though fertilizers is sold at highly subsidized rate, timely payment of the difference between cost price and sale price by the government has helped the sector manage its growth and reduce import dependency.

The only sector, out of the eight core industries, where India has surplus capacity and where it is exporting about 20% of domestic production in petroleum refining. Even though other sectors have done largely better than pre-pandemic level (except crude oil), refining has lagged with production decline of 3.3% over FY20. But this was not because of low domestic demand but continued sluggishness in global market. The Russian attack on Ukraine has created a global mismatch helping refining units ramp up their production and record average growth of 8% over last three months.

While the core sectors are, indeed, the catalyst for growth of other sectors, the production index is not a true reflection of demand for these commodities or industrial activity. This is so because, as mentioned above, Oil, Gas and to some extent, Coal face domestic availability or production constrains. On the other hand, products such as Steel, petroleum refining have a highly integrated global market and domestic production is significantly driven by global demand. A more appropriate measure to gauge underlying domestic demand and in turn, industrial activity, could be production plus net imports of these commodities.

*****

# Public Sector Enterprises – Boon or Bane

Public sector enterprises (PSEs) invariably face criticism as loss making behemoth and for their inefficiency. While there are PSEs which have sunk significant amount of public money, there are also many PSEs which are running professionally and efficiently. These PSEs are making substantial profits even after meeting number of government mandated norms. A brief look at the background and financials of PSEs based on government report.

The Department of Public Enterprises in entrusted with the task of carrying out annual survey of all PSEs. PSEs are companies owned and controlled by the central government. Some of these have been listed but still, a PSE as government is the majority shareholder. Most of them were founded during 1950s-70s in the core industrial sector where India did not have any expertise and private capital was not coming in. PSEs, thus, have strong presence in industries such as heavy engineering, petroleum, steel, power generation, transmission, mining, fertilizers etc. The list here does not include financial sector entities like banks and insurance companies that are separately regulated by bodies such as RBI, IRDAI etc.

There are a total of 366 PSEs at the end of FY21 of which, 108 are under construction. Even though government has expressed its intention to reduce the role of public sector in non-core segments, total number of PSEs has increased in the recent past. This is because many projects in sectors such as power transmission, highways, metros etc. are being executed in partnership with private sector. Managing these projects as a separate company rather than as a part of an existing PSE helps faster decision making.

In terms of financials, PSEs had total sales of Rs 24.3 lakh crore during the year as per the DPE survey. In comparison, total sales of listed private sector, non-financial companies, numbering over 7,000, was close to Rs 50 lakh crore. This implies PSEs are making a significant contribution in total industrial activity. Even though sales have declined marginally by 1% during the year, primarily due to decline in oil prices, it has grown at about 7% CAGR over last ten years. Total capital employed in these enterprises stands at Rs 32.5 lakh crore, increase of 5% over FY20 whereas net worth stood at Rs 13.6 lakh crore. Of this, investment in under construction is about Rs 32,000 crore. Capital employed by private sector is about Rs 62 lakh crore giving almost the same sales to capital employed ratio.

However, a difference between private and PSEs is that PSEs operate primarily in core industrial and capital-intensive sectors which requires significant investment in machinery & equipment. This is reflected in Gross fixed assets (GFA) for these companies which stands at Rs 26.4 lakh crore, over 80% of total capital employed. In comparison, GFA as a percent of total capital is only 57% for private sector listed companies. Sector recording major investments are power generation & transmission, petroleum and coal mining.

However, PSEs were grossly inefficient, bogged down by political interference, favoritism affecting their profitability. The liberalization of 1991 was a watershed movement for them exposing them to market forces and competition. They went through a period of crisis, several of them closing down, but majority of them have re-aligned and improved their profitability. Out of the 255 operating companies, 177 made profits which stood at Rs 1.9 lakh crore, sharp increase from Rs 1.4 lakh crore in FY20. In comparison, private sector entities made aggregate profit of Rs 3.4 lakh crore implying a margin of 6.9%, lower than PSE's margin of 7.4%. The loss-making PSEs, totaling 77, reported loss of Rs 31,000 crore. The number of loss-making companies is down from 81 whereas total loss is down from Rs 45,000 crore in the previous year. Further, average loss is insignificant excluding the top ten which accounted for 85% of losses and therefore, have potential to become profitable. The privatization of Air India, second highest loss-making company, would reduce significant load from the financial report card of PSEs.

However, a handicap PSEs face is the legacy of huge work force as most of them have been running since the time when there was little automation. However, they have been able to correct this anomaly effecting a reduction of nearly 30% in its workforce over the last decade. Current employee strength at PSE is nearly 8.6 lakh, down from over 10.5 lakh in FY21, . The efforts to optimize this resource is evident from the fact that despite a focus on manpower reduction, employees in managerial cadre, who can help drive company's strategy, have increased by 1%.

Even though the issue is highly debatable, PSEs function as a business entity not just with profit motive but also with a larger social objective. They also need to adhere to several guidelines such as reservation in jobs, compulsory procurement from MSE segment and several other requirements which affects profitability. Despite these, if so many of PSEs have managed profitability and created a niche for themselves, that deserves equal applause, just as the private wealth creation receives. Certainly, a PSE is not required to be in the business of making bread or soaps & shampoos or other consumer facing business where the dynamics of operations are entirely different. While the media glare sends a signal of serious inefficiency within the entire PSEs space, it is essential to separate wheat from chaff. What is needed is greater operational and strategic freedom, independent of bureaucratic interference, much like the way Temasek Holdings, Singapore operates.

*****

# India's Logistics Sector – Understanding the Dynamics

Launch of *GatiShakti* and national logistics plan brings to focus issues and inefficiencies related to logistics sector. *Gatishakti* targets development of transport infrastructure integrated across different modes to minimize bottlenecks and gaps in capacity. NLP envisages creation of a digital interface which would integrate information across all concerned ministries, departments and states on real time basis and help users plan movement of their goods. Here is a look at what logistics sector comprises of and related issues.

Logistics essentially refer to movement of input material from source to factories, finished goods from factories to consumption centre and associated infrastructure for storage etc on the way. Unlike a manufacturing process, logistics involve far higher complexity because of dynamic nature of its service, optimization needs arising due to multiple routes, multiple destination, multiple modes of transport, management of empty rakes/ trucks, issues related to inter-state movement and so on. Unfortunately, India's transport infrastructure hasn't kept pace with increasing demand. As a result, logistics cost as a percent of GDP has risen to about 14% against 8-10% in most developed nations.

India's total transportation demand stood at about 4.6 billion tons in terms of quantity and 2.2 trillion tons kilometer in terms of quantity times distance in 2021 as per a NITI Aayog report. This corresponds to movement of almost 4,000 railway rakes per day for close to 20 hours every day (assuming entire quantity was moved by trains). Total tonnage kilometer implies average distance moved by the cargo is 480 km, approx. distance between Mumbai and Ahmedabad, Delhi and Kanpur or Chennai and Mysuru. While the average distance appears less as lot of cargo moves from Northern states to Mumbai or Kolkata, this is so because of significant amount of cargo move short distance within the state also. Average distance for container cargo moved by railways is high; 876 km in FY21 and 928 km in FY20. (Foodgrains cargo move the largest distance at about 1,400 km). Other than the domestic movement, goods totaling about 670 mn tons were moved through ports also as per ministry of ports. (An export cargo moving from Delhi to Mumbai port would be counted as domestic movement as well as port movement).

Out of the total, railways moved nearly 1.2 billion tons or about 25% whereas about 3.2 billion tons was moved through road. An important difference between railways and road traffic is that railways carry bulk of industrial goods whereas finished goods are primarily moved through roads. Among the major items moved through railways, coal accounts for largest share at 540 mn tons (equivalent to almost 400 rakes per day) whereas iron ore accounted for 160 mn tons and cement 120 mn tons, the three accounting for 70% of rail freight traffic.

Average distance moved by railways is 585 km in comparison to 440 km through roads. While the average for roads is lower than railways, it is still high. Roads are considered useful only for distance below 300 km as cost of road movement is significantly higher at Rs 3.6 per ton-km in contrast with Rs 1.6 for railways. (For 2021, actual cost of movement through road was over Rs 5 per ton-km as per the NITI Aayog report). Shifting half of this to rail would imply savings of as much as Rs 2.5 lakh crore besides reduction in pollution and other nuisances caused due to road movement. This excessive dependence on road network lies at the root of the inefficiency in logistics.

Against the international benchmark of 25-30%, roads in India carry as much as 70% of total freight load. Transportation in India has become increasingly dependent on roads over the decades primarily due to lack of planning, inadequate priority to freight traffic leading to significantly higher lead time, storage & warehousing issues at the railway yards and so on. As per a World Bank report, share of railway in total traffic in India stood at as much as 90% in 1951 which came down to 40% in 2005 and is now down to 25%.

Two of the important measures being undertaken to reduce this anomaly are construction of dedicated freight corridor (DFC) and multimodal logistics park (MMLP). The western and Eastern DFC cover a total of 3,400 km, about half of which has been commissioned so far. These two corridors alone handle almost 20% of total freight traffic. Average freight train speed currently stands at just about 24 km/hr (primarily due to significant passenger traffic congestion) which can go up to almost three times as achieved during the trial run over a recently commissioned DFC track. Maximum speed achieved during the trial was 99 km/h.

The other important proposal is development of MMLP. MMLP is nothing but an interchange point for the cargo in a 'hub and spoke' model along with associated storage facility (including cold storage) etc. MMLPs are also expected to help in obtaining clearances and meet other regulatory requirements. Thus, an MMLP would have cargoes coming-in through, say, roads from different factories, getting aggregated at MMLP and would be moved to their destination through rail or where available, waterways. In the same manner, MMLP would distribute the cargo at the consumption center. This would help optimize the network with usage of cheaper modes for longer distance and costlier mode providing only the first mile and last mile connectivity. MMLP would also help reduce the wastage in supply chain of perishable goods. The wastage in fruits & vegetables is around 25-30%. Despite being the second largest producer in the world with fruit production of 90 Mn tons and vegetable production of 180 Mn tons, India has not been able to build its supply chain. The master plan also proposes to map all production centers along with the existing infrastructure so that future projects could be planned based on the demand projection derived from this.

*****

# Real Estate Sector – Down but Not Out!

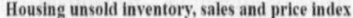

**Housing unsold inventory, sales and price index**

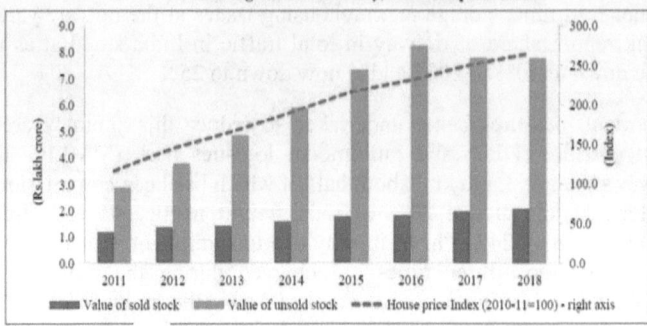

Source - The Economic Survey (quoting Liases Foras, RBI)

Residential property is among the most hit and most talked about sector over the last few years. However, property prices haven't corrected sufficiently despite the stress across all the affected segments, banks, NBFCs and the developers themselves. The stalemate forced the Economic Survey, some years ago, to advise developers to take a 'hair-cut' to revive the market. A look at the market and an analysis of background leading to the current situation.

Housing is unique among all consumer facing segments since 70-80% of the cost is financed through loan. In fact, the segment has grown exponentially after the introduction of EMI scheme. Real estate sector witnessed significant growth during FY08-14 with banking sector's loan to the sector recording growth of 16% CAGR. Bank loan book rose from Rs 63,000 crore to Rs 1.5 lakh crore during the period. Not only were the banks providing funds to the developers, the sector got push from demand side also with retail housing loan growing by as much as 30% during FY10-14 (considering a lag of two years). Total housing loan book of banks to non-priority sector rose from Rs 83,000 crore to Rs 2.4 lakh crore. (Note A. Total housing loan market is nearly double of that; the other half being provided by housing finance companies. B. Priority sector lending comprises of loans up to Rs 20 lakh, major part of which goes towards self-built houses). However, number of projects launched was far higher than market absorption capacity. As a result, while value of stocks sold annually remained in the range of Rs 1-1.4 lakh crore during 2011-15, value of unsold stock rose sharply from less than Rs 3 lakh crore to over Rs 7 lakh crore, as per the Economic Survey figures.

Developers faced their first crisis around this time with drying of credit, a result of stress in the banking sector. Banks' lending to real estate fell sharply to 6% during FY14-19. However, banks continue to lend to retail housing loan, non-priority sector which recorded growth of 25%. Banks were encouraged by the fact that they had very low NPA. Total bank loan to housing sector rose to Rs 11.9 lakh crore at the end of FY19, of which, non-priority loan was Rs 7.3 lakh crore.

If the developers had sat back and let the market inventory clear around this time, possibly the situation would have been different. However, a false belief in the growing size of the market and the desire to make super-normal profits led them to alternate source of funding, NBFCs who made up for decline in banks' lending to the sector. As per RBI data, NBFCs loan book to the segment grew sharply, by as much as 38% during FY16-19. (Data before FY16 was not separately reported). Total outstanding loan by NBFCs to the sector rose from Rs 56,000 crore in FY16 to Rs 1.5 lakh crore in FY19. This is almost comparable with banking sector's exposure of Rs 2 lakh crore.

So, how did the cookie crack, if not crumble? Possibly, a combination of factors such as demonetization, RERA, GST etc led to delays and stalling of many projects. Matter got further complicated with surfacing of funds siphoning and other frauds leading to further scrutiny. Thus, while developers remain saddled with stuck projects, subdued demand did not provide any push to prices. As per the Economic Survey, about 9.4 lakh units worth Rs 7.8 lakh crore (implying unit value of over Rs 80 lakh) were stuck in various stages of completion across top 8 cities at the end of Dec'18.

The core of the problem for the sector is two-fold – large number of stalled projects and lack of demand. The interesting part is that despite such a slowdown, prices as measured by housing price index (HPI), which nearly doubled between 2011 and 2014, have not corrected. This is because builders have chosen to hold back sales rather than reduce the price and sacrifice margin or book losses. The Economic Survey states, "existing unsold housing inventory can be cleared and the balance sheets of both bank/ non-bank lenders cleaned if the real estate developers are willing to take a 'hair-cut' by allowing the house-prices to drop".

Even though housing market for upper middle and high-income group, referred-to in above discussion, are facing significant distress, the affordable housing segment remain robust. The segment has been aided by government incentives such as interest subvention, 100% tax exemption on profits from construction of affordable housing and lower rate of GST and is gaining some attention of market participants. As per a presentation of HDFC Ltd, less than 20% of its borrowers belong to HIG (high income group), not getting benefited from government incentives.

So, what is the way forward? The most important move by the government was to provide corpus of Rs 25,000 crore to fund potentially viable stalled projects in Nov'19. While the initiative has significant potential and can help finish the incomplete project, it still doesn't take care of subdued demand. The funding has to come with conditions related to pricing so that the inventory gets cleared and kick-start a revival.

*****

# Coal Mining – Freed, At Last!

The deregulation of coal mining in 2021 and removing the end use restriction was a water-shed event for the sector. Coal mining was possibly the only regulated sector and it is difficult to understand why this decision took such a long time. A look at the sector and the implications of the decision.

India's coal mining industry is largely a monopoly with nearly 85% of coal being produced by state run company, Coal India Ltd (CIL) (and another 5% by another public sector company). CIL, itself, was formed after nationalization of all privately-run coal mines in 1973. Other than power sector which uses coal for generation of electricity, other large users are Steel, Cement etc where it is used as fuel. Coal accounts for almost 70% of power generation in the country and would continue to drive economy's fuel requirement, at least for next 15-20 years.

Coal mining is the process of extraction of the ore from under the surface of the earth. The extraction, therefore, requires removal of the top surface, called over burden to access the layers of coal. (Indian coal is extracted largely this way, called open-cast mining). However, this is quite a tedious process and entailed removal of close to 1,200 million cu meter of overburden for production of nearly 600 mn tons of coal last year. That is equivalent to depositing the removed waste up to a height of 6 meter across 2,000 football fields! The other method of mining, called underground mining, does not disturb the top layer and is faster method of extraction. However, it has been discouraged over the years for safety reasons.

Despite reserves of over 300 billion tons (equal to over 400 years of production!), coal production has grown at a dismal rate of 4% CAGR all these years. The huge demand-supply gap led to significant increase in imports which reached $26 bn in FY19, almost three times that in FY10. In terms of volume, imports stood at 235 mn tons, one-fourth of domestic requirement. (Even though all of it is not substitutable by domestic variety, more than half of it can be produced domestically).

The scarcity of coal leads to further distortion of the market and sale based on priority allocation. This is possibly the only sector where the buyer chases the seller! About 10% of coal produced is also sold through auction. However, short supply and huge demand lead to high bidding and average sale price works out to nearly 80% above the reserved price.

While the criticality of the resource should have prompted its maximum use and efficient development of the sector, that did not happen. The fact that most other sectors saw significant reforms over last 20-30 years makes it even more surprising and intriguing. The only reform undertaken in early 90s was to allocate coal blocks to private sector companies. However, they were allowed to produce for their own consumption only and barred from selling in the open market leading to inadequate focus. The other lacuna in the reform was lack of transparency in the allocation process ultimately, leading to cancellation of all 204 coal blocks by the Supreme Court in 2014. These blocks were allotted between 1993-2010. A fact giving indication of collusion is that out of the 200 blocks allotted, only 40 blocks were producing whereas the rest had been secured and kept for future use.

The intervention of the Supreme Court triggered reforms in the sector with amendment in policy in 2105 mandating allocation of all mining blocks through auction. The policy was further modified in 2018 permitting 100% FDI in mining industry. Need for these changes was even greater considering the pollution and other nuisance it causes. For instance, washing of coal could reduce the dust emission but is not practiced widely as the regulated price does not allow recovery of additional cost. Further, considering the increasing environmental concerns, coal mines may face global closure in another 20-30 years and the resources may remain unutilized underneath. While government has auctioned only 30 blocks since Supreme Court's decision, large number of blocks are slated to be auctioned soon. The current change in policy, along with the entry of foreign players, would change the landscape with use of advanced technology enabling heavy-duty equipment and faster extraction. This may even enable underground mining without compromising on safety. Government should also break CIL's monopoly by separating all its seven subsidiaries and letting them compete among themselves.

Coal mining industry does not have much time to prove its mettle!

*****

# Telecom Sector – The AGR Crisis

Telecom sector went through a huge crisis with the Supreme Court judgment on AGR. The ruling meant an additional burden of about Rs 60,000 crore on top two companies. While the entry of Jio was itself a big blow, the judgment further compounded the matter. So, what is AGR and what is the current financial state of the companies. A brief look.

The genesis of AGR (Adjusted Gross Revenue) dispute goes back to 1999 when the telecom operators were given the option of paying license fees and spectrum usage charges as a percent of gross revenue instead of a fixed fee. This was done to help them manage their costs. However, a point of contention soon arose on whether AGR includes non-core incomes such as rents, dividends, profit on sale of assets etc or not. Principal of natural justice would possibly conclude that fees should be applied only on the income directly generated from using the resources for which it is being charged, in this case, the spectrum. TDSAT (Telecom Disputes Settlement and Appellate Tribunal) thought so and ruled in favour of the operators in 2015, on the case filed in 2005. However, the Supreme Court has set aside that judgment leading to the current chaos.

The impact of this ruling would not possibly have been so severe but for the upheaval created by the entry of Jio. The entry not only led to exit of players like Tata Tele and R-Com, it also caused severe losses for the existing operators. Bharti Airtel incurred cumulative losses of close to Rs 12,000 crore during FY17-FY19 after profit of over Rs 20,000 crore in the preceding two years (FY15-FY16). For Vodafone idea, two separate entity which merged after the entry of Jio, it was worse with losses of over Rs 19,000 crore after a modest profit of Rs 5,600 crore in FY15-FY16 (on combined basis).

The AGR dues have worked out to about Rs 34,000 crore and Rs 26,000 respectively for Airtel and Vodafone Idea. Interestingly, core dues are only around one-fourth of the total and the rest is interest and penalty for last 14 years. This means, if the companies had sought an escrow arrangement where they could deposit the dues under dispute and kept doing so during the pendency of the case, total liability would have been much less.

The impact of this provisioning reflects in the financial results of Sept'19 quarter. Airtel has recorded losses of Rs 24,500 crore during the quarter, up from Rs 1,300 crore in the previous quarter. Vodafone Idea recorded losses of over Rs 50,000 crore, the highest so far in the corporate history. This has resulted in Vodafone Idea's equity eroding from about Rs 60,000 crore at the end of FY19 to Rs 24,000 crore by Sept'19. (Erosion in equity is not equal to losses due to Rs 25,000 crore of equity raised in April'19). Of the equity raised recently, Rs 18,250 was provided by the promoter groups, the reason why both the promoters look completely dis-inclined to pump-in any more money. A worrying part of its balance sheet is that 'intangible assets' account for Rs 1.3 lakh crore out of total assets of Rs 2.5 lakh crore. Intangibles do not correspond to any actual assets but refer to 'goodwill on merger', trademark etc and have little value in case of liquidation. Other than long-term borrowings of Rs 1.2 lakh crore, company is also facing significant short-term pressure also with current financial liabilities (maturing within next 12 months) of close to Rs 36,000 crore. Against this, its cash & bank balance stands at just about Rs 10,000 crore.

Airtel is reasonably well placed with close to Rs 70,000 crore of equity although down from Rs 91,000 crore a quarter ago. While company also has a huge debt balance of nearly Rs 1.2 lakh crore, it doesn't seem to have serious short-term pressure. To maintain its financial health and credit rating, company has proposed to raise equity of close to Rs 14,000 crore. This is the second equity raising exercise during the year with first rights issue in May'19 mopping up Rs 25,000 crore.

The worst appears to be over for the sector with the recent tariff hike and deferment of dues by two years allowed by the government. However, there is still severe short-term pressure on Vodafone Idea which continues to face an uncertain future.

*****

# Towards An Efficient Electricity Market

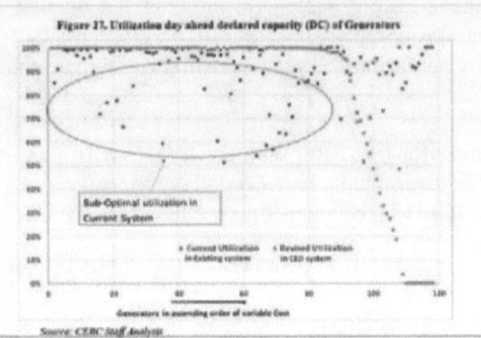

Figure 37. Utilization day ahead declared capacity (DC) of Generators

CERC (Central Electricity Regulatory Commission) released a proposal some time back whereby buyers and sellers would move to a single electronic platform for all the transactions from current bilateral Power Purchase Agreement (PPA). The platform would make sure that power is procured in order of increasing cost of generation with high-cost generators getting last preference irrespective of whether they have a PPA or not. Here is a look at the intricacies of the proposal.

Electricity trade is currently based on long term power purchase agreement between distribution companies (discoms) and the generation companies. The reason for this is that country faced huge power deficit until sometime back and discoms preferred committed power supply even if it came at a higher price. Nearly 87% of total electricity is traded through this mode as per CERC. Further, discoms operate in a limited area mostly within the state. This means even if a low-cost producer has surplus generation capacity in the neighbouring state, it may not be able to purchase the power. There was yet another reason for discom to enter into long term PPA. Discoms who had long term PPAs get first preference for availing the transmission line capacity to carry electricity from generation point to the consumer. The short-term buyers, remaining 17%, are scheduled based on excess transmission capacity available and first come first served basis adding an element of uncertainty.

As per the proposed system, called Market Based Economic Dispatch (MBED), each discom would feed-in its power requirement for the next day in the electronic system which is well developed and working for many years now. The generation companies would also feed-in their generation capacity and the cost at which they are ready to sell. Discoms would also disclose their existing PPAs along with the agreed variable and fixed cost. (As per the PPAs, discoms are required to pay the generator the fixed portion of cost even if they don't purchase the agreed power).

The core job of scheduling is done by the system which calculates the total demand and notifies the generators in order of their cost of generation till the demand is fulfilled. The sale happens at the price quoted by the last generator called market clearing price (MCP). (This means those plants whose cost of generation is even lower would get additional revenue). However, the scheduling is not so simple. There are a number of other factors like transmission constraint, technical minimum capacity at which a plant may need to be run to meet demand spike at a later point in time and so on. While these issues may mean some purchase at higher cost, the optimization still shows substantial reduction in cost of generation. As per CERC study across five states, there would be total reduction of Rs 6,200 crore in the generation cost, approx 11% of total, through MBED. The circled dots in the figure represent the plants that are not running at full capacity even though they have low cost of generation. At the other end are plants which are running at full capacity but would have to shut down their plant after MBED in implemented.

Even though the system seeks to reduce the cost of power produced, it protects the existing bilateral contracts which would get phased out gradually. MBED envisages that buyer would continue to pay the fixed cost (FC) to the generation company. However, it also stipulates generator to pay back to discoms if MCP through MBED is higher than VC through PPA. For example, assume two entities enter a PPA with Variable cost of Rs 2.4 and Fixed Cost of Rs 1.1. Generation Company would continue to get Rs 1.1 from discom even though it is not supplying the power. However, if MCP as per MBED increases to Rs 3.0 per unit (higher than VC of PPA), the concerned generation company would pay back the difference (Rs 3 - Rs 2.4) to the discom. This would protect the discom from any additional burden. Over a period of time, as the PPAs expire, there would be no need for discoms to enter into fresh PPAs. Since market has developed the mechanism to discover the best possible price and provide all the energy consumer needs, discom would not have to worry about reliability of supply.

Another important point of MBED is that not all savings is getting passes on to the consumer but is also being shared with generators. This is quite innovative as it would incentivize generators to invest in efficiency improvement measures and bring down generation cost.

*****

# Power Sector NPAs – A Case Study

Even as power sector evolved from scarcity to surplus, it is besotted with another crisis, sharp increase in NPA estimated at over Rs 1 lakh crore. But how exactly has the sector landed is such a big crisis and what is the way out. An attempt to understand it.

Power sector is a unique sector having transitioned from state monopoly to market driven industry. The industry is going through a turbulent yet interesting phase having overcome the problem of power deficit which has been replaced by problem of excess. The sector's woes can be traced back to the period of FY08-14 when large number of generation projects was initiated. Government's thrust on investment amidst a downturn and a general laxity in due diligence helped them secure funds. As a result, bank loan to power sector rose from just Rs 95,000 crore at the end of FY08 to Rs 4.8 lakh crore in FY14, a five-fold increase! Most of this was being undertaken by private sector companies who added a total of nearly 80,000 mw of generation capacity (mostly thermal). A conservative estimate would put the investment involved in this to the tune of Rs 3.5 lakh crore. Increasing private participation led to its share in total generation capacity rising from 13% in FY07 to 44% in FY17.

In their jest to make business out of scarcity, private sector companies, most of them new to the business, could not fully comprehend the unique structure of the sector. Two important elements were - security of fuel supply and agreement with buyer for purchase for as long as 25 years called Power Purchase Agreement (PPA). Many of them went on adding capacity without PPA or more importantly, coal linkage with a belief that they will find a buyer since there is an aggregate shortage in the economy.

PPAs have another interesting dimension. Increasing generation capacity gave the DISCOMs (State distribution companies), who had always grappled with scarcity, to secure supplies for the future. They entered into large number of Power Purchase Agreement (PPA), even beyond the baseline projections. The economic slowdown meant that there was significant gap between demand and projections and DISCOMs were left with more supplies than needed. As per CEA, PPAs available with DISCOMs is more than 230,000 mw against current peak rated demand of about 165,000 mw only. The problem with PPA is that the buyer must pay the fixed cost portion even if he does not purchase the power adding to the stress on their financials. Having learnt their lessons, DISCOMs have not invited bids for procurement of power since about 2015. Some of them have, in fact, written to the Ministry of Power asking for cancellation of power allotted to them from the central pool. This puts all the plant which did not have PPA until then, without any hope of revival.

Coal linkage or secured fuel supply is another unique feature of power sector. A power plant can secure lending only if it has received coal linkage (other than PPA). The linkage got snapped when the Supreme Court cancelled over 200 coal mine blocks allotted in an opaque manner in 2014. Large number of these plants suddenly became unviable. While coal has been allocated/ auctioned subsequently through various arrangements including government scheme SHAKTI in 2017, it still does not solve the issue completely. Further, precious years were lost during cancellation and re-allotment leading to increase in financial burden.

Despite these issues, several generation plants did get commissioned which was enough to turn the sector from deficit to surplus. As per CEA, total of 110,000 mw of capacity, including 100,000 mw of thermal plants were added in six years till FY18. Fallout of this was that plants which were running well until then became a victim. CEA report states that PLF (capacity utilization) of plants fell sharply from 79% in FY07 to less than 60% in FY18. Lower PLF does not only mean lower recovery of fixed cost but also higher inefficiency in fuel burning and therefore, higher variable cost. Peak power shortage, which is met through peaking sources such as hydel plant or by increasing the output from running plants, has come down from 8.7% in FY13 to 0.7% in FY18.

As per the 40th report of Parliament's Standing Committee on Energy submitted in Aug'18, total of 66,000 mw of capacity owned by independent power producers (IPP) is under stress. This includes 44 coal-based plants with 55,000 mw capacity, nine gas based with 7,000 mw capacity and 13 hydro based with 4,500 mw capacity. Total investment involved could be about Rs 4 lakh crore. The report also states that about 20,000 mw of assets are not having PPAs and will have to wait till the demand revives. Out of this, 11,000 mw do not have coal supply arrangement, even securing that would not do much good in the absence of a buyer. Another 16,000 mw is under construction and it would be a tough call on whether to put-in more money to complete these projects. Some of these have already been taken to National Company Law Tribunal (NCLT) and it is difficult to foresee banks getting anything more than 20% of their money. Cost of these thermal plants has risen to about Rs 8 crore per mw against norm of about 4.5 crore due to delays and increase in interest during construction (IDC). For some of the plants, IDC accounts for over half of project cost. However, gold-plating in some of these cases cannot be ruled out.

So, what next? Demand increase is projected by only about 11,000 MW annually as per CEA. The stressed capacity of over 60,000 mw and under construction projects of NTPC and other financially strong companies of over 20,000 mw means that it could take at least six years to absorb these capacities. Efforts at revival could also get slight boost from retiring old inefficient and high polluting plants. About 7,000 mw of capacity has already been retired as per Ministry of Power and another 10,000 mw are slated to be retired in due course.

The next question is - is it worth waiting that long or the interest is better served by resolving/liquidating these assets by referring to NCLT, as directed by the 12th Feb circular of RBI? The problem in taking them to NCLT is that there are very few buyers in the market (unlike say, in steel industry). Even they have not come forward and have not offered reasonable price in the face of excess supply scenario. This is evident from the fact that bid received for one of the stressed plants was Rs 0.35 crore per mw against construction cost of close to Rs 4.5 crore. A forced sale where no market exists will serve no purpose and cause much higher loss than what would be suffered by spreading the resolution process over a period.

The mechanism put forward by REC, PARIVARTAN, offers the best hope. The scheme envisages formation of an asset reconstruction company, largely owned by the lenders which would take over these assets. It would also involve roping in NTPC which would take care of operational and project execution aspect of the assets. The assets would be put up for sale once the market has stabilized and the asset has all necessary linkages in place. The immediate objective should be to ensure that the machinery lying on the site or partially erected does not deteriorate. Role of NTPC is critical because of its strength in operations as well as project execution.

The problem of excess capacity is not exactly insurmountable. China is facing such a problem for many more industries such as steel and other metals but has allowed them time to stabilize. It may also be noted that USA faced a similar situation after the global financial crisis where government bought equity in several companies. The stakes were sold after the market stabilized over next 4-5 years which also gave government much better price. As the committee noted, "These stressed assets are national assets at the end of the day and need to be preserved, protected and conserved".

\*\*\*\*\*

# Power Distribution Companies – The Elephant in The Room

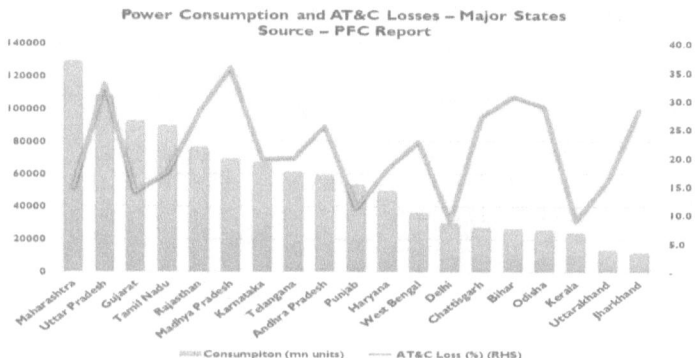

Chairman of the Fifteen Finance Commission called state distribution companies (discoms), "The Elephant in the room", in an interview. Indeed, discoms are in a dire state, operating with AT&C (aggregate transmission & commercial) losses of over 22% and accumulated losses of close to Rs 4 lakh crore. To improve their viability, the finance minister allocated as much as Rs 3.1 lakh crore spread over 5 years, for modernisation. However, not all the discoms are with this level of inefficiency. Discoms in Delhi, Kerala and Gujarat have brought their losses to acceptable level and are making profits. A look at the financial and operational details of various discoms based on a PFC report.

Power distribution operation is largely handled by discoms owned by state governments. Despite the efforts taken over last 15-20 years to improve their operational efficiency, there has been limited success. As per the latest report of PFC (Power Finance Corporation), discoms recorded losses of Rs 86,000 crore (excluding special grants and deferred payments) in FY19, sharp increase from Rs 60,000 crore in the previous year. Sales stood at Rs 5.9 lakh crore including subsidy component of Rs 1.1 lakh crore. Revenue gap (after subsidy received) was Rs 0.72 per unit of power, sharply up from Rs 0.53 in the previous year. Even though state govt are required to reimburse the subsidy, not all the states are prompt in doing that. Actual subsidy paid is less than 90% of dues. Worst among the states is Andhra Pradesh which has paid only 21% of the subsidy claimed by discom.

Major among the loss-making ones are Andhra Pradesh at Rs 16,800 crore, sharply up from Rs 550 crore in FY18, Tamil Nadu at Rs 18,000 crore and Rajasthan - Rs 12,500 crore. However, some of the states have made remarkable turnaround. Among the states which are making profits are Maharashtra which moved from loss of about Rs 4,000 in FY18 to profit of close to Rs 2,000 in FY19. Similarly, Punjab recorded profit of Rs 270 crore against loss of Rs 2,760 crore in the previous year. Among other profitable states are Delhi - Rs 714 crore and Gujarat – Rs 184 crore.

Yet, the annual loss does not reflect the grim state. Most of the discoms have been making losses for most of the years, leading to accumulated deficit of Rs 4.9 lakh crore, despite several write-offs done over the years. Among the worst are Rajasthan with deficit of Rs 90,000 crore, Tamil Nadu - Rs 88,000 crore and UP – Rs 82,000 crore, the three accounting for over half of the total. The few outperformers are Delhi and Gujarat having a surplus at Rs 3,100 crore and Rs 988 crore. It may be noted that Tamil Nadu has not even separated its distribution arm from the generation arm, leading to deficit getting understated.

The deficit is reflected in the borrowings, which is the source of financing. Total borrowings of discoms (including consumer contribution and excluding net worth) stands at Rs 5.6 lakh crore at the end of FY19. The figure hides their dire state as significant amount of loan was waived in FY16 as per a restructuring plan. The debt had reached level of Rs 8.3 lakh crore in FY16 which came down to Rs 5.1 lakh crore after the restructuring. Among the worst are Tamil Nadu at Rs 1.75 lakh crore and Rajasthan at Rs 1.1 lakh crore.

So, what is the cause of such colossal losses? Quite simply – huge inefficiency in distribution. Discoms are incurring AT&C losses of over 22%, meaning they are realising sales from less than 4 units against every 5 units of power they procure. The figure stood at close to 24% in FY16, when the above stated restructuring was done. Even though losses have been coming down over the years, there are some serious laggards. Among these are M.P. - 36%, U.P. - 33.2%, Bihar – 31%, Odisha – 29.2%, Jharkhand – 28.6% and Rajasthan – 28.3%. Among the outperformers are Delhi and Kerala with AT&C losses of only 9% whereas it is 14% for Gujarat.

AT&C losses have two components. Billing losses and collection losses. While a discom may not be able to bill adequately due to lack of metering and may need investment to improve that, high collection losses is purely an administrative issue and points to collusion. Large number of states have achieved 100% efficiency in collection with administrative reforms. Among the states with high collection losses are A.P. at 19.5%, U.P. - 17.7% and Telangana - 14.8%, implying these states continue to supply power to a large number of consumers even though they have not paid their dues.

So, what is the way out? Answers are not difficult to find but politically, very difficult to implement. As per the PFC report, agriculture consumers are paying Rs 0.76 per unit only against unit of over Rs 5. A better option would be to provide direct cash transfer for marginal farmers and bill as per actual cost. The inefficient entities need to engage with the profitable ones and adopt their best practices. While privatization offers the best answer to this consumer facing business as shown in Delhi, state governments need to, at least, segregate the most inefficient pockets and privatize them as done in Maharashtra.

*****

# Nuclear Power – The demonised resource

Nuclear power in India still appears to be moving at a snails' pace despite commissioning the first plant way back in 1969. Nuclear power remains constrained due to huge negative perception related to its operations, long gestation period and until about a decade ago, due to variety of international restrictions. However, it provides huge advantages particularly environmental and its potential needs to be tapped for longer term energy security.

Nuclear Power began its journey in India in 1969 with the commissioning of first commercial power plant. However, even after 50 years of journey, it has reached a capacity of just 6,800 mw so far (and nearly 4,800 mw under construction). The latest, 1,000 mw plant, constructed in collabouration with Russia, was commissioned in Mrach'17. Its contribution to total energy generation in the country is little over 2%. In comparison, some of the countries globally have tapped this resource substantially. While USA has almost 100,000 mw of nuclear power plant, the capacity is 63,000 mw in France. More importantly France generates more than 75% of its energy from nuclear source.

Nuclear power has distinct advantages both environmentally and economically. Nuclear power is actually a non-polluting source of power producing almost no greenhouse gases. Further, it's a highly intensive source of energy with one kg of uranium producing electricity equal to nearly 30 tons of coal. This reduces not only the logistics costs but also associated nuisance such as en-route spillage of coal, ash generation and so on. (30 tons of Indian coal would produce over 10 tons of ash on burning). Intensive source of energy helps construct bigger units of power plants. Against biggest size of 800 mw of thermal power plant in operation, nuclear plant has reached a size of 1,000 mw and plants of 1,600 mw size are under construction.

Biggest advantage with nuclear plant is low cost of fuel which works out to only about Rs 0.7 per unit against about Rs 2 for coal based plants. This does not include the cost of pollution which is intangible. For gas based plant, it is even higher at Rs 3 per unit, based on gas price of $8 per mmbtu. (However, gas based plants suffer even bigger issues in terms of availability of gas).

Nuclear power industry carries considerable baggage because of inadequate understanding of its operations and considerable negative publicity. For instance, an oil spill or a coal mine disaster is looked upon as an isolated accident without questioning the hazards posed by the industry. However, in case of nuclear power, any accident puts a question mark on the operation of the entire industry. (As per Wikipedia, nearly 5,000 people are killed every year in coal mines in China alone). It is interesting to note that the industry still has to defend itself for the Chernobyl accident which happened four decades ago!

However, other than the exaggerated fears related to its operations, nuclear plants do have a disadvantage in terms of huge capital investment and long gestation period. Its capital cost is estimated at around Rs 8-10 crore/MW against Rs 4-4.5 crore for thermal plants. While this still keeps the total cost of generation within reasonable limits, the upfront investment and delayed pay-off does add to the credit risk. Nuclear Power Corporation of India Ltd's (NPCIL) balance sheet of nearly Rs 65,000 crore for running less than 7,000 mw and constructing another 4,800 mw of plants gives a rough indication of the high capital investment. However, an existing debt-equity ratio of 1:1 and cash generation of over Rs 3,000 crore every year means that company can accelerate its construction activity without needing any additional equity capital.

Nuclear Power was expected to get a big boost with the Indo-US nuclear deal. It helped in securing fuel supply for the existing plants with capacity utilization to 80% from about 60% earlier. However, the deal could not expedite initiation of new projects because of issues related to equipment suppliers' liability in case of an accident. With that issue getting sorted out some time back, hopefully, nuclear power would get some more momentum in the years to come.

*****

# Natural Gas Market in India – An Overview

Natural gas market in India, indeed, globally, suffer from significantly volatility in prices. As a result, the market suffers from inadequate investments in exploration, liquefaction, pipeline capacity etc. A major setback for the market was sharp decline in production from K-G basin. Here is a look at India's natural gas market and some of the factors affecting it.

Natural gas is an important source of fuel providing about 25% of total energy consumed globally. It is a cleaner source generating about 52 kg of $CO_2$ per million BTU of energy produced against 80 kg by crude oil and 90-100 kg by coal. It is also cheaper than crude oil having averaged nearly $4 per mmbtu (million British thermal units) over last five years till 2021 against about $10 per mmbtu for crude oil at $60 per barrel (rough figures).

Despite being significantly cheaper, it faces a major drawback as it cannot be transported on bulk basis as easily as oil or coal. While it must be moved through cryogenic ships from one continent to another, it can be moved only through pipeline on land. This requires significant upfront investment, Rs 6-8 crore per km of pipeline, which faces risk in case of drying of gas supplies or reduced demand. For instance, two pipelines totaling 2,400 km and combined annual carrying capacity of 28 mn tons constructed to transport gas from KG basin are operating at 20-25% capacity utilization only as KG basin is not producing gas now.

Natural gas is primarily used for generation of power, as fuel for domestic and automotive and industrial consumption or as raw material for production of fertilizers. Fertilizer and power sector consume nearly 60% of total domestic gas. Despite its varied usage, natural gas in India has not been able to take-off accounting for less than 10% share in total energy consumed. As per PPAC (Petroleum Planning & Analysis Cell), India consumed a total of 49 million tons or 175 mmscmd (million standard cubic meter per day) of natural gas in FY20. In terms of calorific value, this corresponds to 60 mn tons of crude oil. Of this, 23 mn tons was domestically produced whereas the rest was imported.

Domestic production of natural gas in India is marked by discovery of significant gas reserve in 2000s in deep sea waters of KG basin. The discovery and promise of sufficiency in gas supply led to investments in gas pipelines, power generation capacity and associated network. However, gas production could not be sustained due to technical complexity after peaking at nearly 40 mn tons in FY11 with KG basin providing nearly 40%. (To put it in perspective, domestic crude oil production has averaged 30 million tons only over last few years. Total crude oil consumption is over 200 million tons, the rest being imported). With decline in KG basin gas, domestic production has fallen by over 40%.

Natural gas industry also recorded significant investment in LNG terminals projecting sharp increase in domestic demand. India has import capacity of over 40 mtpa with six LNG import terminal, almost double of its domestic production. With the commissioning of these terminals, India's imports increased nearly three times over last ten years which now accounts for 53% of total consumption. Yet, there is a significant scarcity of gas in the country with power sector being hit the hardest. Power sector has total gas-based generation capacity of 24,000 mw. The sector, requiring over 30 mtpa of gas for capacity utilization, is running at just about 25%.

Paradoxically, even though there is a scarcity, LNG import terminals are not utilizing their entire capacity. Average capacity utilization of LNG terminals stands at only 62%, still better than 40% a few years back. While the terminals in Western India are running at over 90%, the ones in southern India are in the range of 11-36%. The reason for the low capacity utilization of LNG terminal is inadequate arrangement for off-take as well as pricing. As per PPAC, India has pipeline network of close to 17,000 km (including partially commissioned lines) with carrying capacity of 94 MTPA. Another 16,000 km of pipeline is under construction. However, as stated earlier, pipelines built to evacuate gas from KG basin are running at less than 25%. This brings down the aggregate capacity utilization of pipelines to less than 50%.

Other than inadequate utilization of LNG terminals, gas pipelines and drying of gas from KG basin, the market has suffered from sharp fluctuation in international prices. Global prices rose from less than $5 per mmbtu in 2006 to over $15 in next two years. LNG importers remained stuck with higher prices as per the terms of contract till about 2014. However, the price of gas produced domestically is fixed by the government as per an administered price mechanism (APM). While the price is linked to international prices, it is fixed for a period of six months and is, therefore, less volatile. APM Price has come down to $1.8 /mmbtu since Oct'20, down 52% over sept'19 and 65% over March'15. Prices have been revised upwards sharply in March'22 due to surge in global prices, from $2.9/mmbtu to $6.1/mmbtu and from $6.1 /mmbtu to $9.9 /mmbtu for gas discovered from difficult basin.

*****

# Food Processing Industry – An Overview

Covid-19 brought greater attention to food processing industry, with increase in consumption of processed food. Fifty years ago, the challenge for the nation was to produce enough to feed its people, the objective now is to help agri-producers move up the value chain. India, at the moment, presents a picture of paradox, being the largest producer of number of food items, yet being the worst in terms of its processing. Here is a look at various components of food processing industry and their dynamics.

Food processing industry (FPI) can be classified into three groups – primary, secondary and tertiary. Primary processing involves cleaning, grading, sorting, packing, etc where the value additions is low and have limited significance except in case of fruits & vegetables processing. Secondary processing primarily includes manufacture of food products like bread, butter, chocolate, dairy products etc, whereas tertiary comprises of manufacture of 'ready to eat' food items. FPI has gained prominence with increasing urbanization, change in taste, greater participation of females in workforce and so on, leading to increased use of ready to cook or eat products. (A roadside Vada-pav stall would be a part of food service industry and not food processing. A floor-mill selling its own product is a part of FPI).

Ministry of Food Processing Industry (MFPI) identifies 18 major groups based on the food item involved. These 18 industries recorded total output of Rs 11.9 lakh crore in FY19 with GVA of Rs 1.36 lakh crore or only 11.5%. The sector has seen a turnaround only recently, growing at 12.7% CAGR (constant price) during 2015-19 in contrast with decline of 3% in the preceding three years. FPI is also an important sector from exports perspective recording exports of $38.3 billion (~Rs 2.9 lakh crore) during 2020-21 (includes both agri-food and processed food). Even though its share in India's total exports is over 10%, its share in global food exports market is only 2.3%, implying significant potential to grow.

Important among these industries are manufacture of grain mill products, manufacture of dairy products, manufacture of vegetable and animal oils and fats (largely edible oils), manufacture of animal feeds, manufacture of soft drinks, bottled water, processing of fruits and vegetables etc. FPI is not restricted to food items grown on soil but also includes categories such as processing of meat & poultry, fish & fish products, manufacture of alcoholic beverages etc. The World Custom Organization has a list of over 450 different processed food and beverages products! Among all the groups, edible oil and grain mill products are the largest category each accounting for almost one-fourth of total food processing industry output. However, they have value addition of only 5.7% and 7.4%. (Consumption of raw material, fuel and power of Rs 100 to produce output worth Rs 125 would imply gross value addition of 25%). Sectors with high value addition are cocoa-based products, processing of fruits & vegetables and manufacture of bakery products, each having GVA of over 20%. However, their share in total output in only 2-3%.

Despite the growth, FPI's has a share of just about 10% in total agriculture sector GVA. This is significantly lower than the level of 30% in China and 60-80% in western countries, as per a RBI report. In case of fruits and vegetables, 65% of total output in USA is processed, 23% in China and barely 2.2% in India. Case of fruits & vegetables, with production of close to 300 million tons, is even more critical as the segment suffers wastage of up to 16% as per a survey cited by RBI. (More so, processing it provides high value addition of over 25%). Wastage of over 10% in case of fisheries and 5-6% even in case of cereals can be reduced by a focused push to FPI. Despite being ranked first in production of several food items such as milk, pulses and jute, second in fruits and vegetables and third in cereals, low level of processing reflects the inability of the economy to leverage the potential.

FPI is important not just from the perspective of its ability to enhance rural income but also because of low capital investment needs and high employment intensity. The sector is also the largest employer accounting for over 10% of manufacturing sector employment and 14% of output. As per Annual Survey of Industries (ASI), FPI provides GVA of 0.65 crore per crore of investment against only 0.42 for the rest of the manufacturing sector. Similarly, persons employed stands at over 10 per crore of investment against 4.4 per crore for rest of the sector. Bakery products is an interesting sector as it has high GVA of 27% and also employs almost 20 person per crore of investment. Since, it doesn't fall under perishable category, the segment makes a perfect case for exports push.

FPI is a vast sector and suffers from lack of quality and timely data on entire range of products and other characteristics. For instance, share of unorganized sector in total output is only about 20% as per NSSO data. However, there are as many as 25 lakh units (with total employment of 50 lakh persons implying average employment of two) in the unorganized sector making it difficult to track their output and other information.

*****

# MSME Sector – Generating Employment or Disguised Unemployment?

MSME sector has been receiving attention from the government and regulators because of its contribution to GDP and employment generation. However, an issue not recognised is - are these jobs for real or they are another form of disguised unemployment. A brief look at the same.

MSME (Micro, Small and Medium Enterprises) sector refers to enterprises operating with capital investments and generating revenue below a threshold. For manufacturing sector, investment limit is Rs 25 lakh for Micro, Rs 5 crore for small and Rs 10 crore for medium enterprises. For Service sector entities, the limit is Rs 10 lakh, Rs 2 crore and Rs 5 crore respectively. As per the National Sample Survey (NSS) during 2015-16 quoted by ministry of MSME, there are 6.34 crore MSME functioning in the country. About 45% of them are in rural area. The pervasive nature of MSME segment is evident from the fact that a person from every fifth household in the country, on an average, runs an MSME. The sectoral breakup shows that nearly 2 crores of them are engaged in manufacturing and services each whereas the rest are engaged in trading. Total people employed is 11.1 crore which works out to just 1.75 person per enterprise. An interesting figure is average employment of 1.83 person for manufacturing units which means many manufacturing MSMEs run with a single person. These could involve running a simple, small machine and outsourcing sales function. For small and medium enterprises, no of employees is 10 and 35 respectively.

Other than the total number of people employed, MSME sector also receives attention because of its contribution to GDP. Gross Value Added (GVA) by the sector stood at Rs 44 lakh crore in FY17, almost 30% of total GDP. MSME in the manufacturing sector have a bigger role as there share in output is 45% and in exports at around 48%. Interestingly, rural India accounts for higher MSMEs in manufacturing segment. Even though per unit GVA for MSMEs is quite low at Rs 6.9 lakh, the aggregate contribution warrants an adequate policy push.

Among the important policies aiding to its growth is compulsory procurement by government agencies of at least 25% of their requirement from MSE (micro and small, not MSME). For FY19, this amounted to Rs 35,000 crore from 90,000 MSEs, or nearly Rs 39 lakh worth of purchase per MSE. Another important policy support has been credit guarantee scheme which has helped nearly 4.3 lakh MSME as per the ministry report. Yet, the sector faces variety of issues in accessing funds from bank, such as absence of proper financials statements, lack of credit history, even lack of separate account of unit and the person running it. Total credit outstanding from banks and NBFCs to the MSME sector was approximately Rs 16.6 lakh crore as at end of Sept'19. Their share of credit is just about 17% against share of 30% in GDP.

Even though MSMEs are making significant contribution, especially in the manufacturing sector, it is probably essential to have a critical look at its structure. There are a large number of MSMEs being run to escape from being unemployed rather than presence of any real opportunity. For instance, an unemployed youth beginning to work as a property dealer even though there are several other such service providers in the neighbourhood or a rural middle-aged person opening a small *kirana* shop as his failing health does not allow him to work in the fields, even though the market is not big enough for another such shop. Some figures need to be considered to understand this issue. First, 99% of the total or 6.3 crore enterprises are micro enterprises implying capital investment of less than Rs 10 lakh in case of service sector. (There are only 5,000 medium enterprises). Almost 96% of the enterprises are proprietary in nature and only 11% are registered with the government. (The NSS survey is field based and involves actual door-to-door engagement to arrive at its findings). This suggests that the job opportunity provided by micro firms, especially in services and trading segments, may not even be sufficient from earnings perspective. It may be useful to identify those earning below a threshold and address their needs separately. The first things would be modification of survey findings bifurcating micro segment into, may be less than Rs 5 lakh and Rs 5-10 lakh category. This could be followed up by analysis of region having maximum enterprises in below Rs 5 lakh category and finding other avenues, helping them develop other skillsets etc. This may also involve bringing out separate policy for manufacturing MSME which definitely has lot more potential. While the task is not easy, the first step is to recognize this problem.

*****

# Understanding the Dynamics of Crude Oil Market

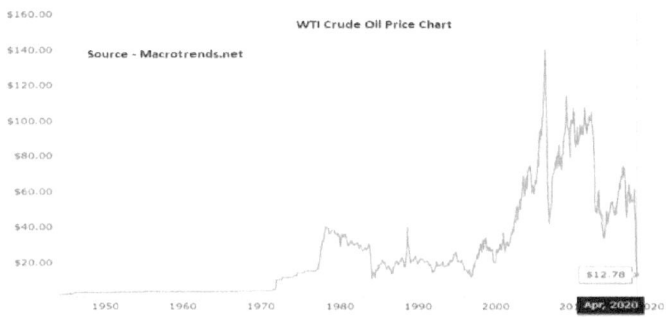

Crude oil had suffered sharp slump with the emergence of the pandemic. The demand crash and lack of timely cut in production had created a situation never seen before – WTI Oil futures turning negative! However, the prices moved up sharply after the initial shock. So, what drives the oil market and who all are the market participants. A look at the same.

Crude oil is possibly the most globalized and most high-profile commodity recording average production of little over 100 mb/d in 2019, as per US EIA (Energy Information Administration) report. Production includes 6 mb/d of unconventional liquid such as shale oil and about 10 mb/d of natural gas liquids (NGL). NGL are produced during extraction of natural gas but have calorific value close to crude oil. At $100 per barrel, this leads to $3.6 trillion of revenue for oil producers. With less than $10 per barrel as cost of production in the gulf region, this serves as source of extraordinary gains for the region.

Crude oil production is concentrated in the gulf region with OPEC (Organization of Petroleum Exporting Countries) accounting for about 35% of global production. (Share of OPEC in total reserves is over 70% indicating their dominance). US has emerged as an important producer, doubling its production over last about a decade. US produced close to 20 mb/d during the year. Of this, Shale oil contributed about 60% up from just about 12% in 2008. Shale oil revolution has changed the dynamics of oil market reducing US's imports from about 15 mb/d in 2005 to less than 3 mb/d by 2019. Among the other important oil producer is Russia at 11.5 mb/d which has become a part of OPEC+. In terms of consumption, US remains the largest consumer at 20.5 mb/d, followed by China and Europe at 14.5 mb/d and 14.1 mb/d. India consumes about 5 mb/d.

Crude oil has hundreds of varieties based on their density, sulphur content etc. The variety produced in USA is called West Texas Intermediate (WTI) and sells at a discount to 'Brent' crude. Brent is the more popular one and used as a benchmark across most markets. Crude oil is not used as fuel alone. Nearly 15% of it is used as raw material or feedstock in petrochemical industry to produce downstream products such as rubber, plastics and a large variety of specialty chemicals. It may be noted that RIL, which refines huge quantity of crude oil, further processes a significant part of it to produce these chemicals.

Despite being a globalized commodity, oil market is not a competitive market and subjected to high volatility. This is because of the presence of Oil cartel, OPEC, which regulates its supply to keep the market on tight leash. OPEC expanded its influence with the formation of OPEC+ in

Dec'16, a group of 24 countries including OPEC and other major producers such as Russia. As a result of production cuts effected by the grouping, oil prices rose from about $50 towards the end of 2016 to over $70 in third quarter of 2018. OPEC had also caused the prices to collapse from over $100 per barrel in 2014 to just about $30 by 2016 by increasing its production. This was done, essentially, to drive shale oil from market. While shale oil production came down during 2014-16, it increased again after the prices started firming up. The inability of OPEC to keep them off the market has diminished its ability to dictate prices especially for US market. OPEC, in fact, has to play second fiddle and reduce its production because of continued increase in non-OPEC supplies to maintain prices (Increase of 2.7 mb/d in 2018 alone).

While the tug of war in the oil market continues, the spread of Covid-19 has led to further complications with massive contraction in demand. As per EIA, the demand is projected to be nearly 30% lower in April'20, a level last seen in 1995. For the entire year, demand is projected to decline by close to 10%, which could still be an under-estimation. Possibly, not anticipating the magnitude of demand disruption, Russia initially (beginning March'20) refused to cut production leading to massive crash in prices. The subsequent agreement, in the beginning of April, to cut production, however, could not save the market.

Problem is more severe with WTI as it is produced far away from sea leading to higher cost of transportation. As a result of demand shrinkage and with existing storage getting filled-up fast, the sudden pressure on prices culminated in WTI 'futures' falling into negative zone. However, the crash in oil prices is a blessing for countries like India and helps reduce government deficits. It has also come up as an opportunity to build its strategic petroleum reserves to reduce the impact of future price shock.

*****

# Highways Construction – Accelerating Momentum

National highways have received much attention in the recent past with the commissioning of some big-ticket projects. The sector had lost way around 2015 when several companies failed to execute and surrendered their projects. The crisis even led to bankruptcy of some of the construction companies and several others referred to NCLT. Here is a look at the dynamics of the sector and current status.

India has a total road network of close to 64 lakh km as per the Ministry of Road Transport & Highways (MoRTH). This comprises of national highways, state highways and other roads network, consisting of city and village roads. Of these, national highways, connecting major cities across different states, play most critical role in providing logistics support. It handles as much as 40% of road traffic with a network of 1.45 lakh km, just 2.2% of total road network. (However, the share would be higher considering the number of lanes). While the share of national highways was close to 5% in 1951, its share fell sharply in the initial decades of freedom when greater attention was paid on improving connectivity at the grass root level. The share fell to 1.4% in 1991, rose to 1.8% by 2004 but declined again till 2013 and now stands at 2.25% at the end of 2022.

The construction of golden quadrilateral, started in 2000, was the turning point for national highways when its critically for boosting the national economy was realized. This was also the time when participation of private sector in highways development was initiated. Construction was undertaken by government agencies alone until then and mired in huge corruption. Total length of highways constructed rose from 4,400 km in FY15 to almost 10,000 km in FY18 and peaked at 13,300 km in FY21. While the construction was lower at 10,500 km in FY22, contracts awarded rose to 12,800 km of length entailing total investment of Rs 1 lakh crore. Since 2013, highways construction has grown at over 6% against about 2% for rest of the road network. Overall, more than 64,000 km length of road projects, costing more than Rs 11 lakh crore, are in progress at the end of FY22 as per MoRTH annual report.

While the construction of highways is relatively easy, the real challenge lies in land acquisition. As per the project status report of government, only 138 out of 895 road development projects are progressing as per schedule and within cost. It may be noted that several road projects were shelved and went into litigation around 2012 due to delays in land acquisition. Yet, some of the highways over last few years have got commissioned in record time. For instance, project commissioning date for Mumbai-Nagpur expressway was *advanced* with successful completion of significant part of land acquisition. Over 20,000 hectares of land have been notified for acquisition for National Highway projects in FY22. Assuming land being acquired to be of 40-meter width (6-lane road would require a iminium of 21 meter width), this would imply acquisition of land over 5,000 km of length.

However, the cost of construction per km has risen sharply over last few years. Average cost of highways construction stood at about Rs 9 crore per km in FY18 which has almost doubled to over Rs 17 crore per km. Some of the reasons for the same is increasing cost of land acquisition, higher number of lanes, overall inflation etc. The recently commissioned (partially) Mumbai-Nagpur expressway is being built at a cost of Rs 55,000 crore or about Rs 78 crore per km! The budget for 2023-24 proposed outlay of Rs 2.7 lakh crore for the ministry, 35% higher than 2022-23 to further accelerate the progress.

As stated earlier, to enable faster construction, private development was encouraged by giving developer ownership for a fixed period of time called BOOT (Build, Own, Operate, Transfer) and BOT. The model received tremendous response around 2006-10 with share of private sector in total investments going up from less than 5% in FY06 to over 40% in FY12. However, projects started getting stuck around this time with issues in land acquisition, difference in interpretation of contract clauses and so on. Projects totaling 8,200 km entailing cost of over Rs 1 lakh crore were stuck causing serious cashflow issues for the developers.

Due to the resultant risk aversion among the project developers, mode of construction was changed to EPC (Engineering, Procurement and Construction) and HAM (hybrid annuity model), introduced in 2016. While contractor was entirely responsible for financing the project in the earlier model, government provides 40% of the project cost in HAM mode. Further, 'traffic risk' has been transferred to the government which pays a fixed annuity to the contractor based on the initial bid, irrespective of the actual toll collection. From a share of less than 10% in FY18, almost all projects are being awarded on EPC and HAM mode now.

With an objective to reduce logistics cost and address the challenge of providing seamless connectivity for goods movement, National Highway Logistics Management Limited (NHLML) was incorporated in 2020. Among the task being undertaken by it is development of Multi-modal Logistics Parks (MMLP), the first and last mile connectivity project for movement of goods. The first project under this is expected to be commissioned by the end of 2023. NHLML is also implementing 40 first/last mile port connectivity road projects with a combined length of 640 km. Average length of these project is only 16 km which signifies how the absence of adequate capacity of feeder routes choke the entire network. Budget for 2023-24 has proposed total 100 first/last mile projects costing about Rs 75,000 crore to be taken up on priority basis.

The development of highways network in North-Eastern region deserves special mention particularly because of the difficult terrain and greater difficulty in laying rail network. Projects totaling 13,000 km worth Rs 1.6 lakh crore are under various stages of planning and construction.

Trivia - India has a road density of 1.7 km per sq km against 0.47 in China and 0.68 in USA. Russia has among the lowest density at 0.08 km/sq km.

*****

# Solar Power in India – An Overview

Solar power in India has recorded exponential increase in total installed capacity over last few years. The segment has got additional boost with offer for total incentives worth Rs 24,000 crore towards building domestic manufacturing capacity. However, despite all the thrust, it still has a long way to go before it can change the total power mix. Here is a look at its current state in India.

India had a Solar power installed capacity of over 61,000 mw at the end of Oct'22, up from 25,000 mw in Dec'18 and just 3,000 mw at the end of FY15. This corresponds to growth rate of 50% CAGR since FY15 and 26% since Dec'18. During FY22 alone, about 14 GW or 23% of total capacity was commissioned. Not just India, globally also, solar generation capacity has increased substantially in 2021, 133 GW or 16% of total capacity of 850 GW.

Solar power has gained momentum with government incentives and increasing global awareness. Among the measures helping the development is assured power off-take, mandatory purchase of renewable power by distribution companies (DISCOM), financing options at lower than market rate and so on. Yet, real breakthrough is significant drop in prices of input material, silicon and polysilicon. As per Bernreuter research, prices of polysilicon have fallen from average of $360 per kg in 2008 to as low as $9 per kg in 2019. The price drop coupled with economies of scale has led to significant decline in price of solar power, from more than Rs 15 per unit about 7-8 years ago to Rs 3-3.5 per unit now. However, polysilicon prices have risen now to over $35 per kg currently.

Solar power is generated by converting sunlight into electrical energy through solar panels. The panels consist of a number of solar cells, 36 to 96 in each. A 60-cell panel would be around 2 meters by 1 meter in size. These solar cells are manufactured by converting metallurgical grade silicon into high purity polycrystalline silicon at over 1,500° C which are further processed to form silicon wafers and then, solar cells. When light particles hit the thin layer of silicon, they cause movement of electrons which creates an electric current. While the power of each solar cell to produce electricity is not enough to be tapped, the cells grouped together provide energy which can be transmitted. As per IREDA (Indian Renewable Energy Development Agency Ltd), total sunlight received by India can produce over 1,600 trillion units of energy assuming eight hours of sunlight. This is a thousand times the total annual electricity consumption of about 1,500 billion units. IREDA is the financing agency which distributed loan worth Rs 16,000 crore in FY22, almost double that in FY21.

IREDA and Solar Energy Corporation of India (SECI) are prime agencies channelizing India's solar initiative. SECI invites bids for projects based on the interest shown by the state government, availability of land etc, along with assurance that it would purchase power generated by the project developer. This power is sold by SECI to power distribution companies through power exchanges. (Private developer or other agencies are free to develop solar plants on their own also). The process has been aided by adoption of online competitive bidding which has helped achieve price discovery. (Te competitive bidding process, along with strong implementing agencies, has helped curb manipulation significantly in all forms of government auctions). On the off-take front, it procured and sold back over 5,000 crore units of power during FY21 at an average price of Rs 3.47 per unit. The price was about 8% lower than in FY20 whereas total traded quantity rose by 18%. Another important initiative taken by SECI is initiation of project involving execution of solar power plant along with setting up of solar module manufacturing facilities having awarded 12 GW of project through this route. This would not just create generation but also, manufacturing capacity while reducing the risk for the project developer.

Another important development in India's quest to harness this source of energy is initiation of PLI (Production Linked Incentives) scheme by the government for manufacture of solar cells and modules. In the first phase, incentives worth Rs 4,500 crore is being offered to four companies for setting up production facility of about 9 GW capacity to manufacture solar cells and modules. However, there were no application for integrated manufacturing - from silicon to modules. Government has allocated greater budget for integrated manufacturing set-up in the second phase with total incentives of as much as Rs 19,500 crore. Bids for the same were invited about a week back. Domestic availability of modules would reduce the price volatility as well as help sustainable development of domestic capacity.

While the benefits from solar power are immense, it faces distinct disadvantages such as high land requirement, high upfront cost, low PLF (capacity utilization) etc. The biggest of these is requirement of huge land, almost five times the land required for a thermal plant. Bhadla solar park in Rajasthan, largest in the world, with capacity of 2,245 MW is spread across 57 sq km, almost 7.5 km by 7.5 km area. Another with 750 mw capacity in Rewa, MP is spread over 6.4 sq km of land, almost 2.5 km by 2.5 km area. The other disadvantage is its low PLF meaning lower generation per mw of installation, further dependent on the intensity of sunlight. Normal PLF of a solar plant in India is 18-20% unlike thermal plants which can achieve PLF of even 100%. The PLF is expected to increase to 22% with advancement in technology.

However, innovation in installation may help overcome the limitation of scarcity of land such as installation of solar panel on canals and rooftop installations. Installation on top and banks of canals has many other benefits such as reduction in evaporation of water, minimal investment of time and money on purchase of land and in creating other basic infrastructure etc. With short commissioning period of 12 months unlike coal-based plant which take up to 4 years, the canal projects can be of great help if pursued judiciously. With its ease of use, rooftop installation has also gained popularity whereby the owner can also sell electricity to the grid. In fact, about 40% of installed capacity is expected to come from rooftop. As per MNRE, India has around 124 GW of solar Rooftop potential. A 5 by 5 meter rooftop can generate about 300-400 units of power per month, sufficient for normal household consumption. The other advantage is its distributed nature which means it can be installed even in hilly terrain, inaccessible regions etc. Solar power can help electrify these remote areas where laying of transmission lines is not only costly but also difficult due to difficult terrain, existence of rivers etc. An area of current research is making solar power 24*7 by use of battery storage system.

Despite all its benefits, the share of solar power in total power generation is just about 1.2% currently. As per National Institute of Solar Energy (NISE), India can add a total of 748 GW of capacity by covering just 3% of waste land area by Solar PV modules. The current installed capacity is less than 10% of that. However, even that would be equivalent to 150 GW of coal-based capacity at 20% plf. India needs to reach that figure to make this source count and anything less than that is underutilization of its potential.

*****

# Wind Power – Regaining the Momentum

Wind power, along with solar, seems to have lost momentum after rapid capacity addition till about 2017. The reason was change in bidding method leading to price risk for the developed which is now being reversed. A look at the broader dynamics of the industry.

Wind energy gained prominence about a decade back with the installed capacity increasing from just 3,000 mw in 2004 to almost 29,000 mw at the end of 2016. This corresponds to growth of over 20% CAGR and average annual addition of more than two-thirds the capacity that existed in 2004. The growth has been facilitated by improvement in technologies leading to more efficient and lower cost installation. The capital cost of wind power installation has come down from over Rs 10 crore/mw to about Rs 6 crore/mw. The height of tower on which the rotor is mounted has reached from about 20 meters to almost 100 meters. As per the government data based on the wind speed conditions, the country has a potential of about 3,00,000 mw capacity at a height of 100 mts concentrated in eight windy states.

However, the growth rate has fallen to just about 6% CAGR after that. The reason was change in the bidding method from 'feed-in tariff' to 'competitive bidding'. Under the feed-in tariff, a developer receives price based on all costs plus return on equity. The competitive bidding method exposes them to project cost risk. While the 'feed-in tariff' is not exactly an ideal system, there have been few takers for government tenders in the revised method. This is so because the project costs are high exposing the developers to high risk, more so, in the current volatile price environment.

A big disadvantage of wind power, indeed, most renewable power, is low capacity utilisation (PLF) at close to 15%. This leads to high fixed cost per unit of power generated even though the running cost is marginal. As per the calculations of CERC, the variable cost of wind power works out to less than 10% of total cost. Low PLF also leads to an anomalous condition where even though renewables have high share in total installation but generate much less power, that too, non-uniformly. For instance, the share of wind power in total power generation is less than 3% share against a share of 9% in total installed capacity.

Even though the execution of wind power is more challenging than solar power, yet, it managed to grow faster since the land requirement is much less. In fact, it does not require exclusive land like in case of solar and can be installed on the sides of a agriculture farm or highway also. Even in exclusive wind parks, the area in between two wind turbine installation can be used for other purposes.

Despite the limelight renewable energy is receiving, these industries are still at rather nascent stage. a lot dependent upon the government support such as compulsory purchase obligation for distribution companies, tax incentives, lower transmission charges etc. Whether they will be able to sustain on their own and compete with the conventional sources of power on equal terms is still to be seen.

***** 

# Industry Analysis – Steel

Steel industry has recorded significant turnaround since its worst around 2016-19 when several companies were making losses. Several of the companies defaulted, including Essar Steel and were sold-off through insolvency court. Here is a look at the dynamics of the industry and latest financial details.

Steel industry is engaged in processing of iron ore to produce finished steel using coking coal as fuel. These go through further value addition such as color coating, galvanizing etc for decorative or strengthening purposes. The products are classified as flat, meaning sheets roiled into coil or long products, meaning rods, bars etc. The industry is capital intensive with significant investment required for setting up blast furnace, coke over batteries and other fixed assets. As a thumb rule, $1 bn of investment is required for setting up 1 million ton of steel capacity. Major consumers of steel are infrastructure sectors such as highways, bridges, construction industry and other sectors like automotive, consumer goods, machinery etc which use specialized steel. Steel is one of the eight core sectors which are monitored closely by the government because of its potential to disrupt the entire economy.

Steel is a global commodity with significant amount of global production getting exported. As per World Steel Association (WSA), global production of steel was close to 2 billion tons in 2021, of which, 460 mn tons or about 25%, was exported. In terms of countries, China is the dominant producer with production of over 1 bn tons or over 50% of global. India stands a distant second with production of close to 120 mn tons or about 6% share. India was a net exporter in 2021 although it imports some grades of specialty steel. Interestingly, China exported only 66 mn tons which means it consumed over 900 mn tons of steel domestically! Global nature of market means scarcity in any market would lead to diversion of production marked for domestic consumption to international market, thus affecting domestic prices also.

Steel industry companies are broadly classified as integrated steel producers (ISPs) or downstream players. ISPs are engaged in the entire value chain whereas downstream players procure steel from ISPs and undertake further value addition only. However, since they procure material from ISPs, their cost structure is higher than ISPs. Raw material to sales ratio stands at around 45% for ISPs against 65-70% for downstream companies. (However, they do have lower fixed assets etc which helps sustain themselves). The downstream segment had a distinct identity earlier. However, entry of ISPs to value added segments over last decade or caused severe erosion of profits of standalone downstream players and closure of several of them. ISPs now account for about 80% of industry's turnover.

Domestic steel industry is fairly consolidated with top five companies accounting for over 75% of sales. Top companies in the sector are Tata Steel, JSW Steel and SAIL, the public sector company. While Tata Steel had sales of Rs 1.3 lakh crore in FY22 (excluding global operations), it was Rs 1.2 lakh crore for JSW and a little over Rs 1 lakh crore for SAIL. For FY22, aggregate domestic sales of listed companies in the sector were Rs 5.4 lakh crore, sharp increase of 65%

over FY21. Raw material cost rose by even sharper 81%, a result of disruption in global supply chain. However, a lower increase in other cost items such as employee cost, sales & distribution etc helped the industry increase its operating profit by 70% which reached Rs 1.6 lakh crore.

Since the industry is capital intensive, borrowings form a significant part of balance sheet. Extent of borrowings and capital intensity are reflected in interest and depreciation (I+D) cost. (Depreciation would be high for a capital-intensive industry). Despite significant increase in sales, these two items remained same, further boosting the bottom line. As a result of sharp increase in sales and favorable movement of some of the cost factors, net profit rose more than two & half times to over Rs 85,000 crore. This corresponds to net margin of 14.5%, sharp increase from 9.3% in FY21. This is also substantially higher than average margin of less than 5% during FY16-19. Improving profit helped industry players bring down their debt level with aggregate debt coming down from Rs 3.1 lakh crore at the end of FY20 to Rs 2.1 lakh crore by FY22.

While the industry would be happy with this margin, pricing power like this in a critical infrastructure industry affects the entire economy through cost push inflation. To blunt their price advantage, finance ministry had imposed additional duties on steel exports in May'22. This helped cool domestic prices. During 2021 (largely corresponding to FY22 which is April'21 to March'22), benchmark steel prices had reached a level of $837 per ton, 72% higher than 2020 as per JSW annual report. The 'spread' or cost of finished product minus cost of raw material rose from just about $200 per ton in 2020 to $386 per ton in 2021, almost double! Even though prices have come down now, domestic steel industry remains on a strong footing with significant momentum in demand and the thrust on 'Make in India'. To reduce dependency on imports, government has initiated production linked incentive (PLI) scheme whereby incentives of about Rs 6,300 crore would be given to 30 selected companies over a five-year period. These companies would be investing about Rs 42,500 crore to add downstream capacity of 26 million tons for production of especially steel.

*****

# Industry Analysis – Cement

Cement Industry had been in the news with acquisition of Ambuja Cement and its Subsidiary, ACC, by Adani group. In another development, Dalmia Bharat announced agreement for acquisition of Jaiprakash Associates. With the current stage of development of India's infrastructure and construction sector, cement industry has a lot to look forward to. Here is a look at the dynamics of the industry.

Cement is produced from limestone which is extracted from mines, crushed and mixed with other materials such as bauxite and heated in kiln at temperature of up to 1,400°C to form clinker. Clinker is then ground with gypsum to produce cement. Cement acts a binding agent and has a critical role in all construction related activities. Unlike other industries, it is invariably located at place where limestone mines are present as transporting the raw material would make the business uneconomical. Despite being a low-key industry, the industry is a part of core sector because of its application across large number of sectors such as housing, building highways, bridges, dams and so on. Housing & real estate accounts for over 50% of cement consumption whereas infrastructure sectors account for about 22%. The industry's performance is actively tracked to gauge the performance of the economy.

Cement industry is largely a domestic industry with very limited trade. Even within the nation, each of the five zones has its own demand-supply dynamics and it is not always economical to transport from one to another. (Yet, there could be some exports from say, North-Eastern region to Bangladesh due to price differential). As per Statista, total global production of cement during 2021 was 4.3 billion tons (steel production is 2 bn tons) of which just about 100-150 million tons was exported. While China leads with production of about 2.5 bn tons, 55% of total, India stands a distant second with production of 380 mn tons. As per Cement Manufacturers Association (CMA). India has a total installed capacity of 565 mn tons. With over 290 operational plants, this corresponds to average capacity of less than 2 mn tons per plant. The largest player, Ultratech, accounts for 20% of total capacity at 120 million tons whereas Ambuja cement, along with ACC, has about 70 mn tons of capacity.

In terms of financials, aggregate sales of all the listed company in the sector was close to Rs 1.8 lakh crore for FY22, increase of 16% over previous year. (It may be noted that aggregate industry sales are just one-fourth that of steel industry). UltraTech and Ambuja Cement had sales of Rs 52,000 crore and Rs 29,000 crore on consolidated basis. However, all the three major cost items, raw material, energy and freight costs rose by about 25% leading to negligible increase in operating profit and operating margin coming down from 24% to 21%. However, decline in interest plus depreciation charges helped net profit grow by 14% to Rs 19,000 crore. In FY21, the peak pandemic year, profits grew by 24% despite sales being constant, aided by decline in most cost items.

For cement industry, energy and freight costs are very high each at about 25% of sales. RM/sales ratio is lower at just about 17%, unlike other industries where it is normally around 50%. Further, the ratio has remained remarkably consistent over last five years between 16-18% as most of the industries have captive mines. This contrasts with other sectors which see significant fluctuation. For instance, RM/sales ratio varied from 43% to 50% during the same period for steel industry. Due to requirement of low investment in fixed assets, aggregate debt is less than Rs 40,000 crore. For industry leader Ultratech, debt-equity ratio is barely 0.2:1.

Over a longer period of FY17-22, industry's performance has been quite impressive. While sales rose by 11% CAGR, net profits recorded an even better rate of as much as 20%. As a result, net profit margin has increased from 7.1% to 10.7% during the period. Profit margin remained consistent in the range of 6-7% during FY14-19 which has increased in the last three years. Most of the gain has come from lower interest and depreciation charges.

Cement is largely a fragmented industry in India with over 40 companies in the listed space, 20 of them having sales of over Rs 1,000 crore. A reason for this is that it is less capital-intensive and is a low value product with each ton of cement costing about Rs 10-12,000 against over Rs 50,000 for steel. Yet, top five players have increased their market share from about 60% in FY14 to 70% now. (This is still lower than share of top five steel industry players). Some of them are acquisition of Binani Cement by Ultratech in 2018 and Reliance Cement by Birla Corp in 2016. Very recently, Dalmia Cement announced its agreement to purchase Jaypee Associates' cement assets. This would increase its capacity by 10 mn tons from about 36 mn tons currently. In another important development, Adani Group has acquired Ambuja Cement and its subsidiary, ACC in Sept'22. While this is merely change of hands and not consolidation, this may lead to further action in the market towards consolidation.

While the capacity utilization for the industry as a whole is about 67%, top companies such as Ambuja Cement had capacity utilization of 86% whereas Ultratech had 77%. Despite capacity utilization being on the lower side, companies do not face any pricing pressure. In fact, average price per ton rose for the top industry players has increased in FY22. The sector has often been accused of engaging in cartelization and is under investigation by CCI (Competition Commission of India).

The sector has made considerable progress in the use of by-products, waste products from other industries. For instance, it can use fly ash generated in power generation plant, slag from steel plants and other such waste products from aluminum, fertilizer, paper & sugar industries as raw material. Other than cost savings, this helps reduce the nuisance caused to environment due to these waste products. For Ultratech, these materials account for 14% of total raw material usage. Cement manufactures have entered several joint ventures with power and other sector companies such as NTPC, SAIL etc to maximize the value from these opportunities.

*****

# Industry Analysis – Pharma

Indian pharmaceutical industry gained huge limelight in the fight against Covid-19. However, the sector is going through deep-rooted structural changes. It is, probably next to food industry, in terms of its sensitivity to socio-political structure and has been subjected to greater price control over last few years. Going a step further, the government is putting a ceiling on margins company offer to the distributors and retailers. Whether these would stifle innovation, a concern raised by the leading companies or it would make the products become accessible to wider section would become clear only in the medium term. Nevertheless, A look at the industry and its dynamics.

Pharmaceuticals are categorized into two groups – generic and patented products. Generic medicines account for 70-80% of the total market. (Large number of generic medicines have also been branded and are sold at a premium). An important characteristic and the reason for government's restriction is that the industry operates with a very high mark-up of 87%, as per NAS data. (Output price - input cost/input cost). This contrast with mark up of 31% for entire manufacturing sector and as low as 12% for dairy and grain mill products.

The high mark-up, a result of disproportionately high cost of medicines, has brought the sector in the limelight, more so, in last 5-6 years. Pharma Policy has proposed significant restrictions to align the prices with their cost of production and make it more affordable to the masses. The policy makes note of the fact that more than 60,000 brand names are present in the market selling 2,500 pharmacopeial salts. This essentially means that companies are giving different brand names to same generic drug and managing to market through aggressive marketing. To mitigate this, the policy proposes the principle of 'one company-one drug-one brand name-one price'. The policy also proposes to restrict "Unethical marketing practices" such as overseas paid trips in a disguised form and such other incentives. It also proposes capping the trade margins. However, the policy doesn't look to be blind to needs for innovation stating that new formulations would be kept out of price control for 5 years. To promote indigenization, it proposes import at peak customs duty for intermediate products which can be indigenously manufactured.

Government has already taken several measures proposed in the policy. Among the first is bringing more medicines, close to 200, under price control with total medicines under control going up to over 850. The move has brought about a reduction of as much as 80% in prices of certain medicines including those for the treatment of cancer. (Slashing of prices of medical devices such as stents and knee implants by NPPA (national pharma pricing authority) in 2017 had also generated severe reactions). The other important move is making it mandatory for medical practitioners to prescribe medicines based on their generic name and not brand names. While the latest move to cap trade margin appear to go against the principle of market freedom, it must be understood that sale of medicines can be undertaken only by license holders and hence, is already a regulated segment. Presence of an entry barriers necessities government intervention to ensure that the players do not enjoy above normal profits.

The actions taken by government seem to having impact on the performance of listed companies, particularly the top ones. The top 5 companies seem to be suffered greater impact of price controls as their net profit margin has come down significantly from 16.2% in FY14 to only 9.9% in FY20. However, rest of the set, who were operating with lower margins of about 10%, remain at the same level. Total sales for the listed companies stand at Rs 2.3 lakh crore in FY20, an increase of 9% over previous year. Sales growth has come down to about 7% during FY17-20 against 12% earlier. Almost one-third of its revenue comes from exports, making it an important segment from the perspective of foreign trade balance also.

So, what does the future look like for the sector. Even though the sector looks reluctant to adapt to changing dynamics, it must understand the gains from low-margin, high-volume model. This has been amply demonstrated by several industries such as telecom, hotels and segments of FMCG. The industry can also increase their focus on exports, particularly untapped African market.

*****

# Industry Analysis - Automobile

Automobile sector continues to be in the throes of a slowdown quite unprecedented in terms of its magnitude. Even though part of the decline is due to impending transition to BS-VI, there are deeper reasons impacting the market. A brief attempt to look at the dynamics of the sector and understand the issues leading to the slowdown.

Automobile sector is classified into 2-wheeler, 3-wheeler, 4-wheeler (PVs) and commercial vehicles (CVs) segments. Despite being clubbed together, each segment has unique dynamics and market drivers. While 2 wheelers derive good amount of demand from rural market, 4-wheelers are almost wholly dependent on urban disposable income. On the other hand, commercial vehicles are driven by industrial activity whereas 3-wheelers are driven by general economic activity, increasing urbanization and lately, entry of app-based aggregators. Even though the industry is dominated by a few large players, it is highly competitive in nature. So much so, that even the attempts by players from one segment to enter another have not been significantly successful.

Industry's sales performance is captured at two levels - manufacturer to distributors (wholesale) tracked by SIAM (Society of Indian Automobile Manufacturers) and retail sales tracked by Federation of Automobile Dealers Association (FADA). Of the two, retail sales give the true picture of market condition as manufactures may resort to inventory build-up at distributors' end to hide any short-term blip. Yet, it is the wholesale data that gets quoted almost everywhere.

So, what is affecting the market and more importantly, whether it is a structural or a cyclical slowdown. The first reason being cited is, of course, transition from BS-IV to BS-VI which will make vehicles less polluting but costlier. Since industry cannot sell BS-IV vehicles after 1st April'20, wholesale dispatch has come down to clear the inventory. However, this would have made perfect sense only if the sales at retail level had not come down. However, that is not so making the crisis more concerning. A bigger reason appears to be changing preference driven by cab and 3-wheeler aggregators. The reason may have some weight as vehicle registrations have come down more sharply in metro cities. For instance, in Delhi, while passenger vehicle and 2-wheelers sales declined by as much as 20% during Jan'20, 3-wheelers actually grew, albeit by a marginal 2%.

Among the important reason for the slump is drying up of finances as significant part of purchase happens through credit financing. This is also corroborated by RBI data. As per the data, growth in bank credit to the sector fell sharply from 28% for the year ending March'18 to 13% for March'19 and has further declined to less than 9% for Sept'19 (year on year). For NBFCs, which are more aggressive in lending to these sectors, growth fell from 31% to 22% and further to about 14%. The NBFC crisis, brought about by the fall of IL&FS, has led to credit squeeze impacting the sectors dependent upon them.

The slowdown has sharply affected the financials of companies in the sector. For the market leader, Maruti Suzuki, while sales declined by 13% for FY20, operating profit declined more sharply by 22%. Net profits registered decline of 26%. For Tata Motors, while consolidated sales decline was the same, company continued to make losses, although lower at Rs 11,000 crore against Rs 25,000 crore in FY19. Excluding Tata Motors, the sector as a whole recorded decline of 12% in sales, 20% in operating profit and sharper decline of 36% in net profit.

Sector stares at a future which doesn't look so bright. For the near term, it is still to be seen whether the companies can pass on the additional cost of BS-VI vehicles. Whether the customers come back also looks quite certain, especially considering the fast-changing preferences. The entry of Electric Vehicles (EVs), with its own set of uncertainties, has further disturbed the market dynamics. Yet, the biggest of all uncertainties is impact of Covid-19 on the supply chain.

*****

# SECTION - V
# CORPORATE

# Welcome Home, Air India!

The sale of Air India to Tata group marks coming of a full circle for the airline. The airline was founded by JRD Tata in 1932 and was nationalized in 1953. Even though the upfront payment for the purchase is not very high, Tatas would have to spend significant amount of money to refurbish and time to make the airline profitable. It faces additional issue of aligning its operations with its other two aviation company, AirAsia and Vistara and avoid cannibalisation of market. A look at the details of sell-off and Air India's finances.

First the details of the deal. As per the agreement, Tata Sons, through its subsidiary, would purchase Air India, Air India express and its stake in the cargo handling subsidiary at an enterprise value (EV) of Rs 18,000 crore. EV implies value of both debt and cash to be invested by Tata. So, Tata would take over debt of Rs 15,300 crore and would pay upfront cash of Rs 2,700 crore to the government. While it may appear that the airline is being sold cheap, it is actually a high-risk investment for Tatas since the airline would need significant amount of additional investment for refurbishment and may incur losses for couple of years before becoming profitable. The sale would not include non-core assets such as land and building, valued at close to Rs 15,000 crore. This would be transferred to a government entity, Air India Asset Holding Ltd (AIAHL). This means Tata would have to vacate the offices and even flats let out to the employees and may be a cause of some short-term discomfort.

The decision is being hailed as landmark because the Airline had been identified as a money guzzler way back in 2000 when the attempt at sale failed. The second attempt in 2017 failed again because government wanted to retain 26% stake in the company. However, no bidder came forward because of the apprehension that government stake could act as a deterrent in smooth functioning of the airline.

Airline's problem could be classified into two categories – Financial and Operational. For last available year ending March'20, the airline recorded consolidated losses of Rs 7,400 crore. With revenue of nearly Rs 33,000 crore, it implies negative margin of 24% indicating the huge distance the new owner would have to cover. As per the Audit report, airline had accumulated losses of over Rs 70,000 crore till FY20, all of this, funded by the government. Despite the infusion of Rs 22,000 crore of funds by the government, airline had negative equity of equivalent amount at the end of FY20.

A part of the problem gets resolved with financial restructuring. The airline had total liabilities of Rs 96,000 crore. Even though some of this is backed by assets such as aircrafts, right of use etc, excess liabilities net of assets was about Rs 54,000 crore. The high level of debt is also reflected in high level of interest cost. Airline's interest cost was Rs 4,100 crore, almost 13% of revenue against just 5% for Indigo, the market leader. As stated earlier, Airline would be transferred with only Rs 15,300 crore of debt and rest of the debt would be transferred to the government entity, AIAHL. This alone may save about Rs 3,000 crore for the new owner.

While the financial restructuring largely takes care of debt, Tata would still have to take care of operational issues such as inefficient utilisation of aircrafts, fleet modernisation and so on. The inefficiency of operations is reflected in the fact that Indigo operated almost 1,400 daily flights in FY20 with its fleet of 274 planes. However, Air India could operate only 400 with half the number of planes. This is an issue that may require investment and the new management would have to handle on priority basis. Another issue, often talked about, is excess manpower. However, contrary to this perception, its employee cost to revenue ratio was only 10.7% which is less than 12.6% for Indigo. In fact, Tata may have to move some of its staff from other aviation businesses to improve the efficiency of service. Yet, it does face the issue of ageing manpower with the airline focussing more on reducing staff rather than recruiting over last ten years. While Tatas are barred from retrenchment for one year, they would, most likely, be offering VRS to the employees after that and going for fresh hiring.

The sale of Air India is culmination of a complex process which must have involved extraordinary amount of deliberations to make the airline attractive for buyer. For instance, the decision to hive-off all non-core assets which would have increased the cost substantially. While Tata has lot of wherewithal to handle the purchase, it is not going to be a cakewalk either.

*****

# Corporate & Financial Sector – Changing Dynamics

Covid-19 pandemic has further added to the woes of corporate and financial sector, already reeling under the impact of subdued economic conditions, NPAs overhang, NFBC crisis etc. Yet, the sectors have shown considerable degree of resilience so far, aided by regulatory and government efforts. The real credit for the same goes to their efforts over last few years to repair their balance sheets and improve their business practices. This is borne out by the Financial Stability Report published by RBI. A look at some of the details.

As per the report, corporate sector has undergone significant amount of 'deleveraging' since the peak in FY16, even though it has stalled over last few quarters. As a result, debt/operating profit ratio for a sample of 3,700 private sector companies has come down from 2.71 in FY16 to 2.32 in FY19. (The report doesn't give figure for FY20 as data for all companies are not available). The ratio, however, is not a strict gauge of debt position as it is also dependent on the profitability. An interesting distinction emerges here between the dynamics of private and public sector undertakings (PSUs). While PSUs also recorded decline in debt/operating profit ratio during FY16-18, the trend diverged subsequently in FY19. So, what could be the reason for this?

A possible reason could be the 'nudge' from the finance ministry to PSUs to step-up their investments. The move is aimed to compensate for the corporate fiscal tightening which has led to significant drop in investments (called gross fixed capital formation, GFCF, in GDP calculations). GFCF grew by 10% in FY19, up from about 7% in FY18, possibly, aided by PSUs spending. Even now, government has been repeatedly prodding PSUs to increase their investment (and to PSBs to increase their lending) to provide a fillip to the economy. While it may help spur the economy, the chances of such assets becoming non-performing are higher, as seen during the spending binge undertaken after global financial crisis in 2008.

Another interesting insight offered by FSR is the difference in the performance of companies rated AAA and those with ratings below that ("others"). While debt/operating profit for AAA rated firms stood at 0.76 times in March'19 (FY19), the same stood at 2.96 times for others, almost four times higher! The significant difference in their debt position reflects in the interest outgo which takes up almost 30% of operating profit for others in comparison to only 6% for AAA rated firms. (Total debt outstanding for the two groups would have given insights on total potential stress for the banking sector). However, while others managed to bring it down from 3.73 in FY18, for AAA firms, it went up from 0.67 to 0.76 between FY18-19. So, what is the reason for this divergence? Going some years further back provides a clue. The ratio stood at 0.73 for AAA in FY16 and 3.99 for others. So, while AAA firms managed to bring it down by FY18 and started doing some investments again, others were still struggling and hence, continued their deleveraging efforts.

Other than the Corporate sector, banking sector, particularly Public Sector Banks (PSBs), have also improved their business practices to reduce their credit risk. It may be noted that PSBs are still reeling under high pile of NPAs. As per FSR, PSBs are lending to borrowers with reasonable ratings only now. As a result, their credit to AA and above group grew at a rate of 22.7% CAGR during FY17-20, even as it declined for those rated below up to -9.5% CAGR. In contrast, Private banks (PVBs) continued their exposure to this group, recording growth of up to 16%. PSBs have also increased their focus towards lending to PSUs which may be less efficient in their operations, but pose lower credit risk as a result of government ownership. PSBs' credit to PSUs grew at over 30% in contrast with decline of 6% for private corporate entities. While private banks' credit to PSUs also rose substantially; by 37%, their lending to non-PSUs also remained high at 12.6%.

Role of RBI to provide stability to the financial sector is evident from the turbulence experienced in the mutual funds industry. Mutual funds industry had total assets of Rs 27.2 lakh crore at the end of Feb'20. The industry witnessed sharp redemption of Rs 15.2 lakh crore (gross) in March, almost double that in February and more than half their total assets, after the breakout of Covid-19. While MF industry did mobilize funds, it was short of the significantly higher redemption, leading to gap of Rs 2.1 lakh crore. RBI came to their rescue by providing the necessary funds, in the absence of which, the industry could have seen several defaults exposing the entire financial sector to the risk of contagion.

*****

# HDFC Ltd - HDFC Bank Merger - The Logic and the Gains

The announced merger of HDFC Ltd and HDFC Bank is an important decision to consolidate businesses and reap benefits of economies of scale. Yet, the move now is dictated more by changing regulations and not just business gains as the business gains were available for many years now. The merger appears to be similar to the merger of ICICI with ICICI bank and IDBI with IDBI bank but is entirely different as the earlier ones were DFIs (Developmental Financial Institutions) and were besotted with an unviable business model. Here is a brief look at this merger and logic behind the move.

First a brief understanding of their businesses. HDFC Ltd is a non-banking finance company (NBFC), founded in 1977, primarily engaged in mortgage or home loan business. HDFC bank is a subsidiary of HDFC ltd and was founded in 1994 subsequent to opening of banking to private sector. The merger is quite unusual as it involves the merger of parent with its subsidiary. It is an all-stock deal. So, there will no monetary transaction. Both the entities are among the top ten profit making companies with profits of Rs 35,000 crore and Rs 21,500 crore for 12 months ended Dec'21. The combined profit makes it the second highest profit-making company in the country.

A look at the financials shows that HDFC bank has grown at a rapid pace and has total asset base of close to Rs 17.5 lakh crore on standalone basis at the end of March'21. In terms of source of funds, deposits account for Rs 13.3 lakh crore whereas equity capital stands at Rs 2 lakh crore. On the other hand, HDFC ltd had total assets of close to Rs 8.8 lakh crore on consolidated basis and Rs 6 lakh crore on standalone basis at the end of Dec'21. The difference is contributed by life insurance, general insurance and asset management subsidiaries. In terms of source of funds, retail deposits account for only Rs 1.6 lakh crore, restricted as per RBI regulations unlike HDFC bank where it accounts for more than 75%. As a result, it has to mobilize funds as debt and other borrowings which accounts for half of its assets and are costlier than public deposits. On simple financial basis, HDFC ltd has a higher cost structure and relatively restricted business as an NBFC.

Despite the gains arising by operating as a bank, the merger was not done all these years because of 'Regulatory Arbitrage' or deriving gains out of regulatory exemptions available to NBFCs. There are two primary requirements that banks are subjected to but NBFCs are exempted from. First, banks have to keep aside 22% (down from 27% some years ago) of their funds as SLR+CRR, investment in government bonds and funds with RBI. These are mandated so as to fund government finances and as a risk capital. The other requirement is 'priority sector lending'. Banks are also required to lend 40% of their funds to sectors identified as priority sector such as agriculture, MSME, low-cost housing etc. An NBFC is free from these. However, it is not all advantage to NBFCs. NBFCs face a disadvantage that they are required to maintain higher level of Capital Adequacy Ratio (CAR) at 15% against 9% for banks. CAR broadly refers to equity funds as a percent of total loan book. Thus, if a bank has reached its limit of CAR, it would have to first generate equity capital before it can expand its business.

The trigger for the merger is the regulatory changes initiated by RBI over last few years, after the collapse of IL&FS. These bring NBFCs, especially the larger ones, on par with banks in terms of regulations. The first is introduction of scale-based regulations (SBR) for NFBCs to be effective from Oct'22. As per SBR, NBFCs have been divided into four buckets whereby the top two layers will be subjected to stricter regulations. An internal committee of RBI has, in fact, recommended mandatory conversion of large NBFCs into banks to mitigate oversight risk. The other is change in NPA norms whereby NBFCs are required to classify a loan account as NPA in case of payment default for more than 90 days, just like banks. NPA classification would mean NBFCs would need to make provisions for that which reduces their equity capital. So far, NBFCs could show lower NPAs by restructuring of such loans. Yet another change is the requirement of LCR (Liquidity coverage ratio) whereby NBFCs are required to keep aside amount equivalent to its payment obligations for the next 30 days reducing its financial manoeuvrability.

Even though it is driven by diminishing regulatory arbitrage, the merger is a big, bold move to consolidate and capture the best of both businesses. The biggest gain would be from the high CAR of over 22% that HDFC brings. (While HDFC Bank also has high CAR of about 18%, the merger would further enhance it). This means the combined entity would have sufficient equity funds to grow its business for may be, even next five years. The consolidation of home loan business would be another big advantage where the bank can combine expertise of its parent and its vast network. While the bank's obligation with regard to priority sector lending would increase, the provision to buy 'PSL certificate' makes it easier to manage this obligation. Another challenge would be to set aside 22% of deposits as SLR, CRR. Based on current figures, this would imply additional investment of about Rs 35,000 crore on these. However, RBI has, generally, taken a liberal view in cases of transition and should allow bank time to meet the obligations.

*****

# Corporate India – The 'Creative Destruction' since Liberalization

The face of Corporate India has changed dramatically in the last 30 years since the economic liberalization began. Liberalization exposed the then established firms to competition, changing corporate mindset of taking markets for granted. Failure to adept to these changes led to what the Economic Survey has called 'creative destruction'. A look at these changes, reflected in the composition of Sensex.

Liberalization changed the economic landscape at two levels – emergence of newer, more efficient companies in the existing sectors and emergence of newer sectors. The same is evident in the composition of Sensex, the stock market index comprising of top 30 domestic companies in terms of size and profitability. As per the Economic Survey, roughly one-third of Sensex firms are overtaken by more efficient firms every five years and removed from the index. Some of the companies which exited the index from the existing sectors are Hindustan Motors & Premiere Auto (Automobiles), Bombay Dyeing & Century Textiles (Apparels & textiles) and many more.

However, that is only a part of the story. Even more profound is the change in sectoral composition with entry of banks and IT, eroding the dominance of manufacturing sector. The share in market-cap for manufacturing companies has dropped sharply from 96% in 1991 to 45% now. More than half of Sensex was composed of materials and consumer discretionary in 1991 which has now come down to just about 20% now. Financial services and IT, which were not existent in early 1990s, account for more than half of Sensex companies now. Interestingly, SBI entered Sensex only in 1996!

Even though manufacturing sector lost its share in Sensex, its share in GDP hasn't declined much. The increase in prominence of services has come about with decline in the share of agriculture sector, down from nearly 30% in 1991 to less than 15% now. The inability of manufacturing sector to take the space vacated by agriculture has been an unfortunate part of India's growth story as this left large number of unskilled workers coming out of agriculture unemployed. Equally unfortunate part is that there is not a single agro-based firm in Sensex, nor was it there is 1991.

Another important change since liberalization is the decline in ratio of size of biggest to smallest firm in Sensex. The market-cap of largest firm in the index was almost 100 times the smallest firm in 1991. This came down to 75 by the turn of century and stood at just 12 times in 2018. This is a result of greater competition within sectors, far cry from 1991 when single company used to dominate the market. The advantage enjoyed by existing firm backed by political class and bureaucracy came to be challenged by newer, more agile firms.

Another interesting change in corporate landscape, mentioned in the report, is the reversal in fortune of "connected" firms, an index created by a brokerage firm, Ambit Capital. The index of the 'connected' firms outperformed the market by about 7% during 2007-10 reflecting profit extracted leveraging their connection. However, the index has underperformed by 7.5% after 2011, as a result of introduction of transparent bidding system for allocation of natural resources.

\*\*\*\*\*

# Shares Pledging - Understanding the Risks

Sale of pledged shares of certain corporate groups by the lenders has once again brought share pledging into focus. The practice had generated lot of controversy over a decade ago during Satyam scam, leading to changes in the regulations governing it. While lender cannot be blamed for the sale, developments leading to the sale and controversy generated subsequently put a question mark over the practice. A look at the concept of share pledging and the risk it poses to the lenders and the company itself.

Shares pledging refers to the practice of borrowing money by the promoter of a company using his shares in the company as collateral. The practice is quite like 'loan against shares' offered by some of the lending institutions. Loan given against pledged shares is normally less half the value of shares and is backed by 'margin call' clause. It means if the share price and thereby, the value of the collateral declines below a threshold, promoter would have to furnish either more shares or pay back a part of the loan. In practice, the margin call is mostly met by pledging of more shares, further increasing the proportion of shares pledged by the promoter. In case the promoter fails to meet the margin call requirement, the lender is free to sell those shares in the market.

While the pledging was intended to meet short term exigencies and working capital needs, it has become an acceptable method to fund even medium-term projects. In fact, most of loans raised through this means are 'rolled over' like in case of commercial papers. As per BSE data, promoters of almost 3,000 listed companies have pledged their shares raising over Rs 2.1 lakh crore. Since law puts no limit on proportion of shares that can be pledged, many promoters have used this method aggressively to raise resources. Nearly 125 companies, involving nearly Rs 50,000 crore of loan exposure, show more than 90% of promoters' holding as pledged.

The 'margin call' clause exposes lenders and other retail investors to disproportionate risk. Since number of shares pledged, as a percent of total supply of shares in the market is substantially high, sale of shares to meet margin call leads to sharp increase in supply of shares. This leads to disproportionate decline in price. So much so, that number of pledged shares remaining with the lender fails to meet the reduced loan amount, triggering another round of margin call requirement. This is quite like chain of events leading to collapse of housing market during global financial crisis.

While decline of up to 50% in share prices is not usual, it is not impossible especially during persistent economic downturn. There have been numerous instances when prices of shares of companies fell sharply. The risk is much higher in cases where the proportion of shares pledged is high. High proportion of shares pledging can even lead to problem of 'moral hazard', implying higher risk-taking behavior by the promoter.

While share pledging is an important tool to raise emergency funds, the practice probably has been taken too far. Lenders have been all too happy since they are able to charge hefty interest on these loans. However, it would not be surprising if some of the regulations related to proportion of shares pledged, utilization of funds, duration etc see changes going forward.

*****

# Corporate Debt Restructuring – Issues Involved

Covid-19 had an unprecedented impact on financials of corporate sector putting at risk very survival of many of them. Other than the cash required to pay salaries etc, companies needed to generate sufficient cash to pay interest and loan instalments. RBI and government undertook variety of measures to keep them afloat. A brief look.

Covid-19 imposed an additional challenge on RBI to keep the borrowers afloat while preserving the soundness of the banking system. As per RBI's Financial Stability Report, 1,640 private non-financial sector companies reported decline of as much as 65% in their aggregate profits for the quarter ended March'20, underlining the seriousness of the crisis.

The first decision taken by RBI was to allow banks to offer moratorium to all categories of borrowers for six months, which was expiring in the last week of September. As per RBI FSR, 48.6% of borrowers accounting for exactly 50% of outstanding loan opted for moratorium (till 30th April'20). MSMEs appeared to be more vulnerable with 65% of loan being under moratorium. A silver lining is that only 31% of large corporate accounting for 42% of total corporate loan opted for moratorium. This possibly implies that either the rest of the companies are not facing severe stress or having sufficient cash balance.

The other important and critical announcement was suspension of IBC (Insolvency & bankruptcy code) by the central government for 12 months. IBC gives lenders the power to file case against a borrower in insolvency court if they default on their loan repayment. If IBC was not suspended, large number of borrowers, who are suffering due to Covid but are, otherwise, financially sound would have landed in IBC.

RBI led MPC has also affected significant reduction in repo rate by 75 basis points in March'20 and another 40 bps in May'20. This was on top of reduction of 90 bps during April'19-Feb'20. While it does give out a positive signal and may help companies/ sectors which are looking for fresh loans, it may not mean much for stressed companies. In fact, total bank loan in June'20 declined over March'20, as per RBI data and banks are parking their surplus funds with RBI.

An issue that arose with moratorium was, how will the interest accumulated during moratorium be treated? Assume a company has outstanding loan of Rs 100 crore from a bank at 10% rate of interest. At the end of six months of moratorium, it would have additional liability of Rs 5 crore as interest accrued. Bank would add this to the principal and charge interest on this also, called 'interest on interest'. The issue has landed at the doors of the Supreme Court and the petitioners are seeking its waiver. The argument is not exactly unreasonable considering the magnanimity of the crisis and the Court appears to be sympathetic to their cause. While this would affect banks' profitability, it is still not a question of survival for them since they would continue to earn interest income from government and from about half of other borrowers.

RBI also set up the Kamath panel to advise on 'restructuring' of bank loans. As per RBI's resolution framework, the restructuring would allow banks to reschedule the payments and grant up to two years of extension in payment. However, only those companies would be eligible for restructuring who had not defaulted in their payment as of 1st March'20 i.e. before the spread of Covid.

As per Kamath panel report, corporate sector had total outstanding loan of Rs 52.7 lakh crore. While Rs 22.2 lakh crore was under stress even before Covid, another Rs 15.5 lakh crore came under stress after that. The panel suggested that both these groups, comprising of 26 industries, should get the benefit. Among the sectors with stress before Covid are Power and Steel with debt of Rs 5.7 and Rs 2.7 lakh crore. Major sectors with high debt, which have come under stress after Covid are retail trade, wholesale trade, roads and textiles with total debt of Rs 2.9, 2.6, 1.9 and 1.9 lakh crore. As mandated by RBI, the panel has recommended that only companies which meet the threshold value for criteria such as debt/equity, debt/EBITDA etc are given this facility. Debt/equity ratio varies across sectors from 3 times to 10 times for commercial real estate

While the restructuring is much called for, there is always an element of subjectivity leading to 'moral hazard' or even collusion. RBI has put in riders such as independent audit, validation by the committee above certain level of debt etc. While the chances of misuse remain significant considering the race against time and number of cases involved, that is still the best option available.

*****

# Yes Bank – Diagnosis of A Failure

The suspension of the board of Yes Bank and appointment of an administrator was almost like a bolt from the blue; but in retrospect, had been coming for quite some time now. The bank had seen a series of defaults in its advances and was unable to raise funds to make up for this. A look at what all was wrong with the bank and how it landed up in the mess.

Yes Bank is a new-age, private sector bank with balance sheet of Rs 3.5 lakh crore at the end of Sept'19, nearly one-tenth the size of SBI. This consists of about Rs 2.1 lakh crore of public deposits, Rs 1.1 lakh crore of borrowings, other liabilities & provisions and Rs 28,000 crore of net worth or equity capital. It is the public deposits, preserving which is the primary reason behind RBI's decision. Net worth got a boost, although not enough for its needs, of about Rs 2,000 during the Sept'19 quarter with a QIP. On the assets side, advances stand at Rs 2.2 lakh crore, investments in bonds etc at Rs 67,000 crore and liquid assets at just about Rs 30,000 crore. The balance sheet has shrunk by about 8% in last six months as a result of its efforts to reduce the risky assets.

The problem with its balance sheet is that it is highly stressed. Whether it was in its pursuit of relentless growth or a relationship involving quid pro quo, bank lent disproportionately to highly leveraged and high risk corporate. It is quite ironic that while most of the private sector banks have gained from their expertise in retail banking, Yes bank's focus was on corporate sector loan which accounted for over 80% of its loan book. During FY15-19, its advances grew by as much as 34% even though equity capital growth did not keep pace, growing by just about 23%. The period coincided with public sector banks reducing their lending activity which helped it gain market share easily. Yet, bigger concern was its exposure to high risk companies with BB and lower rated companies accounting for over Rs 30,000 crore of loan book. Another problem on the assets side is that even its investments, largely considered safe assets, are in high risk bonds, possibly, the other side of quid pro quo, and pose serious risk of mark-down.

Yet, that was a part of the problem. The other part was its questionable accounting practices and deliberate attempt to hide its NPAs. An RBI's Asset Quality Review (AQR) found that bank under-reported its NPAs during FY16 and FY17, almost at about one-fourth of actual. Corporate governance issues became so serious and, possibly, frustrating for RBI that it refused re-appointment of its promoter and managing director whose term ended in Jan'19. Change is management gave bank a chance to clean up its accounts with *gross NPAs going up to 3.2% in March'19, more than double that in March'18 at 1.3%. This doubled again to 7.4% in next six months.* Gross NPA for the bank stood at over Rs 17,000 at the end of Sept'19 which included nearly Rs 6,000 crore of slippage in Sept'19 alone.

While recognition of NPA was the first step, second is to put aside funds against this, called provisioning. However, this reduces bank's equity and bank has to secure additional funds to meet regulatory requirements. (It may be noted that in case of public sector banks, government has infused nearly Rs 3 lakh crore of additional capital in last few years). Bank made provisions of about Rs 5,800 crore in FY19, up from Rs 1,500 crore in FY18 and about Rs 3,100 crore more during half year ended Sept'19.

The provisions made in last eighteen months was nearly one-fourth its net worth, yet, not sufficient. Provision coverage ratio (PCR), or the ratio of provisioning to gross NPA, for the bank was barely 43% in Sept'19. This means if it is not able to recover 57% of money from its NPAs, it would be in deep trouble. That is a big call considering the fact that in most cases of default, recovery works out to less than 50%. The bank postponed declaration of Dec'19 quarter results, scheduled mid-Feb, possibly, due to its inability to find adequate money to provide for NPAs which would, most likely, have risen further.

So, what now? RBI has put forward a 'reconstruction scheme' which entails a new bank, most likely SBI, investing about Rs 11,760 crore for 49% stake. Second and more profound is the proposal to reduce the value of additional tier I capital, valuing about Rs 10,000 crore to zero. (These are interest bearing bonds but investors bear the risk as are considered quasi equity). While this may look unfair to these bondholders, the reasoning would call for much deeper deliberation.

So, will the bank survive? In all likelihood, yes. SBI has the financial, managerial and all experience available with it. While the near-term pain remains, things would be stable in, may be, 12 months from now.

*****

# Lakshmi Vilas Bank (LVB) - The Rescue Plan

The amalgamation of Lakshmi Vilas Bank Ltd (LVB) with DBS India marked the end of the 94-years old bank. Even though the bank is rather small, failure of any bank sends strong negative signal and therefore, calls for RBI's action in case market forces fail to rescue it. (Indeed, in most cases, RBI must come to the rescue). Here is a look at LVB, strategy gone wrong and other aspects of amalgamation.

LVB is a Tamil Nadu based private sector bank with total balance sheet size of nearly Rs 24,400 crore at the end of FY20. Bank had advance (Loans) of Rs 14,000 crore out of this, about half of the which would be corporate loan. On the liabilities side, over Rs 21,000 crore has come from depositors, largely retail. Biggest of RBI's task is to ensure that depositors do not lose their money. LVB's balance sheet has shrunk by as much as 27% over previous year as a result of financial stress and restriction imposed by RBI last year. The bank recorded revenue of Rs 2,200 crore during the year, down 22%.

In comparison, DBS India, the acquirer, had total balance sheet of over Rs 51,000 crore at the end of Feb'19 and revenue of about Rs 1,500 crore. While revenue wise, DBS India is somewhat smaller than LVB, it has a much stronger balance sheet. Further, as a subsidiary of DBS Singapore, with total assets of over $400 billion, DBS India has the ability to play a long inning.

At the core of LVB's problems is, like in case of all other failing financial institutions, sharp increase in non-performing assets (NPA). Its Gross NPA stood at over Rs 4,200 crore at the end of FY20, 70% of it accumulated in last two financial years alone. In percent terms, GNPA stood at over 25%, possibly, the largest for any standalone bank. Bank had to make provisions against these NPA, which totalled over Rs 1,600 crore in the last two years, severely eroding its equity capital. Equity capital stood at about Rs 1,200 crore at the end of FY20, which may have become even zero during the first half of this year. Capital adequacy ratio (CAR) stood at only 1.1% at FY20 end.

So, how did it end up here? For a change, this looks more like a proper business failure, a result of misjudgements rather than a result of any financial misappropriation (based on information available so far)! The previous four in the series - ILFS, PMC Bank, DHFL and Yes Bank - were all a result of fraudulent lending practices. Promoters, chief executives of these four are either in jail/had been to jail and have court cases registered against them. Yet, it is a case of change in focus from retail where it had the experience to corporate lending where it did not. The bank followed the consortium model, taking exposure in loans being given by a group of lenders, reducing the trouble of due diligence. As a result, share of corporate loan went up to 50% of total loan book, up from 40% five years back and possibly, even lower before that. While there was nothing wrong with this practice, per se, the economic downturn, series of corporate failures etc were too much for bank to absorb.

So, was there a possibility to retain bank in its present form? The only option available for bank was to get an investor who could put-in the required equity capital. A suitor was Indiabulls housing finance, whose proposal was rejected by RBI last year, possibly due to governance issues. More recently, Clix group had been pursuing it but could not meet the RBI requirement.

While the amalgamation proposal from RBI has come long after the trouble started, it actually shows RBI's patience to allow market forces to find a solution, of course, to his satisfaction. The proposal is unique since RBI has chosen the domestic subsidiary of a foreign bank for amalgamation of a troubled bank for the first time. This shows its willingness to go off the beaten track. The move would also send out a signal to other foreign banks which want to do business in India but have shown resistance to create a local subsidiary.

As per the scheme, LVB's equity would become zero which means DBS would be taking over only its liabilities to the depositors and bondholders and would be getting all its assets. While this may look harsh to LVB shareholders, it must be noted that bank's equity capital is largely eroded and it is still not certain, how much more NPA may surface from its loan book. (Nevertheless, RBI, which was to declare the final proposal on 20th Nov has deferred the same and if it comes out with a proposal giving some small share to equity holders, it may not be surprising). To that extent, the proposal involves considerable risk for DBS also and would entail significant effort on its part to ensure recovery.

Yet, in the longer run, the potential gain is significant as DBS India gets access to a network of close to 560 branches, with greater concentration in South India, enabling it to access fair share of low-cost deposits. DBS is fairly well placed with GNPA ratio of just 2.6%, down from 3.1% a year ago and CAR of 16%. The parent company would also bring-in additional equity of Rs 2,500 crore which would provide greater comfort to all stake holders.

*****

# Reliance Capital – Tracing the Decline

The supersession of the board of Reliance Capital (R-Cap) by RBI and initiation of bankruptcy resolution process by NCLT (National Company Law Tribunal) marks the end of another of Anil Ambani group company. This is the fifth company of the group under NCLT. The decline of the group is the story of gross mismanagement, diffused focus, failed negotiations and above all, corporate governance issues, as stated by RBI. A brief look at R-Cap and brief financials of group companies.

The decline of R-Cap began some time in 2018/19 with FY18 (ended March'18) being the year when it last made profits; of about Rs 1,200 crore on total income of close to Rs 20,000 crore. Revenue declined sharply to Rs 7,700 crore and Rs 5,200 crore during FY19 and FY20 (March'20, before the pandemic began). This eroded its profitability resulting in cumulative loss of over Rs 2,600 crore in these two years and its equity turning negative to Rs 1,670 crore at the end of FY20 (March'20). This was still not the worst. Company recorded consolidated loss of over Rs 9,000 crore in FY21 with equity turning negative sharply to over Rs 10,000 crore. Yet, the sharp erosion in profits doesn't look very convincing and it won't be surprising if a forensic audit establishes that this was also due to accounting adjustments for previous period.

The annual report for FY21 shows the burden that the company is leaving behind. At the end of FY21, consolidated liabilities of the company stood at over Rs 75,000 crore. While the report also shows loans, investments and other financial assets worth Rs 60,000 crore, how much of it would be recoverable remains highly uncertain. That is more so because of significant related parties' transaction, even involving onward lending to other group entities. Even assuming 50% recovery on these, total loss to lenders, bondholders etc. would be humungous Rs 45,000 crore, almost the same as what Reliance Communication owed to its financiers.

Company's problems, possibly, was linked to IL&FS default also which happened in Oct'18 (FY19), leading to increased attention to the functioning and stoppage of easy money flow to NBFC sector. The writing was on the wall in June'19 when company's auditor resigned citing lack of adequate information. Why none of the lenders, other financiers, institutional shareholders and even regulatory bodies paid attention to the building financial stress within the company is beyond comprehension. To be fair to the company, it did make efforts to sell-off businesses to reduce its debts. However, most of the efforts could not reach successful completion for variety of reasons such as legal issues etc.

However, R-Cap is not alone and as many as five companies of the group are now under NCLT. These are Reliance Communications, Reliance Naval & Engineering (earlier, Pipavav Shipyard, bought by Reliance ADAG group in 2015), Reliance Home and Reliance Commercial. The last two are subsidiaries of R-Cap which have received bids under NCLT and are going through regulatory process. Reliance Communications had debt of close to Rs 47,000 crore when it went bankrupt. Reliance Naval has made losses of almost Rs 14,000 crore between 2016-20. Its total liabilities were Rs 16,600 crore with just Rs 4,000 crore of assets and negative equity of over Rs 12,000 crore at the end of FY20 when it was referred to NCLT. Why the company was not taken to NCLT earlier by the lenders remains a big question.

There was another angle to R-cap, indeed, all group companies' problems which is, high promoter's shares pledging. The declining share prices led to lenders' invoking the pledged shares leading to decline in promoter's holding. (Even here, the group had received very unusual, favorable treatment by the pledgees who had agreed not to sell its pledged shares in the open market in 2019 for six months). As per BSE, promoter group shareholding in R-Cap had come down to only 1.51% at the end of March'20 which was as high as 52.2% at the end of March'18. It is interesting to note that the promoter remained in control of the company with barely 1.5% stake and no one raised any objection!

So, is there anything to salvage from the group? The attention must move to two of the group companies which are still operating although even their financial position remains under cloud. Reliance Power made losses, although marginally of less than Rs 1,000 crore cumulatively for five years ending March'21 and has made losses in the first half of FY22. The other company, Reliance Infrastructure, recorded cumulative consolidated profit of less than Rs 1,000 crore over last five years which includes losses in two of these five years. Even this has made losses in the first half of FY22.

Like in R-Cap, promoters group holding in these two entities has also come down significantly. In Reliance Power, the shareholding declined to 9% by March'21 from a high of 56% in March'19. This has risen subsequently to 25% by Sept'21 with purchase of shares by Reliance Infrastructure, classified as promoter group entity. However, in Reliance Infrastructure itself, the holding is only 5%, down from 49.6% in March'18. It is imperative that institutional shareholders or even SEBI take note of the change in shareholding and initiate the process for management change.

*****

# ArcelorMittal Steel – The Winning Strategy!

ArcelorMittal, along wih its JV partner, Nippon Steel, gained management control of Essar Steel after a long, grueling insolvency process extending over 2½ years. The takeover also marked the entry of the company, promoted by Indian born, Mr Lakshmi Mittal, into India after failing in its organic attempts over a decade ago. A look at the MNC, its businesses and business strategy.

ArcelorMittal is among the world's leading steel company headquartered in Europe. As per its annual report for 2018, it produced close to 85 million tons of steel during the year from its 48 steel making facilities across the world. Of the total, Europe contributes nearly half with American continent accounting for 38% and the remaining, primarily in CIS countries. Other than the core business of steel making, company is also engaged in significant production of iron ore and some amount of other raw material for captive use. Company produced about 58 million tons of iron ore during 2018, nearly half of its iron ore requirements. The backward integration has largely been the result of significant price fluctuations seen in iron ore prices over last decade or so. Almost all of its operations are carried out through subsidiaries and ArcelorMittal is only a holding company.

ArcelorMittal is, itself, a result of much publicized and fiercely opposed in certain quarters merger between Mittal Steel and Arcelor Steel in 2007. The merger was driven by Mr Mittal to bring about consolidation in the steel industry, which is, indeed, highly fragmented. Against iron ore mining industry where the top three players account for over half of the production, top three steel companies would be producing just about 15-20% of steel. While ArcelorMittal has managed to survive the downturn, acquisition of Corus by Tata Steel executed around the same time is going through significant challenges even after selling significant part of the acquired assets.

A look at its financials shows that company recorded sales of $76 bn (nearly Rs 5.6 lakh crore) in 2018, about half of which comes from Europe, its base. Sales is nearly 0.9 times consolidated sales of RIL for FY19. Sales have grown at nearly 16% CAGR during 2016-18, an above normal growth rate for an industry like steel. Operating profit for the year was $6.5 bn, giving it a margin of nearly 8.5%. Despite being its largest market, Europe gives the lowest operating margin averaging about 5% during 2016-18 against over 10% for rest of the world. Net profit for the year was $5.3 bn, sharply up from $1.7 bn in 2016. (Operating profit gets greater attention to understand a company's operational performance as items below this, interest, depreciation, tax, exceptional etc, can show large fluctuations). However, 2019 has turned out to be not-so-good year for the company. For nine months ended Sept'19, its operating profit fell by as much as 49% due to weak steel prices. For the third quarter, company made losses of $0.5 bn, first loss after several years.

Company had total balance sheet of $91 bn (Rs 6.5 lakh crore), nearly $6 bn higher than last year. (RIL's balance sheet crossed Rs 10 lakh crore in FY19). It has a very conservative approach to financial management with debt accounting for only $12.6 billion. Total equity stood at $44.1 bn with debt-equity (net debt/total equity) at just 0.23:1. Another important feature of its finances is trade finance management. Against trade payables of $14 bn, the receivables are only $4.4 bn, getting almost $10 bn of funds to work with. However, inventories are fairly large at $20 bn, almost three months of sales.

Company's core philosophy has been risk-taking and growth through acquisitions. Other than Essar Steel, its recent acquisitions include plant in USA in 2014 through a JV, one in Brazil and another in Italy in 2018. Despite its aggressive approach in acquiring assets, it has also been very agile in its strategy with evolving market conditions. With higher fluctuation in steel market, it has tweaked its acquisition model in recent years and is executing high value acquisition through alliances. It is also very conservative in its financial management. Its current net debt-equity ratio of 0.23:1 would be among the lowest in the industry and far better than Indian companies which go up to over 2:1. While one hand, it is acquiring assets in its core businesses, it is also reducing stake in non-core businesses to maintain financial agility. Against the purchase of Essar Steel, it is selling 50% stake in its shipping business which would give it about $0.5 bn. Company's strategy is broadly similar to that of RIL involving aggressive acquisition/expansion, debt-light and JVs to maintain operational agility.

*****

# Tata Steel - Analyzing the Strategic Re-alignment

The cancellation of joint venture with ThyssenKrupp was a setback for Tata Steel trying to reduce its global exposure. Yet, it is an interesting phase for the company with series of developments reflecting the strategic shift. The focus is shifting back to domestic production in contrasts with the global expansion undertaken during 2004-07. A look at the developments and their impact on the company.

Tata Steel entered the map of global steel producers with almost two-thirds of its revenue coming from global businesses. However, it was never comfortable with its global acquisitions; eventually leading to the decision of divesting them sometime around 2015. However, that was the trough in the steel business cycle which sharply eroded the value of assets on block. After a series of failed negotiations due to prevailing industry conditions, company eventually sold a part of the asset for a nominal sum of €1 in April 2016. The assets at Scunthorpe with 5 mn tons of capacity had estimated value of about $1.4 billion just about two years back. Yet, the sell-off was prudent as the company was making significant operational losses by running them. The sale made earlier sale of Teesside plant in 2010 with 3 mn tons capacity at $500 million look much better. (The Teesside plant was eventually closed down in 2015 after the bankruptcy of its buyer).

The second phase of global divestment involves sale of its South East Asia (SEA) business comprising of assets in Singapore, Thailand and Vietnam. The company had acquired these assets close to the peak of the business cycle and could not make money out of them. The businesses, purchased around 2004-06, accounted for just about 7% of its sales and had negligible share in profits. Company has entered into an agreement to sell these businesses in January this year. This involves transfer of assets into another entity including about Rs 700 crore of debt. Tata Steel would receive close to Rs 2,300 crore and would also hold 30% stake in the entity. The consideration involved implies that it has managed reasonable value from these assets in contrast with the UK sale.

Undaunted by its failure in global businesses, company remains a risk seeker in the domestic space. This was demonstrated by the purchase of Bhushan Steel through NCLT involving substantial sum of Rs 35,000 crore. The purchase of Bhushan Steel was tricky since such assets, coming through bankruptcy, carry certain degree of surprises. Bhushan Steel has a capacity of 5.6 mn tons and the plant is quite efficient as reflected in the turnaround achieved after its purchase. The reason for insolvency was high level of loan, probably a result of malpractices by the earlier promoters including diversion of loan which are being investigated. With its domestic expertise and network, Tata Steel managed to turnaround the company which recorded EBITDA of over Rs 11,000 per ton for quarter ended Dec'18, not very far from EBITDA of about Rs 16,000 per ton for the core domestic business and much higher than that of European business at Rs 4,000.

Result of all these transaction, Sale of high cost global assets at negligible price and domestic purchase, has affected company's balance sheet. The company had to reduce the value of its global assets and write-off nearly Rs 16,000 crore during FY15 and 16. This reduced its equity capital to less than Rs 30,000 crore at the end of FY16. It came with a right issue of Rs 12,800 crore in FY18 which helped take the capital base to Rs 62,000 crore, double what it was two years back. Yet, it has a very high level of debt at over Rs 1 lakh crore at the end of FY19, partially a result of additional borrowings to fund Bhushan steel purchase. It hoped to transfer Rs 20,000 crore of this to the JV which now stands cancelled. Considering the current state of European steel industry, it would be difficult for the company to find a new partner. So, Tata Steel would have to preserve the cash generated from domestic business until the market conditions improve.

*****

# Corporate Battle – L&T Acquires Mindtree

The acquisition of Mindtree consulting by L&T after an intense and interesting boardroom battle generated lot of attention. More so, as such a hostile attempt is being made after a long time in Indian Corporate space. Interestingly, L&T itself was target of two hostile takeover bids in late 1980s and again in 2003, both of which, it successfully thwarted. A look at the deal and the stakes involved.

Mindtree is an IT company founded in late 90s with FY18 revenue of over Rs 5,500 crore. The profit margin has fallen to 11-12% over last two years from 14-15% in FY14-FY15, probably a result of recent pressure on IT sector. L&T, on the other hand, is a diversified conglomerate with major interest in engineering & infrastructure sector. It had revenues of Rs 1.2 lakh crore in FY18, more than 20 times the size of Mindtree. However, its profit margin is lower at about 6%. Low profitability of engineering businesses prompted the company to expand beyond core capital intensive, infrastructure-based segments to people based, asset light service sector. In line with this strategy, company entered IT and financial services business which now account for over 20% of total company revenue. L&T InfoTech had revenues of Rs 7,400 crore in FY18, higher than that of Mindtree, and profits of Rs 1,160 crore implying net margin of close to 16%. L&T has another IT based company in its portfolio, slightly smaller in size than this, both being run independently.

The buyout fits-in quite perfectly for the cash-rich company with its strategy and progression over last about a decade. The purchase should also be attractive for Mindtree as it would get access to the huge clientele of L&T. Unlike in most buy-out cases where buyer seeks emergency funding from lenders for a takeover attempt, money is not an issue here. That is the reason why L&T had proposed to raise its stake to as much as 67%, much beyond what is stipulated by regulatory norms governing takeovers. Rs 10,700 crore needed to fund the buy-out was just 4% of consolidated balance sheet of the company. It had over Rs 7,000 crore of cash & bank balance and around Rs 15,000 crore of liquid financial investment at the end of FY18 which places it very comfortably. The comfort is evident from company's communiqué to the stock exchange mentioning a curt "will be paid in cash" as "nature of consideration", which is in contrast with elaborate details on 'bridge financing', 'share swap' etc in such takeover bids!

L&T is one of the few non-promoters driven companies in the country owned by financial institutions and employee trusts. Mindtree was owned 13.3% by the promoters, 20% by Mr V.G. Siddharth (owned directly and through his other companies) and over 50% by institutional investors. Even though Mr Siddhartha had the largest individual shareholding, he was only a strategic investor and not a promoter. The sell-off plan was necessitated to meet the funding needs of his operating companies such as café coffee day. That became evident when he stepped down from the Board of Mindtree in 2018.

That brings us to why the existing promoters were up against the bid with statements like "snatching child from mother"! Obvious reason is that they had been in control of the company for two decades and did not wish to lose control. Right from the beginning, L&T looked placed comfortable to be able to wrest control. An interesting point that emerged was that promoters of

Mindtree had approached L&T some years back with the offer to sell their stake. If the takeover was not 'culturally different' and 'value destructive' then, how it became so now??!

*****

# BSNL-MTNL Merger - The Lost Opportunity

The proposed merger of BSNL & MTNL announced in 2019 was put on hold by the government in April'22. The deferment is quite a setback as government continues to make significant losses on the operations of BSNL. More so because almost half of the employees had opted for VRS (voluntary retirement scheme) announced by the government to facilitate the merger. A look at the financials and strategic importance of the public sector companies.

Bharat Sanchar Nigam Ltd (BSNL), as the name suggests, provides telephony services, both wireline and wireless in the entire country except Delhi and Mumbai. While it has over 50% share in wireline business, its share in wireless is just about 10%. While high employee cost and outdated technology (company still provides 3G technology only) are the core reason for their sub-par performance, entry of Jio has been the last straw, like for many other telecom companies. With the entry of Jio, its revenue fell sharply from Rs 32,400 crore in FY16 to Rs 12,000 crore in FY19 (provisional). This pushed up losses from Rs 5,000 crore to over Rs 10,000 crore during the period. Cumulative losses, which was just about Rs 12,000 crore till FY15, rose sharply to Rs 40,000 crore by FY19.

In comparison to BSNL, MTNL is a listed entity, much smaller with operations only in the city of Mumbai and Delhi. It had total income of Rs 2,600 crore in FY19, down from close to Rs 4,000 crore in FY16. It made losses of Rs 3,400 crore in the year, increase from Rs 2,000 crore in FY16. Interestingly, even though MTNL is making huge losses, its subsidiary, Mahanagar Telephone (Mauritius) Ltd. (MTML), has made profits for 10th consecutive year in FY19, that too, with monthly revenue per user of less than Rs 250! MTNL's cost structure is even more unfavourable with interest and depreciation, which are relatively fixed, being close to Rs 2,500 crore annually. Interestingly, company's borrowings at almost Rs 20,000 crore is higher than balance sheet of Rs 15,000 crore. (Balance sheet = equity plus liability which includes borrowings). This is because it has a negative net worth of almost Rs 10,000 crore and is surviving because of sovereign backing.

The introduction of VRS, cost borne by the government, was an important element of the revival plan. With nearly 92,000 employees opting for VRS, savings for the combined entity should be over Rs 7,000 crore. At the end of FY19, BSNL had an employee base of 1.67 lakh (down from 1.84 lakh a year ago) whereas MTNL had 22,000. This is in contrast with just about 15,000 for other market players! Employee cost has been close to Rs 15,000 crore for BSNL for most of these years, 45% of its total cost and 60% of total revenue for FY18. In contrast, employee cost for Airtel is one-tenth at less than Rs 1,500 crore!

The other element of revival involves allocation of 4G spectrum, again at the cost of government. Since the company did not have the resources, it could not participate in the spectrum auction. Other than upgradation to 4G, company is also taking other operational measures such as leasing of its tower infrastructure. Towers, totaling 67,000 in numbers, were hived-offed into a subsidiary. Company has earned, on an average, close to Rs 14 lakh per tower by leasing a few thousand towers. The revenue potential, based on this rate, works out to a significant Rs 9,000 crore and realization of even half would be significant. Similar model can be adopted for its manufacturing units also engaged in producing SIM card and other telecom related products.

While the government is making upfront payment for the revival, the same is proposed by paid back through sale of assets by BSNL over the next four years. Its balance sheet shows land & other property valued at over Rs 70,000 crore, Rs 38,000 crore of which is proposed to be sold.

BSNL & MTNL together have a strategic purpose as it provides network connectivity to sensitive segments such as Defence forces as well as government itself and is the reason why they cannot be privatized. The revival still stands a good chance and must be brought back on the agenda. The tariff hike made by private players give more reason for hope. The company would need to make the best use of non-core assets such as tower and manufacturing units. While these cannot be sold-off, again, for strategic reasons, options must be explored to utilize their full capacity by competing in the market.

*****

# Essar Steel Insolvency – Tracing the Saga!

The insolvency process of Essar Steel had been through lot of uncertainty and has generated lot of attention, possibly due to the presence of high-profile international players. The process reached a conclusion with the Supreme Court's decision setting aside the ruling of NCLAT (National Company Law Appellate Tribunal) and awarding the company to the highest bidder. A look at the background of this case.

The Supreme Court's decision comes in response to the petition filed by the Committee of Creditors (CoC) against the order of NCLAT. The NCLAT July'19 order put financial creditor and operational creditor on a par and asked CoC to pay operational creditors in the same proportion as financial creditors. The Supreme Court order has established the seniority of financial creditors, who are secured lenders, and therefore, have a first charge on the money received through sale of the company.

Essar Steel is among the first 12 companies which were referred to NCLT (National Company Law Tribunal) in June'17. These cases were unique since the insolvency was not initiated by any of the lender but directed by RBI as over 60% of the loan outstanding had become NPA for these companies. Loan outstanding in this case is over Rs 50,000 crore and is among the few cases where banks expect to recover full principal amount.

The bids for takeover of the company were invited in Oct'17 after initiation of proceedings in Aug'17. ArcelorMittal and Numetal emerged at the most suited parties at this time. While things looked smooth at that time, a crucial amendment to IBC in Nov'17 upset all the arithmetic. The amendment barred promoters of any defaulting company from bidding for any other insolvent company. This put a question mark on the eligibility of both the bidders as ArcelorMittal was a co-promoter of two defaulting companies, Uttam Galva and KSS Petron. Similarly, Numetal was partially owned by one of the family members of Ruia family, a defaulting group.

To get rid of this handicap, ArcelorMittal sold off its holding in Uttam Galva just before the last date of bid submission on 12th Feb'18. The sale at Rs 24 per share against purchase price of Rs 120 nine years back indicates how aggressively it was fighting this battle. However, even though they ceased to be a promoter, their name was NOT struck off from Stock exchange record as a promoter on the day they submitted their bid..!

The onus fell on the committee of creditors (CoC) which declared both the bids ineligible and called for another round of bidding. Both the parties again made their bids meeting all the eligibility criteria. Ruia's stake in Numetal was sold off to JSW Steel to meet the eligibility criteria. The battle became more interesting with the entry of Vedanta and interest shown by a few more. While the first bids were estimated at Rs 32,000 crore and Rs 18,000 crore by ArcelorMittal and Numetal respectively, the revised bids were estimated at Rs 42,000 and Rs 37,000 crore. Clearly, ArcelorMittal was ready to put in lot more money for the company.

Other than the battle on the financial front, companies also filed cases challenging their disqualification and also challenging other company's eligibility.! ArcelorMittal was asked to deposit Rs 7,000 crore to clear the dues of two defaulting companies even though it had ceased to be a promoter. This tilted the race in favor of ArcelorMittal as Numetal failed to clear its dues, a bid which was accepted by CoC.

While this should have cleared the way for takeover of the company by ArcelorMittal, two more events dragged the process for another year. The first when Ruias, the erstwhile promoters, offered to pay up the entire Rs 54,389 crore. What made this offer interesting was that the offer was made just when CoC had voted in favor of ArcelorMittal's bid! However, their hope was dashed when NCLAT asked them to clear the dues of all of their defaulting companies, estimated at close to Rs 1.4 lakh crore. And the second was NCLAT's decision giving operational creditor equal share and therefore, the Supreme Court's intervention.

*****

# Corporate Governance – Where is India Inc Headed??

India Inc is grappling with unraveling of cases of frauds committed by the top management in the recent past. Cases are not restricted to willful default where lenders' money is at stake but siphoning of company funds or cases of inter-corporate collusion. So, has the corporate India suddenly become so corrupt or there is more to it than that? A look at the some of the developments and the repercussions.

Among the latest is the case of CG power where the promoter and ex-chairman has been charged with siphoning of funds from the company to entities owned by himself. Amount involved is estimated at over Rs 2,000 crore. The case, however, is just one of the series of frauds India Inc has seen in recent times. Among the high profile is conflict of interest charge against former ICICI Bank CEO & MD Chanda Kochhar for the loan sanctioned to Videocon group. These loans subsequently became NPA. The news was so unbelievable that even the board of the bank passed a resolution expressing full faith in her even before details emerged. The allegation of 'quid pro quo' gained weight as Deepak Kochar, husband of Chanda Kochar, was found to have business relationship with Videocon group.

In other instances, the chairman of Jet Airways was stopped from travelling aboard and is being investigated for fund diversion. Another company, DHFL, which has defaulted on several of its loan is facing charges of huge funds diversion and is under investigation by regulatory agency. Corporate governance issues forced RBI to cut short the tenure of chairperson of two of private sector banks although there were no explicit charges. Governance issues are not restricted to large, high-profile companies. There are several cases of frauds related to GST evasion, duty drawback related to exports etc by smaller companies coming to light, lot more than what was seen in earlier times.

Yet, the worst of all is the case related to IL&FS where close to Rs 1 lakh crore of lenders' money is stuck. The wrong doings by IFIN (ILFS financial services), a division of IL&FS, has been termed "nothing short of organized crime" by MCA. It lent close to Rs 10,000 crore, largely to related parties who defaulted on them. To hide these defaults IFIN lent to another set of companies, who, then transferred this money to the first set of companies. They, in turn, paid back to IFIN, thus escaping from becoming NPA. IFIN had a loan book of close to Rs 20,000 crore, most of which is now unrecoverable. IL&FS case is possibly true to the tag of organized crime as even external auditors and rating agencies were bought over and coerced into hiding company's actual financial health. A report by moneylife cites a board meeting incident when an independent director of IL&FS subsidiary was threatened with jail by a company director for raising questions. The IL&FS saga is stark reminder of the comment by a widely respected corporate leader, "I would hire a person with low intellect and high integrity rather than a person with high intellect and low integrity. The potential to cause damage by the second person is far more than the first".

So, are there cases a recent phenomenon or there is more to it than that. There was certainly a steady degeneration in governance standards, quite often, in collusion with regulatory bodies or other government agencies over last decade or so. However, unearthing of these cases does not mean sudden increase but strengthening of monitoring and oversight mechanism. This is being aided by government's tough resolve to break the corporate-bureaucrat-political nexus as promoters, who took advantage of the system, do not find a shelter in government machinery any more. Further, strengthening of punitive measures and plugging of legal loophole such as those related to attachment of property, barring accused from leaving the country, delegation of power to issue lookout notice etc, is closing the escape route for the culprits. Another important legal provision relates to GST empowering officials to arrest the evader if the amount involved is above a certain threshold. A recent case was where a company promoter set up 30 fake units to evade GST! Strong measures being taken for ensuring compliance in the new taxation regime should change the mindset and reduce the urge to evade taxes.

So, are we better-off or worse? While the current situation gives an indication of significant mess, the cleanup is certainly going to make it more level playing field and lead to more equitable and sustainable growth. To that extent, the current phase could be an inflexion point in the evolution of corporate India.

*****

# IL&FS Collapse - Tracking the Developments

The collapse of IL&FS in Sept'18 was a watershed event for India's financial sector. The move by the government to dissolve the company's board and form a new board provided some sanity and saved the stakeholders from the worst. A look at various developments and the current status in the saga involving Rs 95,000 crore of lenders' money.

The default by IL&FS and fear of contagion spreading to the entire NBFCs sector prompted the government to appoint a new board. It was clear right from the beginning that most of its assets will have to sold-off to pay back the lenders. With this as the primary objective, identification of assets for monetization was started involving classification based of their cash flow position - those with sufficient cash flow to meet their debt obligations, those with partial and those with negligible cash flow. Out of the total of 169 Indian subsidiaries, 55 entities with total debt of Rs 11,000 crore have been classified as 'green', 13 with Rs 16,000 crore of debt as 'amber' and as many as 82 with debt of Rs 61,000 crore have been classified as 'red'. Classification of more than half of the companies as 'red' indicates the all pervFSasive nature of fraudulent practices prevalent across the group. However, the due diligence could be conservative, a rather accepted norm, and the realization from sale could be somewhat better than what these numbers suggest. For instance, the first two packages of assets in the area of wind energy and road with total debt of over Rs 21,000 crore have received bids providing nearly 80% recoveries. Many of them are not from 'green' group implying 'amber' group also having significant recovery potential. Other than these two packages, bids have been invited for some more assets which should get finalized in the near term.

Other than the macro level measures, board has also initiated several ground level measures to reduce operational costs and dispose-off non-core assets. Among them are manpower and salary rationalization, office space rationalization/ leasing of such space created. The progress report submitted to NCLT in Aug'19 records 36% reduction in manpower and 47% savings in wage bill between Oct'18 and June'19. An instance of leasing of 50,000 sq ft of space is generating monthly rent income of Rs 1.2 crore. Similarly, disposal of 23 of 36 luxury cars fetched close to Rs 5 crore, averaging over Rs 20 lakh each. While these figures are insignificant in comparison to the total debt, these do play an important role in communicating the honesty of intent. Further, these too involve complicated procedures starting with permission of court to begin the auction process and final approval for accepting the bids received.

The extent of involvement of courts in the operations of the company is so high that it had to approach it even for release of payments from its own cash. In case of a defaulting company, banks refuse to release payments from company's accounts even if there is a cash balance. These payments could relate to statutory payments or salaries etc which are essential for the company to remain classified as 'going concern'. One such case involved Allahabad Bank where the board had to seek intervention of NCLT.

While financial restructuring and keeping the operations going is one aspect of the job, the other involves assessing and establishing the wrong-doings, an enormous task with complex corporate structure involving over 300 subsidiaries. An audit undertaken by Grant and Thornton involving all high value transactions from April'13 onwards showed (interim report) re-routing of over Rs 2,200 crore of funds to IL&FS group companies from the firms which were given loan by IFIN

(IL&FS financial services). IFIN with outstanding of close to Rs 20,000 crore is possibly central to all fraudulent activities. A large part of its funds had been lent through questionable transactions and over 90% of it looks unrecoverable. Accounts of the company and its subsidiaries - IFIN and ITAN are also being re-cast from 2014 onwards. Interestingly and quite understandably, an ex-director of the company had challenged the decision in the court which has been rejected!

The IL&FS fiasco has involved major lapses on part of rating and auditing agencies also with allegations of coercive tactics adopted by the dissolved IL&FS board. Investigations are being carries out by the ministry of corporate affairs (MCA) and investigating agencies such as ED and SFIO. Some of the ex-directors are already in judicial custody. Ministry of Corporate Affairs (MCA) has sought banning of the audit firms for their involvement in cover-up. A fall-out has been that MD of one of the rating agencies has been removed from his job whereas another has been sent on leave. A silver lining is that the lapse is being seen as one-off instance, largely a result of malfeasance of some individuals and not of the rating process itself.

*****

# Reliance Communications – Analyzing the Failure

Reliance Communications' plea to NCLT (National Company Law Tribunal) to proceed with insolvency process marks the demise of another telecom company. The insolvency plea was filed against RCom by Ericson, an operational creditor, in May'18 which has also filed some more cases against the company and its chairman. While the company cannot be blamed for not trying hard enough to save itself, it does seem to lack adequate sense of trade-off involved and maneuver required to survive in a market like India. Its decline, in some ways, is like that of Yahoo! which rejected several offers, only to finally settle for less valuable offer. A brief analysis of how the company went broke.

Reliance Communication or RCom was primarily in the business of mobile telephony until the problems began. Company's woes began, not after the entry of Reliance Jio, but much before when it became clear that Indian telecom industry is soon going to migrate to 4G network. RCom had already spent lot of money for its 2G & 3G services and had substantial debt on its books. Consolidated debt at the end of FY14 was nearly Rs 37,000 crore, not much less than its current debt position of about Rs 47,000 crore. With the onslaught unleashed by Jio, company was fighting to reduce its debt to mitigate the risk arising due to declining revenues, instead of planning investment in 4G.

While it was clear that it cannot survive alone, it made a mess of several opportunities to enter into alliance. (This was unlike the case of Tata Teleservices, which either could not read the market correctly or persisted with its plans despite knowing the risks involved). The only one that it carried out successfully was acquisition of Sistema Shyam Teleservices Limited (SSTL) in Oct'17. However, there was neither any financial gain not outflow for RCom as the merger happened in lieu of issue of equity shares. It had no implication on its objective to reduce debt

The first major failure for the company was calling off the proposed JV with Aircel in Oct'17. The JV with Aircel, proposed in Sept'16, envisaged transfer of substantial part of its debt and its wireless assets to a new entity which was expected to have sufficient cash flow to service the debt. This turned out to be a double whammy as it led to cancellation of the deal to sell part of towers business to Brookfield. The failure of Aircel deal meant RCom's tower assets would not generate revenue as projected earlier forcing a rethink on the part of Brookfield.

Yet, most hurting was the failure to complete the deal with Jio to sell its entire assets related to wireless telephony. While the deal failed as Jio refused to provide guarantee to clear dues of DOT's (Dept of Telecom) estimated at about Rs 3,000 crore, RCom should have managed to find a way around this. Even after provisioning Rs 3,000 crore to DOT, both RCom and Jio would have got significant value from the assets which may have much less value now. For instance, it is highly unlikely that company would get much value for Rs 14,500 crore of intangible assets in the form of telecom licenses.

A related error made by the company was closing its entire 2G and 3G business in Dec'17 losing an estimated 6-7 crore subscribers, apparently to save costs. While there was no substantial decline in costs as bigger part of it is fixed in nature, it deprived the company of revenues, howsoever low it may have been. Further, they could have been moved to Jio's 4G network providing significant additional subscriber base to Jio and giving it additional reason to save the deal.

*****

# Jet Airways – An Avoidable Crash Landing

The grounding of Jet Airways has been a cause of concern for all followers of aviation sector. The sector, despite being a high profile one, hasn't been able to establish itself financially and accounts for several failed businesses over last decade or so. A look at its performance and comparison of the company with a profitable airline.

Jet Airways, with total income of over Rs 25,000 crore in FY18, comes at No 60 in the list of companies in India in terms of sales. However, company recorded loss of Rs 630 crore after making profits of about Rs 1,450 crore in FY17. The company could manage profits in just two out of last five years indicating the inherently unstable nature of its business model looks. It has accumulated losses of close to Rs 10,000 crore till the end of Sept'18. The company has never looked very comfortable financially despite being in operations for 25 years now. The recent crude spike seems to have been the last straw to break the camel's back.

Company's problems can be segregated into two parts - operational reflected in operating margin and post-operational costs reflected in Interest & Depreciation charges (I&D) as a percent of revenue. Company has done very badly on both counts. Besides, the expansion strategy undertaken by company over last five years has not been quite pragmatic considering the stress that was building up.

Average operating profit margin for the company over last three years stands at 6.4% against that of Spicejet at over 10% during the same period. More importantly, company has lower fuel cost, at 30.2% of revenue against 31.2% for Spicejet. The operational inefficiency is reflected in non-fuel operating cost ratio. This stands at 67.5% for the company against 59.2% for Spicejet. This is a smart comeback for Spicejet which was having worse operating ratio five years back. Difference also emerges while accounting for I&D charges. While this has come down over the years from over 10% of revenue to 6.1%in last five years, it is still significantly higher than Spicejet. Average I&D for last five years for Jet stands at 8.2% against 4.5% for Spicejet, almost 4 percentage point difference. If the company had managed even this ratio, it would have saved almost Rs 1,100 crore, significantly higher than the losses.

The other differentiator is company's response when it slipped into red in FY14, a wrong strategic move. With loss of Rs 1,000 crore in FY14, Spicejet began pruning its operations leading to reduction in passenger carrying capacity (defined by available seat kilometers, ASKM) by as much as22%. This also resulted in lower revenues but helped company become more resilient to absorb fuel price shock. Jet Airways, on the contrary, facing worse situation with loss of Rs 3,700 crore in FY14, undertook an expansion strategy, partially to capture the space being left by Spicejet. It was also probably a case of 'adverse selection', having mobilized funds just then by selling stake to Etihad. Its passenger carrying capacity rose by as much as 25% between FY14-16.

However, issues have also emerged related to siphoning of funds, being investigated by regulatory agencies. So, other than the operational mis-management, it could also be a case of governance failure.

*****

# Tata Teleservices - End of the Inning

Tata Teleservices' sale of its consumer mobile business to Airtel marks the end of Tata group's effort to establish itself in the telecom space. Nothing describes the situation better than Ernest Hemingway quote, ""How did you go bankrupt?" Gradually; then suddenly". The extent of loss is reflected by the financials of Tata Tele for FY18. The consolidated balance sheet shows total equity erosion of almost Rs 30,000 crore and additional liability of over Rs 40,000 crore. This is apart from about Rs 7,000 crore that it paid to DOCOMO. So, what all happened and how the group couldn't read the signs. More importantly, did it persist despite the obvious signs against all odds? An attempt to understand the same.

Tata Teleservices is the telecom arm of Tata Sons which began its operations in 2005. Its commencement itself, after a failed alliance with Birla and AT&T, probably was not a good omen to begin with! Company achieved a breakthrough when it managed to rope in NTT DOCOMO, Japan which invested $2.2 bn in the company in 2009. While Tata Tele, probably went all ballistic with this deal, it was a cautious entry for DOCOMO which was not too sure about the market. The market was already showing signs of saturation with large number of recent entrants other than the legal and regulatory uncertainty. To mitigate this, DOCOMO extracted an agreement that if the alliance failed to deliver in five years, Tata Sons would find a buyer for DOCOMS's shares or buy it back at half the prices. Tatas probably did not fully factor-in the fact that they may land up in a situation where they would have to pay back to DOCOMO.

While company's choice of technology, CDMA over GSM, is cited as wrong strategy, that doesn't look like the real problem. While the company was never in a comfortable position, the slide becomes irreversible with the launch of 4G services in India in 2012. The launch of services at nearly the same price as 3G made it clear that 2G and 3G services will not be able to survive. The situation was worsened by the fact that DOCOMO did not appear to share its optimism (and rightly so, as per prudent business practices). So, even when other telecom players were preparing their launch of 4G, Tata Tele was staring at the imminent exit of its partner and searching all over again for another partner.

The extent of stress all through the years of its operations is evident from the financials of its subsidiary, Tata Tele (Maharashtra) Ltd, available with BSE. The company did not make profits in any of the year since 2002 except a marginal profit of Rs 50 crore in FY11. The profitability remained strained even though the revenues moved up from just about a few hundred crore to nearly Rs 3,000 crore, the best in FY16. The stress is also evident from the fact that even when Jio had not started its operations, Tata Tele profitability was considerably low, providing inadequate surplus to reinvest. In FY16, its EBITDA margin was just about 15% (FY15, 20%) in contrast with industry benchmark of at least about 30%. Company recorded as much as Rs 17,000 crore of losses in just the last year.

As per the arrangement, Airtel is taking control of the company on 'no cash, no debt' basis with about 40 million subscribers, majority of its employees and some spectrum. The fixed line, broadband business and enterprise business are being taken over by Tata group companies, Tata Communications and Tata Sky. The company has retained entire debt of about Rs 36,000 crore on its books. While there are assets listed against this including its stake in the tower subsidiary, Tata Sons may have to settle a significant part of this from its own pocket.

*****

# Vodafone Idea – Braving the AGR Crisis

The refusal of Supreme Court to grant any relief on the AGR (Adjusted Gross Revenue) dealt a big blow to the companies, especially for Vodafone Idea. A look at the company, its financials and why things could be tough for it.

Vodafone Idea ltd (VIL) is the third largest telecom company in the country with subscriber base of little over 30 crore and revenue of Rs 38,000 crore (FY19, full year). It is promoted by Aditya Birla group and Vodafone plc, the British telecom company, with total revenue in excess of €44 bn (about Rs 4 lakh crore, FY19). The company was formed after the merger of Vodafone and Idea in Aug'18, a result of price war started with the entry of Reliance Jio. Jio's entry shook the telecom industry, already reeling under the impact of license cancellation a few years ago, with exit of several players such as Reliance Communications, Tata Tele, Aircel etc.

The Feb'20 AGR ruling essentially means that telecom companies are required to include their non-core income also while calculating licensing fees and spectrum usage charge which are paid to the government as a percent of total revenue. The judgment delivered in Oct'19 implies an additional liability of Rs 43,000 crore for VIL. Company made provisions of Rs 23,000 crore in its financials for Sept'19 quarter to meet this liability leading to loss of over Rs 50,000 crore, highest in Indian corporate history.

This shows on its balance sheet, already stretched because of losses accumulated over last few years. At the end of Dec'19, against a balance sheet of Rs 2.4 lakh crore, it had an equity of just Rs 17,600 crore, sharp erosion from close to Rs 80,000 crore in June'19. (Company had completed a rights issue leading to equity infusion of Rs 25,000 crore in May'19). Balance sheet, thus, comprises of over Rs 2.2 lakh crore of liabilities which includes Rs 1.5 lakh crore of borrowings. On the assets side, property, plant & equipment account for only Rs 66,000 crore with over Rs 1.2 lakh crore stated as intangible assets. Clearly, the stakes are high for lenders also, if the company goes bankrupt. It has been trying to monetize its stake of 11% in Indus tower having over 1,25,000 towers but is stuck in regulatory maze.

While Vodafone plc is a successful company globally, its Indian operation has been, possibly, a harrowing experience ever since its entry in 2007. Vodafone plc had written-off €5.5 bn from its Indian investment even before the AGR ruling came. The gravity of the situation is evident from the fact that it has written down the value of all its investment to zero and has made it clear that it is not going to make any further investment in India. However, it continues to remain engaged as India contributes almost half of its 62 crore global subscribers.

So, where does the company go from here? The company has already put aside Rs 43,000 crore towards its AGR liabilities which should help it tide over the crisis. (It is still fighting hard to get some relief as a part of this has to come from Vodafone plc). However, this is an amount calculated by the company and any amount in excess demanded from the telecom department could be the proverbial last straw. The other challenge is current financial liabilities (due in next 12 months) of close to Rs 15,000 crore at the end of Dec'19 against cash & bank balance of just about Rs 8,000 crore. Getting reprieve from the creditors on this would be another challenge.

While the short-term scenario is highly challenging, the worst, in terms of operating environment, is, possibly, over. Company's ARPU has risen almost 23% over last year. (However, the advantage is getting lost with reduction in subscriber base). Further, it has managed significant reduction in its operational expense (over 25% y-o-y) leading to EBITDA margin crossing 30% for April-Dec'19 against less than 15% in the previous year. While the company still made losses in Dec'19 quarter, March'20 quarter would be crucial for its survival if it is able to meet all its operational and fixed cost from the tariff increase effected in Dec'19. The relief announced by telecom authority in Nov'19, deferring FY21 dues for two years, should help it tide over the cashflow mismatch. While the company has a good chance to survive the crisis, fingers are still crossed.

*****

# Telecom Relief Package – Can Vodafone Idea Survive Now?

The reform and relief measures provided to the telecom sector gave Vodafone Idea (Vi) much needed respite. The measures take care of immediate cash needs and should also ensure its survival. However, it is difficult to say whether it would survive as an independent, private entity or would have to issue significant equity to the government. A look at the measures and its impact on Vi.

First the details of the relief provided. Government announced deferment of spectrum and AGR dues payable by the telecom company by four years. However, interest on the dues being deferred would get added to the final liability. The second part of this arrangement is more important as it allows the company to issue equity equivalent to the accumulated interest. Further, in case the telco is unable to pay even the principal amount, government can convert this also into equity. Other than this, government has also abolished spectrum usage charges (SUC) for spectrum acquired in future auction, estimated at 3-5% of total revenue. Further, non-telecom revenue would be removed from the definition of AGR.

So, how does it help the telecom companies, most importantly Vi. To understand that, it would be useful to first look at its financials. The company recorded losses of over Rs 44,000 crore on revenue of about Rs 42,000 crore during FY21. As a result, the accumulated losses stand at close to Rs 1.4 lakh crore, of which, Rs 1.2 lakh crore was recorded in FY20 and FY21 alone. Among the expenses, finance cost at Rs 18,000 crore, over 40% of revenue, stands out.

However, its cash flow for the year wasn't all that bad. (Cash flow statement talks about actual cash transaction only whereas P&L also considers the amount which becomes due but are deferred). Despite the loss and cash of just about Rs 350 crore at the beginning of the year, company did not have to borrow and in fact, managed to meet the scheduled banks' repayment. This is so because actual cash outgo on finance cost and government dues was less than Rs 3,000 crore even though these accounted for about Rs 40,000 crore in P&L. (The rest deferred, to be paid in future). The stressed profitability and reasonable cash flow position together get reflected in its balance sheet. Company has total balance sheet of Rs 2 lakh crore, which includes 'deferred payment obligations' of Rs 1.5 lakh crore, negative equity of Rs 38,200 crore and the rest, other liabilities including bank borrowings of about Rs 25,000 crore.  The deferred obligation arises because of moratorium provided by the government and the Supreme Court on spectrum charges and AGR dues.

This brings us to the recent announcement which should provide further relief of Rs 15,000–20,000 crore annually. However, the most important part from business sustainability perspective is; if the company fails to generate sufficient cash to meet the entire obligation to the government, the difference can be paid in the form of equity, by issue of shares to the government.

At the current stock price, this may involve significant government stake. However, by the end of four years, hopefully, operations should be reasonably stable and company should survive as a private entity albeit with some government holding. What may complicate matters is 5G auction and how market pans out subsequently.

*****

# Vodafone – Another case of costly acquisition and write-off

Vodafone India is to Vodafone plc what Tata Steel Europe is to Tata Steel! Vodafone plc's wrote-off €6.4 billion (nearly Rs 46,000 crore) with respect to Vodafone India's operation some time back. This was the second write-off by Vodafone plc related to India, the first being in 2010 for €2.3 bn and in all, could be eroding more than one-third of the total investment made by the parent. A look at its operations and financial status before its merger with Idea.

Even though Vodafone has faced pressure due to continued low tariffs in the country, the increase in user base has compensated for that. Vodafone India's EBITDA margin at nearly 30% is same as the global average and its share in total operating profit of the company is same as the revenue share at about 11%. The bigger impact to its financials has been due to changes in the regulatory environment specially related to spectrum auction, leading to significant investment in spectrum. It may be noted that spectrum were 'allocated' and not 'auctioned' at the time of acquisition leading to lack of price discovery. As per the company's half yearly report, company's total debt related to spectrum stands at € 5.5 bn. In addition, it purchased € 2.7 bn of spectrum in auction concluded last month which involved upfront payment of € 1.4 bn.

Its cumulative investments in India involves €10 bn for purchase of 67% controlling stake in 2007 and investment in purchase of the remaining stake subsequently. The company also invested about Rs 48,000 crore two months back largely to retire debt and bring down financing cost.

Acquisition of Vodafone India and Tata Steel Europe (then Corus) and their progression thereafter have uncanny similarity. Both the companies were acquired at relatively high valuations amidst tough competition, classic cases of what management books call, winner's curse. However, both suffered sharp reversal in business environment and therefore, significant write-down of their investments. Yet, both the parents have shown lot of commitment to the businesses, failing which, the fate of these acquisition may have been different. The stated reason for the write-off is the increased competition due to entry of Jio. However, it is too early to estimate that since the business model of Jio is such that it can lead to increase in the total revenue pie also rather than sharply reducing the share of incumbents. The move, in some ways, could also be a preparation for its imminent IPO since it is essential to value a company rather conservatively for the success of the IPO. While the amount written-off is significant, it involves only about 7.5% of the total equity of the parent company. So, possibly, this would have limited impact to the consolidated balance sheet.

*****

# DHFL – Tracking the Developments

Appointment of an administrator by RBI to run DHFL would have come as a shock to the promoters as they lose control of the company in one swift move. Yet, that was the easier part. The real challenge would be to bring out its financials more transparently and put it through the insolvency process. The move is also an escape of sorts for the lenders who had been struggling to arrive at a resolution plan. Other than the core issue of financial stability of the company, the complex case also involves investigations into funds siphoning charges and significant court interventions. A look at the developments.

DHFL (Dewan Housing Finance Ltd) is a housing finance company (HFC) with total estimated assets of over Rs 1.2 lakh crore. The tide turned against the company quite suddenly with its reckless growth during FY18 when its total disbursement rose sharply by 56%, a good part of which went to real estate developers. (Questions would remain as to whether it was a genuine business decision gone wrong or a deliberate move aimed to legitimize funds diversion). This was compounded by recourse to short-term financing to fund this expansion which reduced its cost but led to higher risk of asset-liability mismatch (ALM). Yet, the biggest issue and the one leading to RBI's action is the allegations of diversion of funds to related parties, reportedly to the tune of Rs 20,000 crore.

The rumblings of possible issues with company's finances began soon after the surfacing of IL&FS scam. This came to limelight in June this year when company defaulted on its scheduled loan payment prompting lenders to swing into action. While the company tried to raise resources through divestment, these were not enough to meet its immediate needs. These include a loan portfolio worth Rs 12,000 crore, affordable housing subsidiary, Aadhar housing, with assets of close to Rs 10,000 crore and education loan subsidiary with even smaller portfolio. Company's reported discussion to sell majority stake also did not materialize, finally leading to the submission of resolution plan to the lenders, called inter creditors agreement (ICA). The plan sought conversion of part of its debt into equity and transfer of control from the owner to the lenders. While the plan may have had merit, it met with resistance from other stakeholders who feared being treated unfairly. DHFL has large number of mutual funds (MFs) and other bondholders who invested in the company through market instruments such as commercial papers (CPs), certificate of deposits (CDs) etc. Out of the total debt of over Rs 80,000 crore, banks' exposure is close to Rs 40,000 and the rest is owed to retail and other institutional investors.

The uncertainty arising out of the stalemate possibly compelled the government to make changes to the insolvency laws giving RBI the power to take a call on initiation of insolvency proceedings against a financial services company. So far, financial services companies were not included in IBC. The notification, issued just a few days before RBI's action, paved the way for DHFL being put under administrator and thus, getting promoters and Board of Directors out of the control of the company. The administrator can now be expected to carry out a strict due diligence which would form the basis of resolution of the company and end the uncertainty.

*****

# Jaiprakash Associates - What went wrong??

Jaiprakash Associates (JAL) has made losses for four successive years till FY22. The company, once growing at 30% CAGR, finds itself in an irretrievable situation. So, what all went gone for the company. A look.

JAL, a Cement, Power and Civil Construction company around ten years back expanded its business to eight different segments – Real Estate, Infrastructure (Expressways), Fertilizers, Hotels and Healthcare other than the earlier three. Of these, four namely, Cement, Power, Construction and Infrastructure, account for more than 90% of the revenue. The company pursued relentless growth/ diversification, cashing-in on India's growth story during the period around 2007-12. Most of it was related to construction.

A key element of its strategy was that it built its business portfolio around its core business of construction which provided it considerable cost advantage. So, the diversification involved civil construction subsidiary undertaking the project work for expressways/ construction of Hydro-Power plant and so on. The other benefit for the company was that Cement division met all the needs of this important raw material for all these businesses. It may be noted that inter-segmental revenue accounted for more than 25% of total revenue for the company in FY12.

While the strategy was good, the problem was that it spread itself 'too thin, too fast'. As a result of this growth, its balance sheet size grew from less than Rs 10,000 crore (consolidated) in FY06 to more than Rs 100,000 crore in FY15, almost 30% CAGR over nine years! While the revenues had grown at nearly the same pace, the company could not build upon this to improve its profit margins. This was because of some of the projects getting delayed/ some projects failing to take off, leading to write-offs etc an an increasing interest burden.

This started around 2011-12 when the economy almost suddenly went into a decline specially the infrastructure related sectors and many projects started getting stuck. During the period, company's debt level went up manifold, reaching somewhere around Rs 75,000 crore at its peak. This resulted in interest cost rising from barely a few hundred crore to more than Rs 7,500 crore in FY16, nearly 36% CAGR over the ten year period. Profits which peaked in FY11 started declining subsequently, culminating it losses in FY14 which continues to remain so since then.

It also took significantly high exposure in hydro power plants on the back of its civil construction capability and cement making capacity, two important ingredients for hydro projects. However, these projects are highly capital intensive with long gestation period and also subject to stringent regulatory requirement. This often leads to project getting shelved causing write-off of initial project expenditure. At one stage, more than 90% of its total power plant portfolio was 'under implementation' implying a total investment need of more than Rs 50,000 crore and substantial blocking of equity capital also. Clearly, the growth rate targeted by the company was not sustainable.

To be fair to the company, it did try hard to sell-off its assets, trim its businesses and keep itself going. Some of the assets it sold-off early on were Cement business to Ultratech, some power assets to JSW Energy etc. However, the sales also resulted in substantial reduction in its revenues and operating profit which more than offset the reduction in debt level. The real issue for the company is stuck projects for which there are hardly any takers.

*****

# HCC - Too Old to Fail!

HCC (Hindustan Construction Company) got reprieve from the lenders with the invocation of S4A (Scheme for Sustainable Structuring of Stressed Assets) scheme to tide over the bad debt crisis. The invocation of the scheme reflects lenders confidence in the strength of the company. A ninety-year-old company should ideally fall in the category of 'too old to fail', but somehow, it almost lost the plot in the last 6-7 years, going through painful phases of CDR, debt restructuring and now S4A.

HCC's case is, in some ways, a reminder of Nokia CEO words, "We didn't do anything wrong, but somehow, we lost". HCC's strategy can't be termed overly aggressive unlike many of the companies in the similar space, yet it landed in this crisis. Lavasa was a big bet but it was spread over a large time period hence posed lower risk. (However, the limited risk taking strategy helped it save itself from bigger mess and bigger uncertainties that other companies in this space faced).

Yet, Lavasa was among the key factors for the company's woes, further worsened by the economic conditions which quite suddenly turned tough. The change in environment led to fewer projects and hence more pressure on companies to bid at lower margins. Another factor adding to its problems was acquisition of Karl Steiner AG, Switzerland based loss making construction company, not a bad decision but did not come at the right time. These big projects led to significant expansion in company's balance sheet leading to near doubling of borrowings between FY09-11 and tripling by FY15. The fall out of this was fivefold increase in finance cost from Rs 276 crore in FY10 to more than Rs 1,350 crore in FY16.

While the expansion in business did result in higher revenues with sales rising by as much as 80% in FY11, this did not result in higher profits due to reversal in market conditions and increase in fixed cost related to staff, establishment etc. Company posted first loss in FY11 of Rs 65 crore which worsened in FY12 to more than Rs 500 crore, leading to company seeking Corporate Debt Restructuring (CDR). The period after that has remained challenging and company continues to make losses which averaged at Rs 350 crore over the last four years. The company's problems is unique to an extent as it is not only due to profitability issues alone but also due to cash-flow management issues. Its increase in receivables and inventories rose from less than Rs 600 crore in FY09 to Rs 1,200 crore in FY10 and further to Rs 1,800 crore, almost 30% of sales. More importantly, the receivables were not simply slippages but part of claims and arbitration largely with the government agencies. A rough estimate shows company would have saved almost Rs 200-250 crore of interest cost annually, a significant sum for company of this size, if these claims had got settled expeditiously.

The outlook for the company certainly brightens with interest outgo coming down by up to half with S4A clause which would turn the company profitable as per current financials. While the equity dilution would reduce the future earnings available to shareholders, that would a small price to pay for the revival of the company which would hit a century in a decade!

*****

# Lanco Infratech – End of the Road

Lanco Infratech was liquidated by National Company Law Tribunal (NCLT) in 2020. The company had generated revenue (consolidated) of over Rs 8,000 crore in FY17. As per the last annual report (FY17), it had over Rs 27,000 crore of order book in just one segment, not a small change. So, how companies of that size go down and don't even get a buyer?? A brief attempt to understand.

Lanco was primarily engaged in EPC (Engineering, procurement and construction) and Power Generation. The EPC business was partially a backward integration as it derived signification revenue from its Power and other smaller business. Other than that, it also had some presence in natural resources and reality although their contribution is less than 10%.

Lanco is a classic case of an excessive debt fueled expansion going wrong. The company lost not only due to heavy investment beyond its means but also because its commissioned projects did not deliver sufficient return due to litigation, other regulatory hurdles and external circumstances like natural gas shortage. As a result, the commissioned projects which were expected to support the second bunch of ongoing projects actually continued to remain a burden leading to a double whammy.

The company's growth was unbalanced right from the beginning and is evident from the fact that at the end of FY09, it had 500 mw of operating power generation capacity and as much as 4,000 mw of capacity under construction! Investment required for such a large portfolio would be at least about Rs 16,000 crore, Rs 5,000 crore of which would have to come as equity/internal accrual. How company managed to convince its lenders of such large exposure goes beyond normal banking conventions. If there were political influences aiding that, that won't be surprising.

Another statistic that reflects this is its orderbook to revenue ratio. The same stood at about ten times meaning the company is executing orders worth over ten times of what it is delivering in a year. Even the best of the companies can sustain this ratio of no more than 3-4 times. It must be noted that projects based business are high gestation, high working capital intensive business where the company has to make substantial equity investment upfront before it can get paid by its clients or even loan from banks. Lanco is among those few companies which has a high share of operational creditors out of total financial liabilities of over Rs 45,000 crore.

The under-construction projects on which the company took exposure resulted in huge cash outflow during FY10-FY12. Its capital work-in-progress (CWIP) moved up from Rs 1,900 crore in FY10 to Rs 13,800 crore in FY12, more than seven times increase..! CWIP denotes the amount of money blocked in the ongoing projects which would not be generating any output until their completion. Its total debt and interest cost more than tripled in just two years between FY10 and FY12.

The company may have got some breather if its commissioned projects had generated some funds for other ongoing projects. However, its EBITDA remained in the range of around Rs

2,000 crore range during FY10-12 for reasons explained above and slightly rose to Rs 2,650 crore in FY13. With huge funds blocked in CWIP, sharp increase in interest cost and negligible increase in earnings, its interest coverage ratio fell from 4.8 in FY10 to 1.1 in FY13, the year when it reported losses for the first time, from where it could never recover.

While company kept making efforts to sell some assets, it did not get much success as most of the projects were under construction. The problem with ongoing projects is that it commands lower valuation than the cash generating assets hence has lower sale-ability. That is the reason why it could even receive a proper bid during the insolvency proceedings finally leading to the order for liquidation.

*****

# Tata Steel Corus buy – What went wrong

After Struggling for years with Corus, Tata Steel sold-off parts of it to reduce its losses. A painful decision for sure. However, right from the beginning the going was tough for the company. After integration, in the first year itself, company's EBITDA margin fell from about 31% to 14.1%, whereas pre-tax return on capital employed fell from 42% to 19.1% (Annual report, FY08), even though it was expected to improve in the subsequent years. So, what all went wrong? A brief.

The deal seems to have been done on the best-case scenario assumptions, based on the then prevailing growth rate. However, with the slump in global growth, the deal was in for serious trouble. The optimistic view was probably based on the result of its acquisitions/ international JVs in the preceding years where the company was doing reasonably well.

Most importantly, it was an all cash deal causing severe cash outflow for Tata steel on financing cost. Had it been a part cash, part share swap deal, the impact would have been much lesser. For instance, in case of ArcelorMittal, only about 30% of the deal value was paid in cash with the rest being paid in the form of shares of the new company.

To take the previous argument further ahead, Company faced an additional cash outgo on account of interest of as much as $ 900 mn in FY08 over FY07, which came down slightly in FY09. It can be safely assumed that most of it went towards financing of Corus. In contrast, the deal envisaged an annual saving of $ 450 mn only. At the original bid price, cash outgo for interest arising out of the deal would have been almost as much as the expected savings giving company a reasonable chance of succeeding.

The company had been a low-cost producer with access to captive iron ore mines in domestic market. It hoped to repeat the feat by securing mining leases or fixed price contracts for iron ore needs of Corus also which would have resulted in significant savings. However, iron ore and coking coal prices surged beyond all projections very soon after the deal, putting to rest all its plans to achieve savings on this most important cost component.

The aggressive bidding due to the presence of another party made matter that much worse – A classic case of winner's curse. Compare ArcelorMittal. That deal was also stuck at the peak of the cycle, yet it is managing to survive because of not-so-stretched valuation. Yet, nothing takes away the courage shown by the Tata Management and the intangible gains that has come from the deal in terms of raising India's stature in the world business map.

An afterthought - Can we imagine CSN purchasing Corus then and putting it up for sale after 3-4 years, to be purchased by Tata Steel at a much better valuation!

*****

# ABG Shipyard – From Boom to Doom

The insolvency and decision of NCLT to order liquidation of ABG Shipyard puts an end to the future of the company. The fate of the company is similar to that of numerous other ship-building companies going bust globally, especially China. It would be pertinent to look at how company went from boom to bust and it there were any signs to prevent that.

ABG Shipyard, as mentioned above, is a ship building company having two facilities in Gujarat. Company is primarily into rigs and bulk carrier manufactures, the two segments which went through a significant boom during 2005-2008. The boom probably pushed the company into what is called 'risk taking propensity of entrepreneurs'. Banking on this growth, 38% CAGR during FY05-10, company went for significant expansion at an investment, nearly three time its then net worth. A big gamble. The expansion resulted in its borrowings going up from Rs 400 crore in FY07 to almost Rs 1,800 crore in FY09, the year when the first phase of the capacity was commissioned. Ironically, the commissioning of first phase of its shipyard coincided with the crash in freight rates for dry cargo and prices of crude oil.

Despite the signs of reversal in outlook, an optimistic company continued its investment plan for the second phase which was a much bigger risk proposition. Its balance sheet still shows a capital work-in-progress (CWIP) of nearly Rs 2,000 crore stuck due to delay and cost escalation.

The final blow to the company came in the form of cancellation of orders which stood at nearly Rs 10,000 crore in FY12, equal to nearly four years of sales. The cancellation of orders resulted in sales coming down from nearly Rs 2,400 crore in FY12 to Rs 400 crore in FY15 and as low as Rs 34 crore in FY16. It also led to piling up of inventory which went up from nearly Rs 1,000 crore at the end of FY10 to Rs 5,000 crore by FY15 (excluding partial payment received from the customer).

While order cancellations are not in company's hand, yet, from management perspective, a business plan needs to take the worst-case scenario into consideration in a downturn. While companies get some compensation in case of order cancellation, it is not possible to absorb large cancellations. (A recent case is of RIL terminating its contract with Transocean for ultra-deep water drilling for which RIL would compensate Transocean).

The takeover of management would still be a simpler part since the shipping industry is not expected to turnaround anytime soon. Lenders would still have to make more sacrifices including may be, partial divestment for the company to float again.

*****

## Rosneft - Essar Deal - A New Beginning
## for Indian Refining Industry

The buyout of Essar Oil (98% stake) by Rosneft and its partners at a total value of nearly $13 bn is a landmark deal which opens a whole new market for the buyer. The Essar refinery and its retails outlets would become the first to be run by foreign operators and can change the landscape of petroleum refining and retailing industry in the country. For Ruias, the current promoter of Essar Oil, it is a much sought-after deal to save the rest of its businesses.

Rosneft is an integrated petroleum exploration, production and refining company, majority owned by Russian government and BP (British Petroleum) having nearly 20% stake. Size of Rosneft can be estimated by the fact that its total production of more than 250 mmtoe (million tons of oil equivalent) recorded in 2015 is higher than India's total consumption.! However, its refining capacity is quite limited at nearly 100 mtpa and Essar' refinery with 20 mtpa will add significantly to its total capacity. The other factor to consider is that the company has significant debt on its books with debt-equity ratio of nearly 2.3:1. That probably is the reason why company had to sell stake in its exploration businesses recently to Indian public sector oil companies so that its debt level doesn't go up further.

Essar Oil is a part of Ruia group with businesses spanning Steel, Power, Ports, Shipping etc. The group is facing major challenges in most of the segments but more so in the Steel business due to huge investment undertaken which coincided with global downturn. The sale of Oil business is a result of its failure to find a buyer for the Steel business. Oil business is quite profitable with operating profit of Rs 5,800 crore in FY15 estimated to have crossed Rs 10,000 in FY16. As per estimates, the group is sitting on a loan book of almost Rs 90,000 crore which should come down by half or even more, after this deal.

For Rosneft, it can be termed as a prize catch since the refinery is running well, relatively new and most importantly, located in high growth market. In the current scenario, setting up new greenfield capacity has become very challenging with issues such as land acquisition, environmental requirements etc posing much bigger risk to execution. Additional benefit is the presence of Essar Oil in petroleum retailing with nearly 1,500 retail outlets which Rosneft can leverage with its expertise in retailing and current low oil prices.

Yet, the deal has maximum significance from the perspective of petroleum industry so far dominated by public sector companies. How the competition and industry best practices evolve in the medium term would be interesting to watch out for.

*****

# Understanding RIL-ONGC Gas Migration Dispute

Government of India and RIL are locked in a dispute related to migration of gas from ONGC fields to RIL fields in K-G basin leading to undue gains for RIL. While the dispute is going through the legal process, it would be insightful to understand the background and issues raised by the report.

Krishna Godavari (K-G) basin is an oil & natural gas rich area on and off the coast of Andhra Pradesh spread over about 40,000 sq km. Blocks was allocated to RIL, ONGC and various other companies for exploration of recoverable reserves around 2000. Out of these, Godavari PML and KG-DWN-98/2 (D5) are operated by ONGC and KG-DWN-98/3 (D6) which is adjacent to ONGC blocks, is operated by RIL and its partners. Godavari PML is a small block of 112 sq km but with huge concentration of gas. D5 is spread over 9,800 sq km (almost equal to a square of 100 km size) and D6, 7,645 sq km (nearly 90 km square size). While ONGC blocks are not yet developed (and probably cannot be developed also now due to insufficient reserves of gas) whereas RIL started commercial production in 2009.

The issue came to light in 2013 when ONGC wrote to Director General of Hydrocarbon (DGH) raising concerns about continuity and connectivity of its block with RIL's leading to migration of gas. Gas migration is a complex phenomenon occurring at a depth of up to 1000 mtrs. The migration occurs across fractures in rocks due to difference in pressure. This can be loosely compared to two nearby ponds where decrease in level of one pond leads to flow of water from the other pond due to invisible interconnectivity underground. The development of RIL field probably led to reduction in pressure in its block causing flow of gas from the other high pressure blocks.

The ONGC letter finally led to appointment of consultant, DeGolyer & MacNaughton (D&M)in 2015 which confirmed continuity of blocks and considerable migration of gas from ONGC blocks. The consultant reported about 40% of gas migration from the two ONGC blocks which had a total reserves of nearly 26 bn cubic meter. It states that further migration would happen in the subsequent years also since there is no mechanism to plug the connectivity. While the D&M report should have been sufficient for government to impose a penalty, it constituted Justice (Retd) Shah committee to examine the D&M report and make recommendations.

Other than concluding 'unfair enrichment', the committee also noted that 2003 appraisal report prima facie reveals that RIL had prior knowledge about connectivity and continuity of reservoirs. That it did not bring the findings of the report to the notice of is disconcerting. The issue of prior knowledge assumes greater significance since that would have given the opportunity to explore joint development of blocks and higher extraction of precious and scarce fuel. The committee also noted that ONGC also had some prior knowledge about possible continuity in 2007 which is now being investigated by the government.

*****

# Understanding ONGC – GSPC Gas Block Deal

The buyout of Gujarat State Petrochemical Corporation's (GSPC) assets in K-G basin block by ONGC puts an end to GSPC's audacious attempt to establish itself as an important gas producer. GSPC struggled for more than half a decade to extract gas from the field after a high-profile announcement on gas finds in 2005. While there had been issues regarding under estimation of costs, flawed assumption in viability projections etc, as pointed out by Comptroller and Auditor General (CAG), yet the project was an ambitious attempt by GSPC to extract gas from highly difficult and uncertain fields.

The deal relates to gas block allotted to GSPC in K-G basin where it has discovered gas in 2005 and began development of three of the nine fields in subsequent years. However, it could not achieve commercial production from the fields due to difficult nature of high-pressure deep-sea fields despite time over-run and an investment of nearly Rs 20,000 crore. Current production from the fields stand at only about one-tenth of 32 mmscmd expected as per the field development plan (FDP). While there is still possibility of raising the production, that would require additional investment and greater technological expertise, triggering the sale. ONGC would be paying Rs 7,000 crore to GSPC to purchase its 80% stake which stares at a huge write-off now.

From management and risk perspective, a critical lapse on the part of GSPC was its decision to go it alone in this high-risk venture which was further accentuated by its lack of experience. Had the company roped-in ONGC, say in 2010, the field probably would have started commercial production by now and may be, with lower investments. As if that was not enough, it further went ahead and acquired a large number of assets overseas, most of which it has now surrendered, incurring a loss of about Rs 3,000 crore.

GSPC is a State-owned enterprise of Gujarat, engaged primarily in the business of gas trading, transmission and distribution. A logical extension for it was to go for backward integration which led to its bidding for gas exploration. It achieved a breakthrough on highly publicized discovery of gas in the K-G basin in 2005, considered bigger than even the Reliance discovery then. However, in the absence of in-house expertise in development of gas fields and absence of any competent joint venture partner, company probably bungled in developing its prized discovery.

However, all may not be lost yet for GSPC. There are six other fields in the blocks which have the potential to produce gas on commercial basis. However, that may take few more years and probably, would be contingent upon ONGC's ability to start commercial production from the three acquired fields.

*****

# SECTION - VI
# ET CETERA

# Inland Waterways – Tapping the Potential

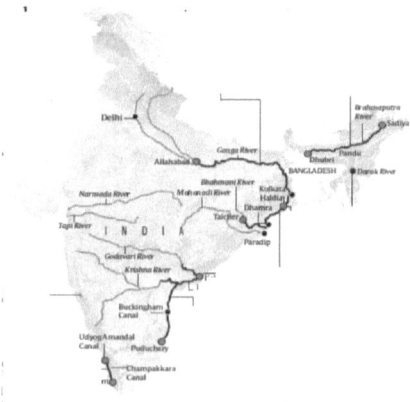

With nearly 14,500 km of waterways, inland waterways transportation system, provide immense potential to change the landscape of goods transportation within the country. These waterways are roughly five times the length from North to South. In fact, the ease of transportation and huge benefits arising out of it leaves one wondering why they have not been developed so far?

Inland waterway is very simple in concept and is nothing but transportation of goods through rivers, subject to certain technical requirements. It is not a new concept and its feasibility was established more than 150 years ago, yet its potential is grossly underutilized in the country. As per Wikipedia, the total cargo moved by the inland waterway is just 0.1% of the total inland traffic in India compared to 21% in US.

The most important benefit of waterways is its cost effectiveness and ease of use. Low cost of transportation is very important for high volume, low value products such as fly ash, coal, cement etc. It is also easier for movement of bulky and over dimensional cargo (ODC) such as Cars, project items such as machinery etc. (Successful movement of cars from its plant in North India to Kolkata about two years back gave much fillip to waterways development). Other than the operating cost, the investment required for development of waterway is also significantly lower than road or rail network. More importantly, it doesn't require land acquisition and associated displacement, the biggest cause of delays and cost escalation of projects in the country. That is not all. The most outstanding benefit is significant reduction in vehicular pollution, an issue being debated intensely but little concrete measures to mitigate it in place, yet. On the flip side, the travel time through waterways is higher than through roads or railways.

While country does have a few operating waterways, the passage of National Waterways Act in April'16 brought forward an action plan to harness its potential. The act notified a total of 111 waterways as National Waterway (five of them already operating), totaling nearly 20,000 km of length. The Act gave the central government power to develop and commercialize them which rested with the state government until then. Among the longest of these is the waterway on River Ganga (NW-1) from Allahabad to Kolkata totaling 1,620 km, on River Godavari (NW-4) covering the states of AP, Telangana and TN and on River Yamuna (NW-110) covering UP, Delhi and Haryana. These two waterways have a length of over 1,000 km. Of special mention is

NW-6 in the North-East region which is only 121 km long but covers a hilly terrain, otherwise difficult to navigate through roads.

The most important parameter for navigation through water channels is least available depth (LAD) which should be a minimum of 3 meters for navigation of vessels with carrying capacity of 1,500 ton. (Ports work with draft going beyond 12 meters, loosely equivalent to LAD, which allows them to handle ships with capacity of up to 100,000 tons). It may be noted that NW-1 is constrained by low LAD of 1.2 meters limiting its potential. Government has taken up a project, aided by World Bank, to increase it to 3 meter which would provide boost to movement of export bound goods from North and Eastern region to the port city of Kolkata.

While the government efforts are laudable, the nation is still at least a decade away from realizing the proper potential of waterways. Innovative model for development as tried out in highways development may help reap its huge economic benefits.

(Image Source - Wikipedia)

*****

# Ken Betwa River Linking – A Tough, Ambitious Project

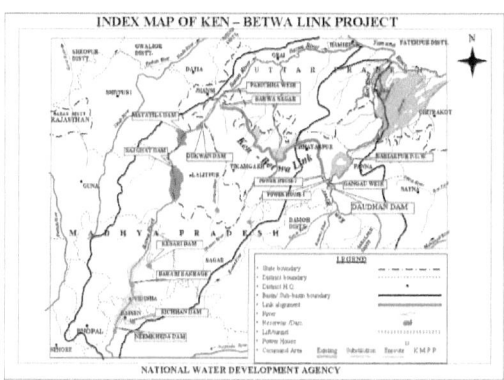

Ken-Betwa River linking project is an ambitious project with considerable benefits. The project, if successfully executed, will pave the way for taking up many more such projects, crucial to meet country's irrigation needs and change the face of Indian agriculture.

River linking projects essentially provide a channel for the transfer of water from a surplus river to a deficit river. Globally, there are many examples like Rhine–Main–Danube Canal, Tennessee–Tombigbee Waterway etc which have been built successfully. In Indian context, the benefits are even greater since there is wide difference in rainfall pattern across the country causing rain deficit in some region and floods in some other region. The river linking will not only feed the deficit region but also provide an outlet to the excess water, otherwise cause of severe floods. Further, it would reduce the country's dependence on monsoon which provides water not only for a short duration but is also erratic in nature.

Ken is a river flowing through M.P. and U.P. and has water surplus of about 1,000 Mn m$^3$. Betwa is another river mainly flowing through water scarce region of MP. The project proposes to link the two rivers by a canal 230 km long, equal to the distance between Delhi and Agra. The relatively short distance of the canal makes the project quite favourable from the cost perspective. In contrast, the Indira Gandhi canal, built to feed the deserts of Rajasthan, covers a total distance of 650 km. The impact of canal on the agrarian economy of Rajasthan is a case study on water transfer projects which has helped irrigate nearly 4,000 sq km of barren land in the desert district of Jaislmer.

The K-B project will not only meet the irrigation needs of the area in the route of the canal but a much larger area on the basin of river Betwa. Total area estimated to receive water for irrigation is 4,500sq km, much larger than 470 sq km of area on the route. It may be noted that this area is larger than the area covered by the Indira Gandhi canal mentioned above. Currently, irrigation covers only 30% of cultivable area in the region.

Like any other developmental project, this project also involves certain sacrifices. The project would submerge about 10% area of the national park in the region reducing the space available to the animals and also cause partial loss of habitat for the vulture species. Yet, the benefits arriving out of the project linked to basic human needs, unlike industrial or highway projects, compel the policymakers to attempt a way out. Hope, the project management team finds a way to keep the damage to manageable level and the project sees the light of the day.

(Image courtesy of National Water Development Agency)

*****

# Understanding Indus Water Treaty

Indus River water system often finds mentions during conversation around tackling the menace of terrorism originating from neighboring nation. Here is a look at Indus Water treaty (IWT), over half a century old agreement between India and Pakistan to share water flowing through these rivers.

The Indus Water Treaty (IWT) deals with sharing of water of six rivers flowing from India into the Pakistan. These are Indus, Chenab and Jhelum called "western" rivers and Beas, Ravi and Sutlej called "eastern" rivers. Despite the classification, all the rivers flow from North India to Pakistan running almost parallel for some distance. However, none of them originate in India but in Tibet, Afghanistan and the Himalayas. Before meeting the Arabian Sea in Pakistan, all of them merge into Indus making it the largest of all and giving the treaty its name. Average annual flow estimated in Western River is about 166 km$^3$ in and about 41 km$^3$ in eastern river. (1 km$^3$ is equal to about 114,000 m$^3$ per hour of water flow).

Before partition, almost all the water from these rivers used to flow towards Pakistan area. After the partition, claim on this water became open. After initial years of temporary arrangement which both the partiers were not satisfied with and after a grueling nine year negotiation brokered by the World Bank, an agreement was reached in Sept' 1960. The agreement divides usage of water into two categories – consumptive and non-consumptive. Non consumptive use refers to purposes such as generation of power, navigation, fishing etc. As per the agreement, India got the right to use water from eastern rivers for consumption whereas water from western rivers was given to Pakistan. This meant sharing in 20:80 ratio between India and Pakistan. However, India had the right to use water from western rivers for non consumptive purpose, most important being, generation of power. Some amount of water was also available to India for irrigation purpose. The treaty also envisaged constitution of a permanent water commission which would be given the right to visit other country's facilities once in five years. Incidentally, members from Pakistan visited Indian side of Indus water system very recently in January.

The treaty also envisaged ten year transition period during which India was required to supply water from the eastern rivers also to Pakistan. This was incorporated to allow Pakistan to build adequate facilities, dams, canals etc so that areas supplied by eastern rivers could also be connected with western rives. The deal made sense as volume of water in western rivers was sufficient to meet the needs. Almost two-thirds of Pakistan now lies in the basin of Indus water system. While India had the right to use this water after the transition period, it did not build sufficient dams, canal system etc in its territory to divert the water flow. India is using only about 94% of its share. To make up for this, government approved one of the projects in Dec'18, under planning for over a decade. However, it would still be 3-4 years before the project is completed.

While the stoppage of water supply after such a long time is certain to meet with lot of resistance, a clause in the agreement gives India the freedom to do so. The clause specifically states that no country can claim right over other's share even if the other country was not utilizing its share fully. It is this clause which India would use even though Pakistan had been getting India's share of water for decades. While the impact may not be too heavy, it is not ignorable either.

*****

# Cauvery River Dispute - A Brief History

The more than 100 years old Cauvery River dispute relates to sharing of water from River Cauvery mainly between Karnataka and Tamil Nadu although Puducherry and Kerala are also a party. The issue, though agrarian, has become a sensitive issue over the decades and taken a political colour.

River Cauvery is probably the most important river of South India originating in Karnataka and meeting Bay of Bengal in Tamil Nadu. Its total length is nearly 765 km of which approx. 320 km lies in Karnataka and 416 km in Tamil Nadu. The difference arising out of the river water sharing had been recognized in the 19th century itself leading to agreement between the two states (One, a princely state and another under British control) in the year 1892 and 1924. The second agreement defined quantity of water to be shared between the riparian states giving more share to Tamil Nadu. The other important clause of the agreement was that it prohibited the upstream areas from undertaking any dam construction which can affect the water availability to other areas downstream. The agreement also provided for reviewing the provision after fifty years to distribute any surplus water, if available.

However, soon after the reorganization and formation of Karnataka state in 1956 (earlier, state of Mysore), it started constructions of dams citing increased needs of the newly formed state. It constructed four dams which could cut water supplies to Tamil Nadu substantially. The basic premise of Karnataka is that the original agreement gave undue favor to Tamil Nadu and it can release water only after meeting its own needs.

Despite Tamil Nadu's constant follow up and attempt at finding a solution throughout 70s and 80s the matter could not be resolved. A judicial tribunal was finally set up in 1989 which gave its interim order in 1991 and final order in 2007 giving almost 60% of water (419 billion cubic ft out of total of 726 billion cubic ft) to Tamil Nadu. While the order has taken care of distribution in normal years it has given no direction on sharing of water during drought years. This remains a point of dispute between the states and Supreme Court had, some time back, directed Karnataka to release water from River Cauvery.

*****

# Indian Legal System - Justice Delayed is Justice Denied

Even though Indian Legal System has stood the test of times for its rule-based judgment process and fair trial, there is one adage on which it has possibly, failed to deliver. And that is, "Justice delayed is justice denied". The same applies not only to civil or criminal cases but also to business cases. Indeed, while India has improved its ranking on World Bank's ease of doing business ranking from No 142 to No 63, its ranking stands at very low No 163 in 'enforcement of legal contract', one of the parameters used for World bank ranking. A look at the status and measure taken to improve the judicial process.

As per the Economic Survey, there were nearly 35 lakh economic/ commercial cases pending at five important High Courts at the end of 2017. Other than that, nearly 1.8 lakh cases are pending across six appellate tribunals. (Yet, pendency of commercial cases is far better than civil and criminal cases where the total pendency across all level of Courts stands at about 5 crore). Commercial cases are largely disputes between two business entities or between a business entity and government. Tribunals are special courts across sectors such as Telecom and Electricity and for dealing with high value direct and indirect taxes. Of the total cases pending with High Courts, almost 70% of cases relate to taxation disputes putting the onus of faster disposal on government. Taxation cases also have higher pendency averaging 6 years against 4 years for the rest. Interestingly, just 0.2% of these cases constituted nearly 56% of the total demand value.

While the general perception is that the delays are due to lengthy process of justice, a closer look reveals that there are a number of avoidable reasons. *One important reason for the delay is frequent adjournments, meaning deferment of the hearing*. Even though the law permits only three adjournments, the rule has not been followed in at least half of the cases. Not only does it delay the process of justice, it also works as a tool in corporate battles. The Economic Survey states, "The extraordinary alacrity with which the courts grant adjournments have ensured that the powerful will always outlast the weak, making a mockery of justice". As per the World Bank report, average time taken for resolution of a legal dispute is more than 4 years. This also involves expenses of almost 30% of amount under dispute, most of which goes towards lawyers' fees. The silver lining is that the quality of judicial process is rated above average.

While the Supreme Court has made note of the fact, concerted effort to reduce such adjournments are still needed. To curb this tendency, the Supreme Court in a recent judgment imposed fine on all the parties in a corporate case dating back to 1998, calling it "abuse of judicial process by the rich and the powerful, wasting enormous amount of court's time". (The book "How Corporations, Government, and Trial Lawyers Abuse the Judicial Process" by Robert A. Levy, gives a glimpse of the same with actual cases, although, the cases are from USA).

Another factor responsible for increasing delay in court cases is use of special provisions such as Special Leave Petition (SLP) or Writ petition to approach the higher courts. As per the Survey, SLP admitted at the Supreme Court increased from around 25% in 2008 to nearly 40% in 2016. In contrast, the Supreme Court of USA and Canada admit 3% and 9% of the cases filed before it. SLP is a provision available in the constitution to approach Supreme Court directly in rare cases when a 'substantial question of law' is involved. Similarly, use of writ petition which applies to civil and criminal cases leads to lower amount of time available with the High Court leading to delay of other cases. As per the Survey, almost 10 lakh writ petition cases are pending across the

High Courts. The Survey suggests the Courts to revisit their jurisdictions and avoid resorting to special provisions.

The judicial reforms have gained momentum over last few years. Some of the important decisions taken by the government recently are scrapping of over 1,400 redundant laws, changes in taxation laws, passage of bills related to arbitration council and formation of commercial courts at district level. In a important change of taxation laws and to reduce the pendency, government increased the minimum amount under dispute for filing a petition in case of tax dispute in July'18. This increased threshold from Rs 10 lakh to Rs 20 lakh for filing cases in lower court, from Rs 20 lakh to Rs 50 lakh in high courts and from Rs 25 lakh to Rs 1 crore in Supreme Court. This is estimated to have reduced the number of cases by about one-third at lower courts; the pendency has come down more sharply, almost half in case of both High Court and Supreme Court (Direct tax cases). In case of indirect taxes, pendency has come down by about one-fourth. Interestingly, amount foregone by government was only Rs 6,000 crore, not even 1% of annual tax revenues. Government has also formed commercial courts at district level which would hear commercial disputes of value between Rs 3 lakh and 1 crore. (Disputes above Rs 1 crore can are directly filed at High Courts whereas below Rs 3 lakh are filed in regular civil courts).

While the current state of legal system appears too bleak, the reality may not be so bad. One of the hopes being that case disposal rate stands at close to 90%, almost the same as other major countries. Total backlog of cases is equal to just about two years and nearly 80% of cases are disposed-off within three years of being filed which is quite acceptable. While a number of reforms are being initiated, an initiative that can be taken is to raise an alert after a case crosses a threshold, say, 24 months, after which the case must be put on fast track and provisions such as adjournments etc is made stricter.

*****

# HDI – Increasing Divergence

The Human Development Index (HDI) report by United Nations Development Programme (UNDP) paints a stark picture of inequality across the globe. While humanity has managed to bring many people out of extreme poverty, newer forms of inequality have emerged. More worryingly, countries with low HDI not only have a low level of income, but also lower life expectancy which is as much as 20 years. A look at some of the details and India's standing.

UNDP measures three essential parameters to arrive at HDI – Life expectancy, level of education measured by number of years of schooling and standard of living measured as per capita income. The report looks at the statistics for a total of 189 countries. Norway tops the list with HDI of 0.954 which corresponds to life expectancy of 82.3 years, average schooling of 18.1 years and per capita income of $68,000 (PPP). Niger stands the last with score of 0.377 and has expectancy of 62 years, schooling of 6.5 years and income of $912. India stands at No 129, one notch above last year, with expectancy of 69.4, schooling of 12.3 and income $6,829.

Other than individual countries, report looks at regional HDI also which gives a better view. As per this, OECD (Organization for Economic Co-operation & Development) countries have life expectancy of 80.4 years, schooling of 16.3 years and income of $40,000. In contrast, LDCs (Least Developed Countries) have expectancy of 65 years, schooling of 9.8 years and income of $2,630. for Sub-Saharan Africa has the worst life expectancy at 61.2 years.

However, the above figures provide very simplistic view of the data generated by HDI which runs into over 50 data points spread across ten tables! Some of these are inequality adjusted HDI (IHDI), Gender Development Index and Gender Inequality Index (GII) and Multidimensional Poverty Index (MPI), each based on variety of parameters. For instance, IHDI measures inequality within the country in level of life expectancy, education, income share of poorest 20%, top 10%, top 1% and Gini coefficient. Other tables look at factors leading to better score on the three core parameters such as number of physician and hospital beds per thousand population, pupil-teacher ratio, trained teachers, subject score for 15-year-olds (!), percent population with vulnerable employment, population with access to electricity, sanitation etc. Yet another set of tables look at environment and socio-economic sustainability, each measuring 10-12 parameters. It may be noted that many of these parameters correspond to sustainable development goals (SDG).

IHDI captures variation within the country for all the three parameters separately. For instance, Hong Kong SAR (China) stands No 4 but is placed much lower at No 21 in terms of IHDI. Norway tops the chart even on this count. Surprisingly, India ranks one notch above on this although all the countries have lower value for IHDI. For Norway, inequality in life expectancy is only 3% which is 20% for India and goes beyond 30% for low HDI countries. While the inequality in education is in low single digits for high HDI countries, it goes beyond 40% for LDCs and is disappointing for India at 38.7%.

In terms of GII, Switzerland tops the list with higher life expectancy for female and nearly same level of schooling. However, per capita income differs significantly at $50,000 and $70,000. India is ranked slightly better at No 122 on this count with higher life expectancy and more years of schooling for female. However, income for female is much lower at $2,600 against $10,700 for male. Even the global average is $11,200 for female against $20,200 for male. The report, however, says that these are crude estimates. Multidimensional poverty index measures percent of population below the poverty line, intensity of deprivation, population vulnerable to poverty etc. While Europe and East Asia has only 1.1% below poverty line, it is as high as 57.5% for Sub-Saharan Africa, that too, with a high intensity of deprivation at 55%. India ranks quite poorly on this with poverty figure of 27.9% and severity of deprivation of 44%

Other than the country wise ranking on specific parameters, the report also looks at the development in a holistic manner. It has spent considerable amount of space on how children from poor families remain in the vicious cycle of development. They may not be able to afford an education and are at a disadvantage when they try to find work. These children are likely to earn less than those in higher income families when they enter the labour market, when penalized by compounding layers of disadvantage. The report rues, "They watch from society's side-lines as they see others pull ahead to ever greater prosperity and people well empowered today appear set to get even farther ahead tomorrow".

Other than the basic capability, the development also takes into account the enhanced capability, such as life expectancy at 70 years of age, which requires advance medical care, level of tertiary education which requires certain level of prosperity and of course, access to broadband. While mobile penetration has reached a level of 67% in low HDI against 137% for high HDI, there is a huge gap in the related enhanced capability - broadband penetration. This stands at less than 1% for low against 28% for high HDI. Worse, the chances are that the gap would increase over time.

An important point mentioned by the report is that policies to tackle economic inequality require much more than a mechanistic transfer of income corroborated by an interesting figure related to impact of income distribution across countries with different HDI. While taxes & transfers led to 17-point reduction in the Gini coefficient across the developed countries, the same was only 4 point in case of developing countries, a result of inefficient government mechanism and leakages.

*****

# OXFAM Inequality Report- Sign of Economic Health or An Economic Crisis??

The annual OXFAM report makes for another distressing reading with world's billionaire, totaling just 2,153, owing more wealth than 460 crore or 60% of humanity on earth! Further, wealth owned by top 1% is twice that of 690 crore or 90% of humanity. What makes it worse is that governments across the world are in no way, equipped to arrest the increasing concentration.

And if that doesn't help you visualize the concentration of wealth, consider this. Even if an individual (or his/her forefathers) was saving as much as $10,000 per day since the building of pyramids in Egypt, his accumulated wealth would still be only 1/5th the average of five richest billionaires! While a small part of this would be innovation and hard work, 1/3rd of it is inheritance and another part, a result of monopolies (at global level) accentuated by cronyism. The ability of private interests to influence privatization deals, to secure natural resources at throw away prices, corrupt public procurement, tax exemptions and loopholes are all ways in which well-connected private interests can enrich themselves at the expense of the public.

The inequality gets further accentuated as a result of collapse in taxation of the super-rich individuals and the corporations owned by them and deliberate tax dodging. As per the report, only 4% of total taxes is contributed by wealth tax. The report states that super-rich avoid as much as 30% of their tax liability. While the middle class would be happy receiving a generous dividend with low corporate tax rates, they do not realize that better part of this has gone to the top 1%, something that should have gone to the government or the wage earners. As per the report, during 2011-17, average wages in G7 countries increased by 3%, while dividends grew by 31%. The report quotes the study by Thomas Piketty and his team which shows that between 1980 and 2016, the richest 1% received 27% of global income growth against only 12% secured by bottom 50%.

In their pursuit by finding ways and loopholes to avoid and evade taxes, they are aided, willy-nilly, by the armies of tax advisers at their service. Multinational corporations exploit loopholes in tax codes to shift profits to tax havens and avoid taxes, costing developing countries an estimated $100bn. It is pertinent to note that just 0.5% of additional tax on top 1% for next 10 years could help create nearly 12 crore additional jobs and meet education, healthcare and similar needs.

Tax dodging by the wealthy deprives governments of resources leading to reduction in social programmes and other development activities. Increasingly, they are relying on the advice of agencies like IMF which is further perpetuating the inequality. Oxfam quotes an IMF program of relying on VAT to raise resources, which has hit poor the hardest.

Other than the aggregate inequality, the report rues over increasing gender inequality with majority of females having to bear a large part of unpaid work. As per the report, women & girls spend over 12 billion hours of unpaid work every day. This could still be an under-estimation as it corresponds to just 4 hours of such work with world population of 7.7 billion. The work corresponds to over $10 trillion of value addition worth a modest $2.4 per hour. The report also notes the impact of childcare support on productive engagement of females. Countries where the government provides childcare support, either through direct provision or subsidies, 30% of women are in waged employment, compared with just 12% in countries without such policies.

So, what are the options left for the humanity? The first is to stop celebrating wealth as a sign of economic growth but a malaise. The economic growth parameters must be changed from the size of the economy to the size of wealth held by the bottom 50%. While the billionaires could be running the engines of economy, the same should not scare governments from taking harsh decisions and cracking down on loopholes. The narrative needs to move from the problem of 'tax terrorism' to 'wealth terrorism'. While global co-operation has made some progress lately, it has happened, possibly, a few decades too late. Yet, there are still inadequate global tax rules which need to fixed urgently.

*****

# Beyond GDP - Measuring Happiness!

Every new year brings with it hopes of a happy new year. But are we really becoming happier? The World Happiness Report for 2022 shows divergent trends in happiness score across countries. However, what gives lot of hopes for humanity is the surge seen in social support as the world battled pain and suffering caused due to the pandemic. Here is a look at some of the findings and methodology of the report.

The growing international efforts to evaluate happiness and bringing it to mainstream can be attributed to the UN resolution in 2011 sponsored by Bhutan. The resolution proposed giving more importance to happiness and well-being in determining how to achieve social and economic development. Supported by the UN, the first edition of World Happiness Report was released in 2012. The report is based on the survey carried out primarily by Gallup World Poll. It lists out countries using six measures - life evaluation score, GDP per capita, social support, healthy life expectancy, freedom of choice and corruption. The life evaluation score is arrived at as net of frequency of experiencing positive emotions such as laughter, enjoyment etc and frequency of experiencing negative emotions such as worry, sadness, anger. However, the sample size of survey is quite limited at 1,000-3,000 per country and whether that can give a true representation can be debated.

At one level, the report gives lot of hopes since average life evaluation score has remained largely same during 2020 and 2021 as its pre-pandemic level. However, the average value masks the deviation in the movement of score across nations and for young & the old. While some of the nations have seen their happiness score increase by one full point (in a scale of 10), others have recorded increase in stress, worry, and sadness. Even in terms of inequality within the nation, regions such as Sub-Saharan Africa and MENA have seen significant increase. On the other hand, life satisfaction has fallen for the young whereas it has risen for those over 60.

However, not all is gloomy. The most remarkable change is global upsurge in compassion which acted as a support for caregivers during the pandemic. There has also been large increase in the proportion of people who gave money to charity, helped strangers and did voluntary work over last two years. Average value of these three measures has risen by 0.25 points compared with the level before the pandemic. Whether this sustains after the pandemic would be eagerly observed.

In terms of specific countries, Finland tops the chart with a score of 7.82 (maximum - 10), followed by Denmark, Iceland and Switzerland. The top two countries were the same in first report of 2012 also but the places have changed. Even though per capita GDP is not the sole determinant, it plays a distinct role as evident from regional difference in score shown in the image. Scores for other European countries have remained largely same although it might change this year due to adverse impact of war. For USA, the happiness score has declined by about 0.25 points with fall in rank from 11 to 16. India is placed at No 136 with score of 3.78. It is placed even lower than countries like Chad, Ethiopia and Yemen which gives credence to the view that sample may not be representative. An indicator where India ranks high at No 34 is freedom to make life choices. Further, confidence in national government in India has increased from 0.53 in 2013 to 0.79 in 2021. For India, the residual value has score of -1 which reduces its rank. This is loosely the value that cannot be explained by the individual findings and hence, added or deducted from the aggregate score of the nation.

Even though the level of happiness has not changed across all the nations, references to happiness in text across both books and social media has increased sharply. Parallelly, references to income and GDP have fallen which might mean changing priorities of life.

And what is the role of governments in improving the happiness of its people. The report notes that public feels angry with political leaders who are perceived as being unable to solve growing inequalities, corruption, violence and insecurity. It mentions four deliverables for the governments - rule of law, quality of regulations, control of corruption and effectiveness of governance. For individuals, it doesn't provide any prescription but generosity, extending social support and volunteer work are some of the ways individuals can add to the collective happiness.

\*\*\*\*\*

# End Note – My Favorite Quotes

I never worried about money. I grew up in a middle-class family, so I never thought I would starve. And I learned at Atari that I could be an okay engineer, so I always knew I could get by. I was voluntarily poor when I was in college and India, and I lived a pretty simple life even when I was working. So, I went from fairly poor, which was wonderful because I didn't have to worry about money, to being incredibly rich, when I also didn't have to worry about money. I watched people at Apple who made a lot of money and felt they had to live differently. Some of them bought Rolls-Royce and various houses, each with a house manager and then someone to manage the house managers. Their wives got plastic surgery and turned into these bizarre people. This was not how I wanted to live. It's crazy. I made a promise to myself that I'm not going to let this money ruin my life. - Steve Jobs

You have to be empathetic to reality. You can bend reality but you cannot break it. On cash in India, my team here worked on me for a long time to make that happen. If you get stuck too much with the way you want the world to be, you'll find that the world passes you by. As an entrepreneur and as a startup, you have to find a balance between where you want the world to go and where it actually is. Hopefully it will follow the path you think it will, but sometimes unexpectedly, it bends the other way and takes the fork on the road. That's part of the fun. So yes, we accept cash in India – Travis Kalanich, Uber.

To assume that all who are entrusted with the task of administering, will do so flawlessly and then to blame them when the system fails; is not the mark of a good policy. The effective strategy is to take people to be the way they are and then craft incentive-compatible interventions – The Economic Survey.

India operates on fuzzy logic and there is ambiguity in the way people do things so Indians can cope with ambiguity better. In a European environment, managers are unwilling to cope with situations when things go wrong. If you have been working in a growth situation and then you hit the brick wall people surrender; so, I think the ability to think on their feet and cope with the uncertainty of the future has given me a positive impression of Indian managers. Indians working outside of India have turned around tough situations in a different cultural situation. (James Douglas, EMA Partners International)

"Whatever limit us, we call fate"- whoever says this, hasn't seen enough of life.

The greatest conflicts are not between two people, but between a person and himself.

A fool gets annoyed at the slightest provocation. A wise man overlooks an insult – Bible.

Towering genius disdains a beaten path. It seeks regions hitherto unexplored.

For a general about to fight an enemy, it is important to know the enemy's numbers, but still more important to know the enemy's philosophy.

The man who is a pessimist before 48 knows too much; if he is an optimist after that, he knows too little – Mark Twain

To withdraw is not to run away and to stay is no wise decision when there is more reason to fear than to hope.

Every morning in Africa, a Gazelle wakes up. It knows it must run faster than the fastest lion or it will be killed. Every morning a Lion wakes up. It knows it must outrun the slowest Gazelle or it will starve to death. It doesn't matter whether you are a Lion or a Gazelle. When the sun comes up; you'd better be running.

Knowledge workers cannot be controlled; they must be motivated. They must serve a purpose more meaningful than personal profit - Peter Drucker.

If it's 20 per cent left in your body, just give that 20 per cent.

------- X -------